The Making of the United Kingdom, 1660–1800

BRITISH ISLES SERIES

The Emergence of the British Isles
1450–1650
Steve Ellis

THE MAKING OF THE UNITED KINGDOM, 1660–1800

State, Religion and Identity in Britain and Ireland

Jim Smyth

An imprint of **Pearson Education**

Harlow, England · London · New York · Reading, Massachusetts · San Francisco · Toronto · Don Mills, Ontario · Sydney
Tokyo · Singapore · Hong Kong · Seoul · Taipei · Cape Town · Madrid · Mexico City · Amsterdam · Munich · Paris · Milan

Pearson Education Limited

Head Office:
Edinburgh Gate
Harlow CM20 2JE
Tel: +44 (0)1279 623623
Fax: +44 (0)1279 431059

London Office:
128 Long Acre
London WC2E 9AN
Tel: +44 (0)20 7447 2000
Fax: +44 (0)20 7240 5771
Website: www.history-minds.com

First published in the United Kingdom in 2001

© Pearson Education Limited 2001

The right of Jim Smyth to be identified as Author
of this Work has been asserted by him in accordance
with the Copyright, Designs and Patents Act 1988.

ISBN 0 582 08998 0

British Library Cataloguing in Publication Data
A CIP catalogue record for this book can be obtained from the British Library

Library of Congress Cataloging in Publication Data
A CIP catalog record for this book can be obtained from the Library of Congress

10   9   8   7   6   5   4   3   2   1

Produced by Pearson Education Asia Pte Ltd
Printed in Singapore (mpm)

The Publishers' policy is to use paper manufactured from sustainable forests.

071502-1496H5

CONTENTS

CONTENTS

SERIES EDITOR'S PREFACE

The last few years have witnessed an explosion of interest in what is now generally known as 'the New British history'. By this is meant a holistic approach to the history of the British Isles, in which the familiar story of the rise of an English, later British, nation is replaced by a more comparative account focusing on interaction between the archipelago's different peoples, countries and cultures, particularly in the context of state formation. If we look for the reasons behind this change of emphasis, they apparently have most to do with very modern developments, reflecting changed political circumstances. In particular, the recent readjustments in internal relations between the constituent parts of the British Isles and also parallel changes in relations with continental Europe have reminded both historians and the general public of different, less familiar aspects of their past. Most obviously, Britain's retreat from empire in the two decades after World War II inaugurated a period of introspection and a reconsideration of traditional imperial perspectives in which the United Kingdom appeared as the civilising centre of a large and successful empire. Where previously there had been a remarkably unanimous belief in the homogeneity of the British political system, following the collapse of the imperial mission, the 'home nations' began to rediscover their differences. Thus, the last thirty years have seen a marked growth of separatist parties, the Scottish National Party and Plaid Cymru, and most recently the establishment of Scottish and Welsh assemblies. In the case of Ireland, separatism has had a rather longer history, but the Northern troubles since 1969 and the chequered history of the Stormont regime also underline the recent tensions in the union. And alongside this partial reversal of earlier centralising initiatives within the archipelago, the period has also witnessed successive moves at European level in the direction of integration into an embryonic, quasi-federal superstate, the European Union, with a consequent loss of national sovereignty.

There have of course been earlier attempts to look at particular aspects of British history from this kind of state-centred, archipelagic perspective. For instance, the origins of the various unions (1536, 1707, 1801) which marked the development of the modern British state have long attracted the historian's attention, and more recently the implications of an archipelagic approach have been discussed in essays of a more theoretical, historiographical bent. Yet only in the past decade has the New British history attracted the kind of attention associated with a major departure in history writing. In essence, this has involved a distinct shift in focus from nation-building to state formation as an interpretative principle of British historiography. It is reflected both in the growing number of scholars writing from this perspective and also in the increased numbers of historical conferences given over to discussion of the subject. Among members of the general public and in the media, moreover, suggestions that modern nations are themselves a product of state formation have recently sparked a debate about other fundamental questions like the characteristics of Englishness or Britishness, and the differences between them – matters that had previously been considered so self-evident as to occasion scarcely any debate.

Recent indications of instability in the modern British state have perhaps served as a reminder about its composite, multinational character and the problematic nature of British identity; but until very recently the historiography of the British Isles had in practice remained resolutely nation-based in character. Following Leopold von Ranke in the nineteenth century, historians were long content to chart the origins of the modern nations within the archipelago, dividing the British Isles into separate national territories, England, Ireland, Scotland and Wales. Thus, for instance, English history charted the growth of the modern English nation, in England, ignoring for the most part those English communities established in medieval Ireland or Wales which – above all because they were not destined to remain English – were the preserve of Irish or Welsh historians. Similarly, Scottish historians focused on those *Gaedhil* and *Gaill* living in Scotland, as Scots in the making, but the similar process of interaction between those *Gaedhil* and *Gaill* living in the Gaelic parts of Ireland and the Englishries there supplied a quite separate story of national development told by Irish historians. Paradoxically, only when the union in its post-1920 form seemed in danger of collapse did British historians begin seriously to address the question of how it had been established and how it actually operated in the first place.

Perhaps a more deep-seated reason for the emergence of the New British history has to do with the phenomenon known as revisionism. Revisionism first emerged in the 1970s, at a time when debates about the concepts of modernity and modernisation in the scientific community were beginning to influence the writing of history. As faith was eroded in such ideas as scientific progress, social and technological development, and civilisation by education, so the notion of history as grand narrative was increasingly challenged. Revisionism marked a reaction to what has been described as 'present-centred' history and a refocusing of the historical agenda on contemporary problems and concerns – history 'as it actually was', so Leopold von Ranke most famously described it. Von Ranke, however, was ultimately responsible for another extremely tenacious assumption of which revisionism was critical, the idea of the rise of the nation and the growth of the nation-state. This idea reflected his belief that nations were the divinely appointed unit at work in history and that each nation had its own appointed moment of destiny. Thus the initial impact of revisionism was to challenge traditional perspectives on the rise of four modern nations in the archipelago.

In this context, the crucial revisions were to English history, since England was the dominant and historically best-documented of the four nations. In particular, English revisionism sought to challenge the grand narrative known as Whig history, viz. an interpretation of the English past which served to validate a set of present-day political beliefs and goals, notably a belief in England's natural progress towards liberty and prosperity, together with the assumption that English history was quite unique, its main

patterns of development owing nothing to outside influences. Contemporary developments, particularly Britain's membership of the European Union and EU initiatives
towards closer economic and political integration, have also seemed to undermine this
English grand narrative, transposing England from its dominant position in the British
Isles to the periphery of an expanding Europe. Moreover, the revisionist shift from vert-
ical to horizontal presentations of history has meant that critiques of exceptionalism
(and a renewed interest in comparative history) have also been a feature of revisionist-
style writings in the other national historical accounts. Yet English revisionism was
also critical of the formerly dominant social interpretation of the English Civil War as a
proto-modern event, one of the bourgeois revolutions that, by overthrowing feudalism
and advancing socialism, ushered in the modern world. Again, events in eastern Europe
since the mid-1980s have likewise seemed to discredit these Marxist perspectives.

For all these reasons, traditional nation-centred perspectives on the British past have
no longer seemed quite so convincing in recent years. Yet the step from nation-based
history to an alternative view based on New British perspectives was by no means
obvious. Once again, European developments have been influential in pointing the way.
Partly this reflects the decline of the nation-state, at least in western Europe, even
though in eastern Europe the disintegration of the Soviet Union and Yugoslavia have
seemed to reverse this trend. Perhaps more important historiographically, however,
has been the influence of continental European historians, particularly given the renewed
interest in comparative history which followed the revisionist emphasis on problems
and perspectives as they appeared to contemporaries. Although, allegedly, the nation
achieved modernity in the nation-state, the typical political entity of the pre-modern
period was in fact the composite monarchy, viz. monarchies ruling territories with more
than one people and culture, and originally distinct kingdoms and principalities with
a common king. In other European historiographies a state-centred approach had in
practice long been common currency, despite the continued preoccupation here with
nations rising. For instance, the work of British-based continental specialists on
European composite states and multiple monarchies offered convenient models with
which the Anglo-Norman empire or the Tudor–Stuart kingdoms might be compared.
The problems surrounding the Habsburg monarchy, Denmark–Norway, or the Polish–
Lithuanian commonwealth might not exactly match the British kingdoms, but they
underlined the point that pre-modern states were frequently composite and multinational. Thus, for instance, once revisionism had undermined social-change explanations
of the English Civil War, a European-style three-kingdom approach supplied an obvious alternative, and in point of fact royal authority did collapse first in the Scottish and
Irish kingdoms of the British multiple monarchy. Moreover, English revisionists soon
discovered that, besides offering a new perspective on the Civil War, analyses of the
British kingdoms as a multiple monarchy had other applications, notably in terms of
charting both the origins of empire and also of the modern British state.

The discovery of the New British history thus promised a quite radical revision of the
historical agenda, particularly in terms of periodisation, which is only now being gradually worked out. For instance, in a British context, 1066 was chiefly important because it
inaugurated a period of expansion which saw the transformation of the Anglo-Saxon
kingdom over the following 250 years into a multinational entity covering large parts of

Ireland, Scotland and Wales and in which the English kingdom was also closely linked to French territories, latterly as a dual monarchy. In this context, too, the collapse of the Anglo-French dual monarchy (1449–53) seems more of a watershed than the advent of the Tudor dynasty in 1485. The Anglo-Scottish diplomatic realignments of 1558–60 created for the first time a British state system: even though 1603 remains important, this was more for the Anglo-Scottish dynastic union heralded by these realignments, together with the completion of the Tudor conquest of Ireland, than for the replacement of a Tudor by a Stuart on the English throne. Similarly, the high points in the Stuart century were not so much the successive political crises between king and parliament as the various union projects and proposals that prefigured 1707, notably the 1652 Cromwellian union. And in the last century, earlier moves towards the consolidation of a multinational British state have seemed to unravel, first in Ireland and more recently in other Celtic countries. In short, grand narrative has reappeared after a decent interval, but this time the organising principle is state formation rather than nation building. Admittedly, in some respects the New British history appears to mark a retreat from postmodernism, but more by way of highlighting inconvenient facts about the present (partition in Ireland, for instance, and the problematic character of the present United Kingdom of Great Britain and Northern Ireland – to give it its full, but revealingly awkward title) than as a simple reinstatement of modernisation theories. Particularly for the early modern period, the focus on interaction between four nations and three king-doms also includes a strong, characteristically revisionist, comparative dimension. In any event, the new synthesis does, at least, have the merit of explaining how people in Ireland, Scotland and Wales also happen to be part of the modern British state.

The Longman History of the British Isles is a series of four volumes, written by leading British historians, which has been devised specifically with this new perspective in mind. It covers the development of the British Isles over the last millennium, from Norman times to the present. The series will offer a substantial grounding in the subject, an overall interpretation of the period covered, and an assessment of the latest historio-graphical developments. Yet, beyond the requirement that each volume should offer an exposé of the period's main developments in a transnational, archipelagic context, no attempt has been made to impose a 'house style'. The New British history has an obvious political dimension to it, and we are so far at present from achieving a consensus among historians about its strengths and weaknesses that even key terms like 'the British Isles' are contested. Each volume develops its own range of topics as determined by the author. Yet broadly, the aim has been to offer a shorter, interpretative survey, focusing on those areas in which the new approach provides a more obvious departure from traditional histories, rather than to provide a comprehensive account intended to sup-plant the national histories. In addition to the main chapters of narrative and analysis, each volume has an extensive critical apparatus. This includes a glossary of technical terms, numerous maps or illustrations, tables of officials and institutions, a critical guide to further reading, and a full index. It is hoped that these aids may also prove useful to those more familiar with the subject.

Steven G. Ellis

INTRODUCTION
The British problem

A s he set out to write the twentieth-century volume of the canonical *Oxford History of England*, A.J.P. Taylor encountered a conceptual and organisational puzzle: 'Ireland, Scotland and Wales all raised problems,' he recalled, 'for a series officially dedicated to the history of England. No previous contributor to the series had thought of this difficulty nor had G.N. Clark, the editor. Somehow I sorted it out: the lesser breeds were allowed in when they made a difference in English affairs as they often did.'[1] As a brief flick through the contents tables of the earlier volumes confirms, Taylor's dilemma – and his solution – was not quite the discovery he claimed. Clark's own volume *The Later Stuarts* had chapters entitled 'Relations with Ireland' and 'Relations with Scotland'. Other contributors, though not all of them, had chapters on 'Scotland and Ireland' (though not Wales) or on 'The Celtic Fringe'. That marginalisation of the other nations, on the 'fringe' or periphery, reflects certain hard historical and political facts. The peoples of these islands have shared histories; but they have not shared these equally. Introducing his long poem 'Cromwell', Brendan Kennelly observes that 'because of history, an Irish poet, to realize himself, must turn the full attention of his imagination to the English tradition. An English poet committed to the same task need hardly give the smallest thought to things Irish.'[2] In short, the histories of early modern Scotland, Ireland and Wales would be unintelligible without reference to their larger neighbour. English history on the other hand, is more obviously – though not entirely – self-contained. Even the most intellectually compelling advocate of 'multicultural' and 'pluralist' British history concedes that England remained the locus of 'the effective determinants of power' within these islands.[3] Thus, just as English poets may safely ignore the Irish literary inheritance, English historians of the eighteenth century can, by and large, neglect Scotland after 1707. They can, but they should not. The lesser breeds, after all, did not merely make 'a difference in English affairs'; in a variety of ways they also helped shape 'the state structure' which provides 'the core of the institutional story' of these islands.[4]

English dominance rested, in the first instance, on economic power. Access to English and colonial markets played a pivotal role in 'selling' a union to the Scots in 1707. Conversely, English (after 1707, British) mercantilist restrictions on Irish exports fuelled Irish 'patriot' resentment throughout the eighteenth century. Demography also helps to explain England's preeminent position within these islands. Precise figures are notoriously difficult to pin down, of course, but the outlines are clear enough. During the seventeenth century the English population rose from around four million to five million, in Ireland it doubled from one million to two million and in Scotland it hung around the one million mark. The population of Wales did not cross the half million threshold until after 1750. By the end of this period – 1800 – England had over eight million, Ireland almost four and a half million and Scotland just over one and a half million inhabitants.[5] Finally, before reading the documents or examining the statistics, the careful historian will do well to look at the map. Core-and-periphery relationships are spatial as well as economic, political and cultural. The so-called 'Celtic Fringe' pre-supposes an English 'centre' and uneven development is often, among other things, a function of distance, of physical remoteness. It is no accident that the Gaelic and Welsh languages held out longest against the relentless march of English in the Highlands and western edges of these islands. The same holds for Basque and Catalan in relation to Spanish or Breton in relation to French.

The technical and conceptual challenges entailed in constructing a more integrated, or even a more synchronised, history of the British Isles are formidable, begin with the lack of an agreed terminology, and mount as the untidy conglomerate which became the United Kingdom of Great Britain and Ireland resists all ready-made classification. The very term 'British' is part of the problem, particularly in respect of Ireland. In Ireland in the late seventeenth and early eighteenth centuries it might denote Protestants of English and Scottish extraction, or, more narrowly, the Ulster Scots; it never extended to the 'native' Catholic population. By the late eighteenth century many Scots had come to embrace the term 'North Britons' with some enthusiasm, but at the time of the union in 1707 just as many, perhaps, rejected the name. South of the border, little Englander self-regard, Scotophobia, Paddywackery and 'Taffy'-baiting remained as robust as ever.[6] Only to the Welsh, the descendants, as they saw it, of the 'ancient Britons', did the concept of Britishness seem comparatively unproblematic. Partly with predictable Irish scepticism in mind, J.G.A. Pocock floated the idea of an 'Atlantic archipelago' as an in-offensive alternative to the 'Britain Isles'.[7] However, though value-free and geographic-ally precise, the term is too anachronistic, too much an historian's coinage, and to date shows little sign of catching on. Hugh Kearney proposes 'Britannic', but that too is open to similar objections, even if the seventeenth-century English historian, Laurence Echard, claimed that Ireland was known to the Romans as Britannia Minor.[8] The 'long eighteenth century' is the crucial period for the formation of British identities. But, although senses of Britishness did take hold, these never won universal acceptance or completely supplanted older national and regional allegiances. Indeed the British problem may be conceived in terms of the resilience of cultural self-identification within the so-called Celtic Fringe. Britishness, in other words, can be viewed as a construct or fiction which failed, ultimately, to absorb or homogenise the Scots or Irish, just as 'Spanishness' failed to integrate fully the Basques or Catalans.

The issue of which conceptual framework best integrates the histories of the multi-national British polity is equally unlikely to be settled to everyone's satisfaction. Kingdoms (unitary, multiple and composite), colonies (functional, *de facto* and *de jure*), provinces, regions, peripheries, nations (real or imagined), states (confessional, modernising or *ancien régime*), societies and empires overlap and jostle for the beleaguered – or bewildered – historian's attention. While remaining alert to the various conceptualisations of the relationships in which these islands have been imbricated, and proceeding from the premise that there are processes at work here 'whose history can and should be studied',[9] this book does not offer any sort of 'total history' of Britain and Ireland in the long eighteenth century. Rather, beginning with the restoration of the monarchy in the three kingdoms in 1660, it attends to certain themes, events and institutions which, it is argued, are better understood when restored to their 'British'-wide 'forgotten contexts'.[10] These include the Restoration itself; the intersections between politics and religion; identity formation, national and supranational; and constitutional relations between the three kingdoms, with particular reference to the two acts of union in 1707 and 1800.

Chapters 1 and 2 examine the Restoration and the political and ecclesiastical settlements that followed in some detail: first, because the three-kingdom dynamics of the Restoration crisis serves as a kind of case study for these islands' history; and in that significant case at least it soon becomes apparent that an anglocentric approach simply will not do. Second, the Restoration and Restoration settlements are treated in such detail because, as much as the revolution settlements of 1689–91, the political and ecclesiastical arrangements of 1660–62 shaped the structures of governance and experience in Britain and Ireland for well over a century. Thus in both English and Irish history, for example, scholars are pushing back the beginning of the 'long eighteenth century' to 1660.[11] Nothing illustrates the foundational character of that year better perhaps than the history of religion. After the proliferation of Protestant sects during the interregnum, the re-establishment of the Church of England, and of the episcopal churches in Ireland and Scotland, had enormous legal and political consequences. At the level of official theory, and in many ways in practice, Church and state interpenetrated and throughout this period confessional affiliation continued to shape politics, to define the legal status of individuals and groups, especially Catholics, and to undergird senses of identity. In fact it might be argued that the legal and political centrality of the 'Church by law established' places it alongside the English monarchy at the 'core of the institutional story of the state structure' which J.M. Roberts sees running, like a spine, through the histories of these islands.[12]

Chapters 3 and 4 explore the interactions of politics and religion during the Restoration era. In Chapter 3 we see how the ecclesiastical settlement of 1660–62 not only excluded Protestant Nonconformists from the state Church, but backed them into political opposition as well. This is true of all three kingdoms, but the scale and intensity of conflict varied. Thousands of Dissenters, notably English Quakers, suffered imprisonment, but nothing in the English or Irish experience compared to the resistance of the Covenanters or to the ferocity of the 'Killing Times' in Scotland. Chapter 4 treats another special case in the annals of religious strife: the Catholic Question. Again the power of religion to shape and even to define politics is demonstrated, as wave upon wave of anti-popery swept the ruling elites and Protestant populations of the three kingdoms.

After the constitutional experiment with union during the mostly unlamented interregnum, England, Scotland and Ireland were restored to their pre-1649 status as distinct kingdoms under the one king (but not, importantly, under the one 'crown'). Chapter 5 examines constitutional relationships between England and Ireland and between England and Scotland, and how they changed. Both of 'John Bull's other kingdoms' were drawn into tighter central, London-based, control: Ireland by the imposition, increasingly marked after 1688, of Westminster legislation; Scotland in 1707 by legislative union. However, closer political integration was not accompanied by uniform cultural assimilation or anglicisation. Like religious conflict, constitutional dispute between the constituent kingdoms of the late Stuart composite monarchy were intimately connected to issues of identity. Chapter 6 turns to a phenomenon in which the themes addressed in this book – constitutions, identities and religion – converge. Jacobitism posed the single biggest threat to the revolution settlement (1688–91), the union, the British state and the Hanoverian succession (1714) in the eighteenth century; and, although in one respect it was an anti-British movement – it sought to dismantle the union – in a geographical sense its British-wide credentials are beyond question. Jacobite sentiment and Jacobite organisation were present to varying degrees in Wales, England, Ireland and, above all, Scotland. And in each country, moreover, the traditional bases of support for the pretender had a nationalist and confessional – Catholic and episcopal – complexion.

Jacobite dynastic nationalism failed both to oust the House of Hanover and to undo the British state. Chapter 7 looks at a partial 'success story': the consolidation of the British state and the fabrication of a British identity. 'Success' was not only partial, as in Scotland and Wales, but uneven. In *Britons*[13] Linda Colley simply evades the problem of Irish exceptionalism; and avoidance, perhaps, is the wisest strategy! Nevertheless, it is argued here that by the last quarter of the eighteenth century 'Britishness' did represent something more than a pious fiction. Senses of identity, to be sure, were complicated. For instance, after 1707 English politicians continued unselfconsciously to conflate the British with the 'English' parliament, or government, or king; and yet by this time certain structures and institutions, such as the army and the empire, can only be described as British.

Colley's decision to exclude Ireland from her analysis in *Britons* stemmed from the crucial role she assigns to Protestantism in her account of British identity formation. The evidence for the overtly Protestant dimension of the British project is indeed substantial, but recent work on religion and identity in eighteenth-century Britain has tended to emphasise the diversity of Protestantism, and hence its potential to divide politically, rather than, as Colley stresses, its capacity to unite.[14] Chapter 8 offers an account of religion and politics in the eighteenth century which likewise focuses on the varieties of Protestantism, as well as the mixed fortunes of Catholics in a Protestant state. The 'Catholic Question', of course, loomed largest in Ireland, but the political potency of anti-popery in Britain should never be underestimated. London's anti-Catholic Gordon riots in 1780 underlined spectacularly the continuing vitality in this period of sectarian categories inherited from the sixteenth and seventeenth centuries.

The explosive passions detonated in Scotland and England in 1778–80 by the attempt – sponsored in parliament by Edmund Burke – to repeal some of the anti-Catholic penal laws anticipated the 'No Popery' general election of 1807 and the political crisis provoked by the Catholic emancipation in the late 1820s. It was the Act of Union, between Great Britain and Ireland, which came into force on 1 January 1801, that forced the Catholic Question back to the forefront of British politics. Chapter 9 examines how that fateful union came about, both in its long-term intellectual, and in its more immediate political, contexts. The architects of the union hoped to resolve finally one of the great political problems of the age, rooted, like many of the problems in

1660, in issues of religion. Irish Catholics, they believed, might safely be admitted to [x v] near-full political rights within the framework of a United Kingdom parliament with a guaranteed Protestant majority. It was not to be. The plan to accompany union with Catholic emancipation was scuppered by the 'king's friends' in Ireland, led by the Earl of Clare, and by the king himself. Protestant Ireland's Catholic Question became Britain's Irish Question. Thus, with the Scots and Welsh by and large at ease with their British identity Ireland in 1801 had become the British problem.

Notes

1. Taylor, A.J.P., 1985, *A Personal History*, London, 302.

2. Kennelly, B., 1987, *Cromwell*, Newcastle, vi.

3. Pocock, J.G.A., 1982, 'The limits and divisions of British history: in search of the unknown subject', *American Historical Review*, 87: 2, 313.

4. J.M. Roberts's general editor's preface to Langford, Paul, 1992, *A Polite and Commercial People: England 1727–1783*, Oxford.

5. These figures are drawn mainly from Wrigley, E.A. and Schofield, R.S., 1981, *The Population History of England, 1541–1871: A Reconstruction*, Cambridge, Mass.; Daultrey, Stuart, Dickson, David and O'Grada, Cormac, 1982, 'Hearth tax, household size and Irish population change, 1672–1850', *Proceedings of the Royal Irish Academy* C, 82/6; and Smout, T.C., 1969, *A History of the Scottish People, 1560–1830*, London.

6. See the section on 'English nationalism and the Celt' in Langford, *Polite and Commercial People*, 323–9.

7. Pocock, 'Limits and divisions of British history', 318.

8. Kearney, Hugh, 1989, *The British Isles: A History of Four Nations*, Cambridge; Echard, Laurence, 1691, *An Exact Description of Ireland*, London, 1.

9. Pocock, 'Limits and divisions of British history', 317.

10. The phrase is J.C.D. Clark's: 1989, 'English history's forgotten contexts', *HJ*, 32.

11. For example, Dickson, David, 1987, 1999, *New Foundations: Ireland 1660–1800*, Dublin; the edition of J.C.D. Clark's *English Society*, Cambridge, 1985, starts at 1688, the second edition – 2000 – at 1660.

12. See note 4.

13. Colley, Linda, 1992, *Britons: Forging the Nation 1714–1837*, New Haven and London.

14. Many of the essays in Clayton, Tony and McBride, Ian (eds) 1998, *Protestantism and National Identity: Britain and Ireland c. 1650–c. 1850*, Cambridge, can be read as either explicit or implicit critiques of the Colley thesis.

ACKNOWLEDGEMENTS

The origins of this book are in teaching. My interest in 'British' history was deepened by teaching the 'British Problem' course at Cambridge in the early 1990s. My colleagues, Brendan Bradshaw, John Morrill and David Smith brought a sense of intellectual energy and engagement to that task which has stayed with me. I would also like to thank another pioneer in British history, Steven Ellis, Editor of the 'Four Nations' series, for staying on during the preparation of this book long after it was reasonable to expect. The Paul M. and Barbara Henkels Fund of the Institute for Scholarship and Liberal Arts at the University of Notre Dame generously financed part of the research, for which I am grateful. Stephen Smyth and Katie Keogh helped enormously with my usual computer problems. Jonathan Clark, James McGuire and Jonathan Steinberg read all or part of the manuscript and offered many perceptive comments and suggestions. I am in all of their debts. I am also in the debt of the staff at the National Library of Scotland, the National Library of Ireland, the Bodleian Library, University of Oxford and Cambridge University Library where most of my research was conducted.

I am Irish. My wife, Mary, is a Scot. Our children, Michael and Eilis, were born in England. They now live in America, and have attended school in Dublin. The University of Notre Dame's football team, many of whose players are African-American, is nicknamed 'The Fighting Irish'. Questions of 'national' identity, which I explore in this book, endure.

The publishers are grateful to the following for permission to reproduce copyright material:

Map 1 redrawn from *Atlas of Irish History*, published and reprinted by permission of Gill and Macmillan Ltd (Duffy, S. 1997); Map 2 adapted from Map 2 and Map 3 from *Jacobitism and the English People*, published and reprinted by permission of Cambridge University Press (Monod, P. K. 1989).

LIST OF ABBREVIATIONS

Bodl.	Bodleian Library, Oxford
Cal. S.P. (dom.)	*Calendar of State Papers (Domestic)*
Cal. S.P. (Ire.)	*Calendar of State Papers (Ireland)*
CUL	Cambridge University Library
EHR	*English Historical Review*
HJ	*Historical Journal*
HMC	*Historical Manuscripts Commission*
IHS	*Irish Historical Studies*
NLI	National Library of Ireland
NLS	National Library of Scotland
PRONI	Public Record Office of Northern Ireland
P&P	*Past and Present*
SHR	*Scottish Historical Review*
SHS	Scottish Historical Society

LIST OF ILLUSTRATIONS

MAPS

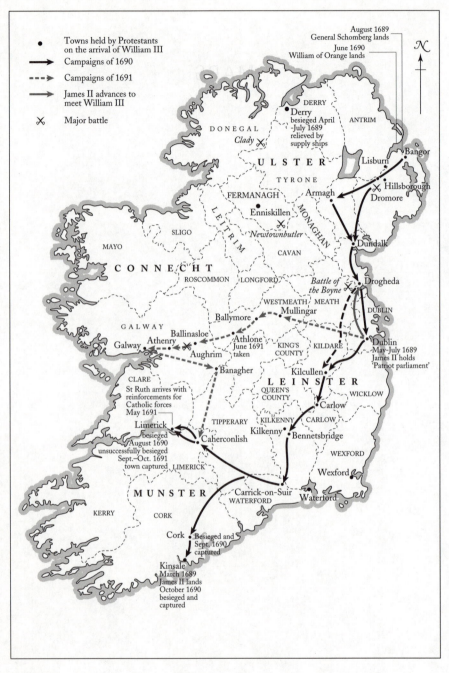

Towns held by Protestants on the arrival of William III

Campaigns of 1690

Campaigns of 1691

James II advances to meet William III

✕ Major battle

August 1689
General Schomberg lands

June 1690
William of Orange lands

N

DERRY

Derry besieged April –July 1689 relieved by supply ships

DONEGAL

Clady ✕

ANTRIM

Bangor

Lisburn

✕ Hillsborough

Dromore

U L S T E R

T Y R O N E

FERMANAGH

Armagh

MONAGHAN

Dundalk

Enniskillen

Newtownbutler

CAVAN

LEITRIM

SLIGO

MAYO

C O N N E C H T

ROSCOMMON

LONGFORD

Battle of the Boyne ✕

Drogheda

WESTMEATH

MEATH

DUBLIN

Ballymore

Mullingar

Dublin
May–July 1689
James II holds
'Patriot parliament'

GALWAY

Ballinasloe

Athenry

Galway

Athlone
June 1691
taken

KING'S COUNTY

KILDARE

Aughrim ✕

Banagher

Kilcullen

L E I N S T E R

CLARE

St Ruth arrives with reinforcements for Catholic forces May 1691

QUEEN'S COUNTY

WICKLOW

Carlow

TIPPERARY

Caherconlish

KILKENNY

Kilkenny

CARLOW

Bennetsbridge

Limerick
besieged August 1690 unsuccessfully besieged Sept.–Oct. 1691 town captured

LIMERICK

WEXFORD

Wexford

M U N S T E R

Carrick-on-Suir

WATERFORD

Waterford

KERRY

CORK

Cork
Besieged and Sept. 1690 captured

Kinsale
March 1689
James II lands
October 1690
besieged and captured

Map 1
The Williamite War in Ireland, 1689–91

- ○ Oxford   Riot on 29 May 1715
- **London**   Riot or demonstration, 29 May and 10 June 1715
- Leeds   Riot or demonstration, 10 June 1715

N

Oldham
Blackley
Eccles   Failsworth
Stand   Manchester
Platt

Congleton
Leek
Newcastle-under-Lyme
Stone   Uttoxeter
Stafford   Burton-on-Trent
Lichfield
Wolverhampton   Walsall
Kingswinford   West Bromwich
  Oldbury
Dudley   Birminghman
Halesowen
Stourbridge   King's Norton
Worcester

Leeds
Manchester
Warrington   Sheffield
Congleton
Wrexham
Whitchurch
Wem   Stamford   Norwich
Shrewsbury   Peterborough
Bridgnorth   Nuneaton
Cleobury Mortimer   Cambridge
Worcester
Gloucester   Oxford
London
Bristol
Bath   Marlborough
Norton St Phillip
Yeovil

Map 2

Anti-Hanoverian riots and demonstrations in England, May to August, 1715.

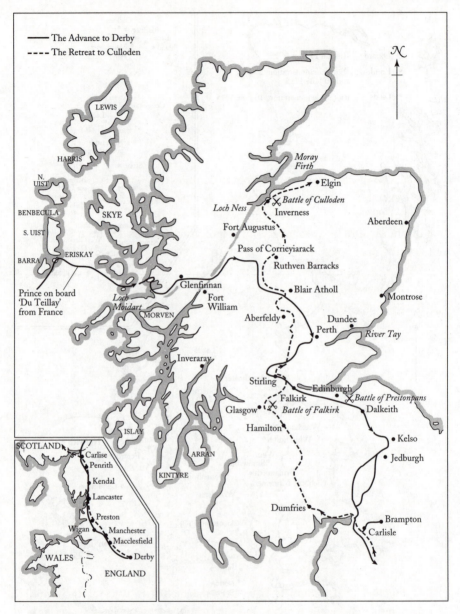

Map 3
The Jacobite campaign in Scotland and England, 1745–46
Source: Redrawn from Maclean (1989)

THE RESTORATION
Four nations in search of a king

On 28 December 1659 – days before crossing the border into England – General George Monck's army was encamped at the Scottish village of Coldstream when Captain John Campbell arrived from Ireland. He brought good news. On 13 December a group of army officers, supported by Sir Charles Coote in Connaught and by Lord Broghill in Munster, had seized Dublin Castle and declared for Parliament. Monck marked the occasion by ordering the discharge of the 'great guns' at Berwick and by holding a day of prayer in thanksgiving. Campbell then returned to Dublin carrying a request from the general for reinforcements. Six regiments of foot marched into Ulster for embarkation to Scotland, but in the event they were not needed.[1]

At the close of 1659 the fate of the 'four nations' hung in the balance. Over twenty years had passed since the great crisis, detonated in 1637 by Charles I's attempt to impose the English prayer-book upon the Scots, had plunged the three kingdoms first into war, then into unprecedented constitutional innovation.[2] The English civil wars, 1642–49, culminated in the victory of the parliamentary forces and the New Model Army under the command of Oliver Cromwell, the execution of Charles on 31 January 1649, and the declaration of an English republic, whose jurisdiction extended *de jure*, if not yet in fact, to Ireland. Scotland was another matter, and while the English parliament was prepared to execute the king of Scotland, the Act for 'abolishing the kingly office of England and Ireland' omitted reference to the Scottish crown.[3] Civil wars and wars of religion also raged in Ireland and Scotland during the 1640s and so interpenetrated with events in England, that together these conflicts have been labelled 'the wars of the three kingdoms'.[4] Thus while regicide and the creation of a republic settled affairs in England – for the time being – conflict in Ireland and Scotland was only resolved by English military conquest. Cromwell's Godly regime could not allow the persistence of an armed Catholic threat on England's western flank, nor, after the Scots had crowned Charles II as a covenanted king in 1650, could it permit a Stuart on the throne north of the border. Political

[2] union followed military subjugation and during the 1650s 'Irish' and 'Scottish' MPs (who were often in fact English) sat in the London parliaments. But, by the time Cromwell died in 1658 the fragility of this startling new political dispensation – the abolition of monarchy, the disestablishment of the Church, greater religious pluralism, the maintenance of a standing army and union – soon became apparent. Equally apparently, there was no consensus about what should replace the Cromwellian Protectorate. Monck forced the issue by breaking rank with his fellow generals in defence of parliament's authority. However, the big questions remained unanswered: who would rule? What form would a new government take? And, most importantly perhaps, how would that government be legitimated?

Monck's request for extra troops on 28 December was wholly characteristic. He was nothing if not cautious. By maintaining allegiance to the expelled parliament – the so-called 'Rump' – the previous October, he had split the army and threatened to precipitate a 'fourth civil war'. But, rather than rush into confrontation with his erstwhile comrades, he played for time. Exploiting skilfully the English army's reluctance to fight by opening negotiations and thereby keeping alive hopes of compromise, he meanwhile purged the regiments under his command of politically suspect officers, and used the time to woo the support of the Scottish political nation. The longer he stalled, the further the balance of forces shifted in his favour. Now the turn of events in Ireland vindicated these delaying tactics. The Irish officers had at first remained neutral between Monck and Generals Lambert and Fleetwood, on the grounds that an army divided against itself would let in the common royalist enemy. Their offer of support, contained in Captain Campbell's letter, gave Monck a decisive advantage: taken together the armies of Scotland and Ireland actually outnumbered the army in England.[5] What is more, Monck could by then also count on the support of the fleet under Vice-Admiral Lawson, of the garrison at Portsmouth and of General Fairfax – 'retired', but with a formidable local power base in Yorkshire.

Still he proceeded with caution. He wrote to the officers of the Irish brigade stationed in the north of England. Consisting of 1,000 foot and 500 horse, the brigade, drafted in August to help quell Colonel Booth's royalist uprising, had served under Lambert in Cheshire. Whose side would they now take? After appealing to them to join him in his 'just undertaking', Monck warned of the consequences of their not doing so:

> [of] this you may be assured, that unless you join with me in defence of the parliament, though you should conquer this army, yet you must be necessitated

to fight once more for your interests in Ireland . . . join with me, you shall be
heartily welcome . . . and all your interests in Ireland secured.[6]

Some Irish brigaders, such as Colonel Zanchey and the regicide, Colonel Axtell, stuck by Lambert; most defected to Monck. One, Major Godfrey, assisted Fairfax in the occupation of York city on 1 January; another, the brigade commander, Daniel Redmond, was afterwards knighted by Charles II for services rendered during the crisis.[7]

Facing superior forces and encirclement, psychological attrition and growing political isolation, the morale of Lambert's troops cracked. The English army drawn up at Newcastle disintegrated. Monck marched south unopposed. The restoration of monarchy, if not, even at that late stage, intended, was now perhaps inevitable.

Polycentric, rather than anglocentric, British history clearly works better – offers more useful and appropriate perspectives – for some periods, events or phenomena than for others. The Restoration is one of those events. The entire crisis, from Monck's refusal to endorse his fellow generals' expulsion of the Rump Parliament in October 1659, until Charles Stuart's arrival at Dover in May 1660, can be viewed as a successful revolt of the peripheries against the centre. Similarly, the leading actor in the complex and protracted endgame which brought back monarchy is best understood in a 'four nations' context.

Born in Devonshire, George Monck fought for the king against parliament in England and for parliament against the Confederate Catholics in Ireland, where he soldiered with Sir Charles Coote. He campaigned in Scotland in the early 1650s and later helped to govern it with Broghill. As a land grantee of the Cromwellian settlement, with an agent in Wexford and a cousin, Cornet Henry Monck, stationed in Dublin,[8] and as an old associate of many of the leading political and military figures there, Monck was exceptionally well informed about developments in Ireland during the critical winter of 1659–60. His adroit cultivation of the Scottish estates, designed to secure his rear before marching south, displayed a firm grasp – based on experience – of local political realities, as well as sound military strategy. When he reached London, and addressed parliament as its deliverer on 6 February, he urged the members to attend to Scottish and Irish concerns. Silently conflating Wales with England in the style of the time, his correspondence during this period is peppered with references to 'the three nations'. The king, whose return he did so much to bring about, succeeded to three kingdoms.

[4]   The fact that in February Monck singled out Scottish and Irish concerns, the former respecting the Anglo-Scottish union, the latter the uncertain legal status of land confiscations, is instructive. For all the interaction and connections between the nations, the political elites of each confronted different circumstances, had different problems and, as Monck's address shows, different agendas. The fact too, that these distinct Scottish and Irish issues were raised in the English parliament, sitting in London, is equally instructive. The English locus of power in these islands was never more apparent than in the 1650s, when Scotland and Ireland were subject to English military rule. Ultimately, the overturning of the Cromwellian settlement at the peripheries resulted from the collapse of political authority at the centre. It is in England that the story of the Restoration must begin.

In the absence of the institution of kingship the Cromwellian regime was held together by the person of Oliver Cromwell. As Lord Protector his authority rested on his personal prestige with the army. But prestige, unlike crowns, cannot be inherited and so, when he died on 3 September 1658, the regime did not long survive his passing. While his son, Richard, became Lord Protector, political power shifted, ever more nakedly, to the army. Neither the army nor Richard, however, was able to solve the problem of legitimacy or settle upon an agreed form of government. In addition to bringing the army back to the forefront of politics, the uncertainties unleashed by Cromwell's death stimulated revivals of religious and political 'radicalism'.[9] During 1659 'Anabaptists', Quakers and the Godly of all sorts assumed more visible profiles in public life, particularly and significantly in the ranks of the army, 'a battle-axe in the hands of the lord'.[10] The anti-Protectorate republican, or commonwealth, minority formed a vocal and assertive opposition to the 'court' in Richard's parliament.[11]

On 22 April Richard's Parliament, the 'civil authority', was dismissed by the army, which then took effective – but as soon became clear, precarious – control. A bewildering sequence of events followed: the recall (in May) and expulsion (in October) of the Rump, royalist plots and political divisions within the army, the recall (at the end of December) of the Rump for the second time, the readmission (on 20 February 1660) of the 'secluded members' – those so-called moderates purged in 1648, and the final dissolution (on 16 March), of the Long Parliament, military coups and attempted counter-coups in Dublin, popular unrest on the streets of London. . . . The overall effect of those events, of what Milton called this 'strange aftergame of folly',[12] are not hard to discern. The alternation of formal authority between the army and the Rump together with the resurgence of the religious 'radicals' had an enormous destabilising impact on British society and politics. Two great fears, of instability – or anarchy – and of religious 'fanaticism', fuelled an inexorable anti-republican reaction, and helped to shape the eventual settlement in Church and state. It is important to remember, too, that the adherents of the 'Good Old Cause' were a (shrinking) minority; that John Evelyn's *Apology for the Royalist Party*, which foreshadowed the post-Restoration crack-down on the sectaries, almost certainly reflected public opinion more closely than John Milton's coruscating assault on kingship, *The Readie and Easie Way to Establish a Free Commonwealth*.

No sequence of events is more richly endowed with those 'decisive turning points' so beloved of historians than that which led to the restoration of Charles Stuart. One such juncture was Monck's fateful decision to oppose his fellow generals and to uphold the authority of the Rump. From that point onwards he became the key player in the unfolding drama. The second recall of the Rump, the readmission of the secluded members, who voted to dissolve the Long Parliament, the election of a Convention Parliament and finally, and certainly not least, the unconditional character of the Convention Parliament's invitation to Charles, all owed much, if not all, to Monck's interventions.

In retrospect the step-by-step stages by which the Restoration came about seem to possess a coherence and a logic that lend the entire episode an aura of inevitability, and this, in turn, has led some historians to conclude that, from start to finish, Monck planned and orchestrated the whole thing.[13] But that is to credit the general with implausible qualities of foresight and consistency of purpose. It is more likely that his actions – and masterly inaction – were improvisations in response to rapidly changing circumstances. In so far as they can ever be determined, Monck's actual motives are more interesting, because emblematic of wider public anxieties, than the single-minded covert royalism of 'radical' accusation and post-Restoration legend.

Preeminently a professional soldier, he believed that soldiers should obey the civil power and not, ironically, meddle in politics. Thus, whatever his views on the content of the Derby petition – effectively an ultimatum – presented by army officers to the Rump Parliament may have been, Monck disapproved of armies petitioning parliaments *per se*. Generals Fleetwood and Lambert should not have been overly surprised, then, when after they had 'interrupted' parliament in October 1659, the commander-in-chief in Scotland refused to comply with their action, insisting instead that they had dangerously exceeded their legitimate authority. Monck had no love for the Rump. Behind his intervention on its behalf lay deeper concerns for stable

[6]   government and public order. He had, for example, like Broghill, another former royalist and an important Irish ally in the months ahead, earlier supported the kingship petition offering Cromwell the throne. Now the political turmoil caused by the army's actions and by the re-emergence of the religious 'fanatics', not least within the ranks of the army, prompted Monck to take a stand, and others to follow suit.

The general's hostility towards the sects was well founded, shared by many of his contemporaries, and reciprocated. The Anabaptist and Quaker officers imposed upon the army in Scotland during the summer of 1659 constituted the bulk of the political unreliables purged between October and December. Edmund Ludlow had conducted a parallel remodelling of the army in Ireland that summer, to the extent that it became identified as a refuge for the republican and the Godly. These new Irish officers reacted with fury to the Scottish purge, it being 'impossible to believe how most shamefully these A[na] B[aptists] do reproach my Lord General Monck, saying that he intends to bring in the king of Scotts, and that he hath put out all the Godly'. On 3 November Henry Monck reported from Dublin that while the Irish army remained neutral 'all that are inclinable to Anabaptism do declare against the parliament'.[14] In England the leading Quakers George Bishop, Anthony Pearson, Isaac Pennington and George Fox the younger, all sided with the army against the Rump. Not for nothing did the printed propaganda, the pamphlets and newsletter circulated among Monck's troops attack the sects as it invoked the justice of parliament's cause.[15]

The spectre that haunted men like Monck, Fairfax, Broghill and Coote was 'social' as well as religious. To the men of property religious fanaticism, 'levelling', licence and disorder were inextricably linked. The lessons of recent experience, when Ranters and Diggers had, it seemed, almost turned the world upside down, were not lightly discarded. Public order, security and political stability were imperatives which surfaced at each turn of events, driving them on in a definite direction; if not towards monarchy and episcopacy, then certainly towards strong government in Church and state, and even the reintroduction of 'a single person'.

The public order problem presented Monck with a particular dilemma in Scotland. Under the Cromwellian regime Scotland was garrisoned and more closely policed than at any time in its history, leading one English defender of the union to boast that it was now possible, as never before, for a man to travel the length of the country unmolested with £100 in his pocket.[16] Monck's projected march south therefore ran huge risks in terms of local policing. When he met the representatives of the Scottish nobility, gentry and burghs summoned to Edinburgh on 15 November, he enjoined them to keep the peace in the shires, and to desist from communicating with the party of Charles Stuart. The Scots, in turn, wished to arm, specifying the danger of 'highland raids'. The general, as ever, proved cautious. While he needed the Scots' goodwill, he remained alert to the threat of a national or royalist uprising. Scotland was bitterly divided, it was true, between 'Protestors' or 'Remonstrants' who were republican, anti-covenanting 'Malignants' who were royalist, and 'Resolutioners' who remained committed to a covenanted king. The Protestors, however, were a minority. The majority were pro-Stuart. Arms were issued, but rationed to shires adjacent to the highlands.[17]

The Scots also faced constitutional uncertainties. Whereas Scotland, or at any rate the English interest and English army in Scotland, had been represented in the Protectorate parliaments, the Rump, recalled in May 1659, was exclusively an English (and Welsh) legislature. As the Protectoral ordinance of union lapsed, it compromised the legal status of judges, magistrates, revenue officers and other officers of the state. Over the coming months no new appointments were made, nor, in contrast to the case of Ireland, were parliamentary commissioners appointed for Scotland. Soundings of Scottish opinion as to the future of the union were taken in late May, but the 'sample' was unrepresentative and the results inconclusive. As James Sharp, the Resolutioner (or moderate Presbyterian) agent in London reported, on the question of union his countrymen 'are not of a mind'. A leading 'Protestor' (or hardline Presbyterian) James Guthrie, even proposed a distinct Scottish republic.[18] A parliamentary committee established in June prevaricated. By October, and the second 'interruption' of the Rump, the constitutional problem remained unresolved.

It is tempting to view these constitutional and legal uncertainties as having a similar unsettling effect upon the propertied and respectable classes as the spectre of disorder and the sectaries resurgent. Significantly, in his speech to parliament on 6 February 1660 Monck called for the implementation of the 'intended union' with Scotland, proportionate taxation and 'a speedy provision of civil government, of which they have been destitute near a year, to the ruin of many families'.[19] Yet according to one modern expert, the impact of this suspended legality was 'greater in theory than in practice'. If magistrates and burgh courts lacked legal authority, they nonetheless continued to function as if nothing had changed. Local government did not collapse, nor did the fabric of the law disintegrate. Indeed Scotland's stability throughout the crisis of 1659–60 testifies not only to

[8] Monck's careful management but to the earlier 'success of English republican rule'.[20]

In Ireland constitutional uncertainty generated more profound anxieties
within the political nation because more was at stake. Monck succinctly
summarised the position in the February speech:

> Ireland is in an ill-settled condition, and made worse by your interruptions,
> which prevented the passing an act for settlement of the estates of adventurers
> and soldiers there, which I heard you intended to have done in a few days;
> and I presume will now quickly be done, being so necessary at this time, when
> the wants of the commonwealth call for supplies: and people will unwillingly
> pay taxes for their estates, of which they have no legal assurance.[21]

Religious issues and forms of government mattered less to the Protestant
community in Ireland than did the urgent need to obtain formal, enforce-
able, ratification of titles to property confiscated under the (legally?) defunct
Protectorate regime. 'Powers have made laws,' declared the Munster officers,
'and subsequent powers disowned and nulled what the preceding powers
had acted; that now the questions are not so many, what is the meaning of
the law, as what is law; whereby that is become a subject of debate, which
formerly was a rule for ending it.'[22] The shape of any new parliament was
less important, that is, than its ability to validate and secure the massive land
transfers of the 1650s.

At first Ireland's Protestants merely reacted to events in England, and in
conjunction with Monck. 'The first part is always acted on the English
stage,' observed the anti-Ludlow officers, and 'the Irish and Scottish nations
are so far influenced thereby, that they become participants more or less in
her peace or war, in her prosperity and adversity.' For his part Ludlow
accused the officers of 'moving not a step without his [Monck's] orders
and directions'.[23] However, events 'off stage' soon gained a momentum of
their own.

As he marched south Monck received numerous addresses calling for
the restoration of the Long Parliament by the readmission of the 'secluded
members' who had been purged in 1648. As 'moderates' who had favoured a
compromise with King Charles I, the readmission of this group could only
bring the restoration of monarchy closer. Monck responded, however, by
damping expectations. He wrote to the gentlemen petitioners of his native
Devon, for example, defending the republic and counselling obedience to
the Rump. At about the same time he urged Broghill to 'discountenance' the
petitions reportedly being framed in support of the secluded members by

their 'eager abettors' in Ireland. Parliament, he advised, had 'given judgement against their readmission' and in favour of filling up its vacancies with new or 'recruiter' members.[24] Monck lagged behind public opinion. Yorkshire, Norfolk, Oxford, Warwickshire, Cheshire and, crucially, the citizens of London, all petitioned for readmission. Yet, despite the unmistakable and 'general defection of the misguided and abus'd multitude'[25] from the Rump, the general, apparently with the power to make or break it, held back.

A declaration of intent composed by James Sharp, and distributed among the soldiers at Coldstream, envisaged 'a free parliament, chosen by the people and protected from violence to settle civil government'.[26] In his address to the Rump five weeks later, Monck accepted its decision on readmission but encouraged its members to increase their number by filling up the vacancies. Monck fell out of step with public opinion because he served two constituencies: 'the people', clamouring for readmission, and the army, more wary, and for good reason. Everyone understood that readmission would bring restoration nearer. Sir Hardress Waller, regicide and nominal commander of the army in Ireland, certainly understood that. 'To bring in a free parliament,' he noted, 'would be to bring in the king; and that to bring in the king would be to endanger his [i.e. Waller's] and all their heads.'[27] Milton, too, foresaw the danger of slipping back into the 'detested thraldom of kingship'.[28] Only the army stood in the way, and that is why the general moved more circumspectly than the political nations: he had to carry the army with him.

In Ireland Waller canvassed his fellow officers to enter an 'engagement' against recalling the secluded members. When the majority refused to subscribe Waller and his supporters took control of Dublin Castle.[29] But for him history repeated itself as farce. The next day, 16 February, Coote and the Dublin-based officers declared for a free parliament, followed two days later by Broghill and the Munster officers and by the city. The garrison bowed to the inevitable, effectively abandoning Waller to his fate and compelling him to surrender. In Yorkshire the county grandees threatened to withhold taxes from the discredited Rump; the streets of London simmered with discontent.[30] Anthony Ashley Cooper and others, using Sharp as go-between, pressed Monck to act. On 21 February the secluded members were readmitted.

Monck promised the returning MPs freedom to transact their business, set out the need for a broadly Presbyterian Church settlement, the payment of soldiers' arrears and so on, and instructed them to issue writs for elections to a new parliament 'to represent the three nations'. The sense that any

[1 0]   settlement a future parliament might effect concerned all three nations and not merely England, reflected the general's recent experience and drew on the precedent of the Cromwellian union. The Long Parliament, now instructed to dissolve itself, represented England and Wales only, whereas the successor Convention Parliament would, according to the original instruction, be based on the Protectorate constituencies of 1654, including thirty seats each for Scotland and Ireland. However, it is difficult, as so often, to ascertain Monck's intentions because elections to the Convention Parliament proceeded in England and Wales alone.

Scots were divided on the desirability of maintaining the union. At a convention of the burghs and, meeting separately, the shires, held in Edinburgh in February, delegates drew up a list of grievances for the consideration of parliament. These dealt with mainly economic and practical affairs, such as levels of taxation and the quartering of troops, but one proposed that 'a way should be found for uniting the nations', with the retention of Scottish law. The union clause emerged from the burghs, which seems to indicate that the merchant interest had benefited from free trade. The union had generally benefited the Protestors too, by underwriting their uncompromising stance, and it is not surprising that the Protestor and republican, Johnston of Warriston, wanted Scotland represented at the forthcoming parliament. The shires, on the other hand, objected to the union clause, and when the convention agent, William Thompson, travelled to London union did not figure in his brief.

That silence represented a victory for the nobility and for the Resolutioners. An 'independent' Scotland would afford the nobility its best chance of reasserting its traditional authority and, so the Resolutioners thought, of securing an orthodox, and national, Presbyterian Church.[31] The evidence suggests, though, that purely Scottish considerations already counted for little with Monck. English attitudes to Anglo-Scottish relations were brutally pragmatic, and Monck, as Sharp noted, was surrounded by English advisers. As Sharp also noted, the English would 'either incorporate, or make us distinct, as they should find most serviceable to their interest'. Presumably then the union was no longer deemed serviceable because Monck effectively dissolved it by excluding the Scots from the Convention Parliament.[32]

If for the Protestant community in Ireland the defence of the land settlement took precedence over politics or religion, for the Scottish elites constitutional relations and even the economy mattered less, perhaps, than the Kirk. Sharp arrived in London days after Monck to promote the Resolutioner case. There he enjoyed access to the general and the general's confidence, but his influence over him, or over the course of events, appears to have been negligible. Sharp had to steer a course between 'independency', tolerating doctrinal pluralism among individual congregations, and the return of episcopacy, and in many ways the signs were encouraging. Monck seemingly favoured an ecclesiastical settlement based on 'presbyterianism, not rigid',[33] and, as one of its last acts, the Long Parliament had the Solemn League and Covenant reprinted and read from every pulpit.

The reaction against political and religious 'radicalism' had marginalised 'independency' and, as an anxious Warriston realised, its Scottish variant, the Protestors. Episcopacy, 'moderate' or otherwise, was another matter. Recognising England as the most likely incubator of any episcopalian *revanche*, Sharp's senior colleague in Edinburgh, Robert Douglas, insisted that the forthcoming ecclesiastical settlement must win the consent of each of the three nations. Fears of an English reversion to prelacy also accounts for the Resolutioners' preference for greater constitutional autonomy for Scotland. A similar strategy to Douglas's was probably in Broghill's mind when he wrote to his old Resolutioner allies in Edinburgh, asking them to send an agent, either Sharp or James Wood, to Ireland. Interestingly, Monck prevented Sharp from going. As far as he was concerned the ecclesiastical settlement would be made in England and nowhere else. Sharp, the future Archbishop of St Andrews, has been demonised in Presbyterian legend as an opportunist who betrayed the Kirk. But the overriding impression conveyed by his most recent biographer's careful reconstruction of his activities in London between February and May 1660 is of impotence in the face of momentous political events. Monck ignored the Resolutioner agenda for a Presbyterian Church in three kingdoms, because he could.

Sharp's failure is emblematic. As Godfrey Davies observed, 'in Scotland the Restoration was mainly accomplished by alien hands'.[34] In Ireland, by contrast, the Restoration was mainly made by local hands. Nothing demonstrates that more clearly than the unilateral meeting of a convention at Dublin in March 1660. Where the Scots were divided, the English Interest in Ireland, composed of 'old Protestants' established there before 1641 and of Cromwellian officer-settlers, began to fuse in a common defence of the land transfers. Yet viewed in a longer perspective the contrast is surprising. Scotland, wrote the Earl of Newcastle in 1658, was 'an antient kingdome' which under the union of crowns had retained its laws and parliament; Ireland was a 'subordinate kingdome to England', governed by English law, its own parliament notwithstanding.[35] Newcastle's view, typical of seventeenth-century Englishmen, was far from typical of seventeenth-century Irishmen,

[1 2]   Protestant or Catholic, and the convention duly 'declared' and 'asserted'
that:

> as for several hundreds of years last past, by the laws and laudable customs
> of this nation, parliaments have ben usually held in Ireland, and that those
> parliaments laws have been enacted, and laws repealed, and subsidys granted . . .
> so that right of having parliaments held in Ireland is still justly and lawfully due
> and belonging to Ireland, and that the parliament of England never charged
> Ireland in any age with any subsidys, or other public taxes or assessments,
> until the violence offered in December, 1648.[36]

The convention also commissioned a 'disquisition' from Sir William
Domville which delineated the legal and historical bases of Ireland's ancient
constitution. Irish historians used to approach that 'startling assertion of
independence' as part of a larger pattern, relating it to earlier Old English
(Catholic) defences of legislative autonomy and to later Protestant patriot
aspirations, from Molyneux's *Case of Ireland Being Bound by Acts of Parliament
in England Stated*, in 1698, to the 'constitution of 1782'. Viewed from that
perspective the convention features as a staging-post on the forward march
of 'colonial nationalism'. But recent, more tightly focused and detailed
studies, by restoring the convention to its immediate political context, attach
less significance to the high-flying rhetoric of self-government.[37] The
real point of the claim to legislative competence was not any principle of
'national' autonomy, but as a means of safeguarding the land settlement.

The convention, consisting of 137 'old' and 'new' Protestants, met
in Dublin on 2 March. That act, in itself, as effectively repudiated the
Cromwellian union in practice as did Domville's subsequent disquisition
in theory. But the main purpose was to manage the prospective restoration
on the Protestant community's own terms. These insubordinate proceedings
generated deep hostility and suspicion in England. From January onwards
when the idea of a convention was first mooted as a means of raising sub-
sidies to pay army arrears, Protestant leaders in Ireland had to rebut the
accusations and rumour-mongering of Ludlow and other republican officers
that they 'intended to set up for themselves'.[38] On the contrary, they
declared, that was a 'foul and unjust calumny'; indeed

> the people of Ireland are so far from designing or intending to divide or
> separate from England, as they conclude such a division or separation would be
> absolutely destructive to the nation . . . they being generally bone of their bone
> and flesh of their flesh . . . the welfare and interests of England and Ireland are
> so inseparably interwoven as the good or evil of either must necessarily become
> common to both.[39]

Ludlow's suspicions went beyond the alleged separatist tendencies of the Irish Protestants. As early as 1 February Warriston reported that Miles Corbet and Ludlow were accusing Waller, Coote and Broghill of trying to 'bring in Charles Stewart'.[40] They could hardly have been more wrong about Waller, or more right about Coote. About a week later Coote dispatched Sir Arthur Forbes on a secret mission to the court in exile, pledging his allegiance, and briefly opening up the intriguing possibility of an Irish Restoration preceding an English one. But with a firm grasp on the geography of political power, Charles deemed it 'more necessary that I go for England' first,[41] and Forbes returned with the king-in-waiting's thanks and two blank royal commissions for Coote to fill in as he wished.

In politics timing is all, and as the options rapidly narrowed from commonwealth or king to king on what conditions, Coote displayed an immaculate sense of timing. With the army purged of committed republicans, religious 'radicalism' in retreat and the ascendancy of the old Protestants, or as Monck called them, 'the sober party', the Irish convention had a more conservative complexion than the Long Parliament, with whose closing days its proceedings overlapped. Unlike the English parliament the convention did not resurrect the Solemn League and Covenant; rather, despite a substantial Presbyterian contingent, including Sir John Clotworthy (and, perhaps, Broghill), it laid the foundation of an untrammelled episcopalian Church settlement. On that score, as in its incipient royalism, the Irish convention anticipated the English Convention Parliament to be called on 25 April. The Long Parliament dissolved on 16 March. 'And now,' wrote Samuel Pepys that evening, 'they begin to talk loud of the king.'[42]

In the six weeks between the dissolution of the Long Parliament and the meeting of its successor, as the anti-republican, anti-military, anti-sectary reaction gathered unstoppable force, 'they' also wrote much of the king. Royalist tracts rolled off the presses. Suspected of writing one of the handful of pamphlets opposing the king's return, Marchamont Nedham was dismissed as the editor of the official newsletter *Mercurius Britannicus*. Milton's publisher, Livewell Chapman, went into hiding. And, even at that late stage, Monck continued to purge the army of politically tainted officers. Yet though the commonwealth's days were clearly numbered, royalist triumphalism could still prove premature. Buoyed up by the turning tide, on 25 March a former chaplain of Charles I, Matthew Griffith, managed to land himself in Newgate by preaching a sermon, 'My son fear God and the King'. Griffith's vengeful tirade drew a reply from Milton, *Notes on a Late Sermon*, his last political pamphlet. But the clergyman's timing was only slightly misjudged; the poet wrote for a defeated cause.

[1 4]   In Brussels Charles and his chief advisers, Sir Edward Hyde, Sir Edward Nichols and James Butler, Marquis of Ormonde, were busy making preparations. Soon after the dissolution of England's Long Parliament Monck met the king's agent, Sir John Grenville, to whom he set out his modest terms for supporting a restoration of the monarchy: payment of army arrears, confirmation of title to confiscated Church lands, religious toleration and an act of indemnity. He further advised Charles to remove himself out of Catholic Spain's jurisdiction. Finally, the king's 'invitation' would have to come from the new parliament.[43] Coote might have got there first with his offer of loyalty, but it was Monck, the real power-broker in the senior kingdom, with whom Charles negotiated.

The results of the elections to the Convention Parliament were conclusive. Not a single known republican secured a seat. The new parliament consisted of 'Presbyterians' (defined loosely as those who had favoured a compromise with Charles I in 1648), royalist Cavaliers or the sons of Cavaliers, and those, like Ashley Cooper, Monck and Fairfax, who had faced down the English army and the Rump. Nothing more clearly signalled the mood of the country, perhaps, than the return of Sir Charles Booth and of his Welsh fellow conspirator, Sir Thomas Middleton, who had taken up arms against the republic only eight months before. The only issue that remained to be settled was the conditions that the Presbyterians hoped to attach to the king's restoration.

Charles now offered his own 'conditions'. From his new base in the impeccably Protestant Dutch republic the king and his advisers crafted the 'Declaration of Breda', dated 4 April. The declaration shrewdly devolved the problems of indemnity, arrears and title to the deliberation of the forthcoming parliament, and promised religious toleration for 'tender consciences'. On 8 April Sir John Grenville left for England with copies of the declaration and a royal commission for Monck as commander-in-chief. On 29 April Grenville presented copies of the declaration to the Council of State, and these were in turn presented to the speakers of both Houses two days later. In reply the assembled members voted that by the 'fundamental laws' of England, government was by king, lords and commons. The restoration was assured.

On 8 May the Presbyterian MP Sir Matthew Hale moved that a committee be appointed to consider which clauses of the Newport Treaty negotiated with the king's father should be presented to the king. Monck opposed the motion and opposed further delay. That day parliament proclaimed Charles king. At this delicate juncture the Irish convention had felt secure enough to defer to English sensibilities by adjourning. As Coote informed Monck, 'the Convention and the English gentry of Ireland that are not of the army . . . expect a good settlement of the three nations from the wise consultations of the parliament of England'.[44] The king was duly proclaimed in Ireland on 14 May. Charles landed at Dover on 25 May and began his journey, not to Edinburgh or Dublin, but to London.

Notes

1. Sir Hardress Waller to Monck, 16 December, Monck to Waller, 28 December 1659, Officers in Ireland to Speaker Lenthall, 11 January 1660, in Firth, C.H. (ed.) 1901, *The Clarke Papers*, London, iv, 202–3, 225–7, 241–3; Gumble, Thomas, 1671, *The Life of General Monck, Duke of Albemarle, with Remarks upon his Actions*, London, 182–4. The most detailed accounts of events leading to the restoration of Charles II are in Davies, G., 1955, *The Restoration of Charles II, 1658–1660*, Oxford; Hutton, R., 1987, *The Restoration in England and Wales 1658–1667*, Oxford; Dow, F.D., 1979, *Cromwellian Scotland 1651–1660*, Edinburgh; and Clarke, Aidan, '1659 and the road to Restoration', in Ohlmeyer, Jane (ed.) 1995, *Ireland from Independence to Occupation 1641–1660*, Cambridge.

2. For a sustained analysis of the crisis of the late 1630s from a three-kingdom perspective see Russell, Conrad, 1991, *The Fall of the British Monarchies 1637–1642*, Oxford.

3. Firth, C.H. and Rait, R.S. (eds) 1911, *Acts and Ordinances of the Interregnum, 1642–1660*, London, iii, 18–20.

4. The coinage of the phrase 'wars of the three kingdoms' is sometimes attributed to J.C. Beckett, significantly perhaps, an Irish historian, e.g. Pocock, J.G.A., 1982, 'The limits and divisions of British history: in search of the unknown subject', *American Historical Review*, 87: 326; Clark, J.C.D., 1989, 'English history's forgotten contexts', *HJ*, 212 n. 4. However, it can be traced back earlier, to Edmund Curtis (an English historian of Ireland, based in Trinity College Dublin) who in turn attributes it to 'the Irish' of the 1640s: Curtis, 1936, *A History of Ireland*, London, 242.

5. Davies, *The Restoration of Charles II*, 187.

6. Monck to the officers of the Irish brigade, 28 December 1659, Firth, *Clarke Papers*, iv, 228–9.

7. Davies, *Restoration*, 240.

[1 6]   8. Monck to Broghill, January 1660, *HMC Various Collections*, vi, 438–9.

9. 'Radicalism' is an anachronistic term. It did not begin to evolve its modern sense until the second decade of the nineteenth century. I confess, however, that like 'Anglo-Irish', I have found it very difficult to dispense with. Moreover, in context its broad meaning is usually clear enough. Thus in the 1650s 'religious and army radicalism' denotes opposition to the restoration of monarchy, to the re-establishment of the Church and to bishops.

10. The phrase is cited in Hill, C., 1984, *The Experience of Defeat: Milton and Some Contemporaries*, London, 151.

11. Roots, I., 'The tactics of the commonwealthmen in Richard Cromwell's parliament', in Pennington, D. (ed.) 1978, *Puritans and Revolutionaries*, Oxford; Hirst, D., 1987, 'Concord and discord in Richard Cromwell's house of commons', *EHR*. clll, 407: 339–58.

12. Milton, J., *The Readie and Easie Way to Establish a Free Commonwealth* in Ayers, R.W. (ed.) (with an historical introduction by Austin Woolrych) 1980, *Complete Prose Works of John Milton*, vii, *1659–60*, Yale, 358.

13. The 'dissembling royalist' interpretation of Monck's actions is most pronounced in Ashley, M., 1977, *General Monck*, London, which in turn relies heavily on the contemporary account and apologia of Monck's chaplain Thomas Gumble (see note 1).

14. Henry Monck to William Clarke (?) 3 November 1659 *Clarke Papers* iv, 91, 95.

15. Hill, *Experience of Defeat*, 133–4; Hutton, *The Restoration in England and Wales*, 73.

16. Rutt, J.T. (ed.) 1828, *The Diary of John Burton*, iv, London, 168.

17. Dow, *Cromwellian Scotland*, 254–6.

18. James Sharp to Robert Douglas, 28 May 1659, in Staples, Rev. W. (ed.) 1930, *Register of the Consultations of the Ministers of Edinburgh and Some Other Brethren of the Ministry*, ii, *1657–1660*, SHS, Edinburgh, 184–5.

19. The speech is reprinted in Gumble, *Life of General Monck*, 230–3.

20. Dow, *Cromwellian Scotland*, 231–2.

21. Gumble, *Life of General Monck*, 230–3.

22. *A Declaration of the Lord Broghill and the Other Officers of the Army of Ireland, in the Province of Munster* in Birch, Thomas (ed.) 1742, *A Collection of the State Papers of John Thurloe*, London, vii, 817–20.

23. Bridges, John, Warren, A. and Warren, E., 1660, *A Perfect Narrative of the Grounds and Reasons Moving Some Officers in Ireland to the Securing of the Castle in Dublin for the Parliament*, London, 1, Clarke, '1659 and the road to Restoration', 257.

24. Monck to Broghill, January 1660 in *HMC Various Collections*, vi, 438–9; Davies, *Restoration*, 269–72.

25. The phrase is Milton's, *Readie and Easy Way to Establish a Free Commonwealth* in Ayers, *Complete Prose Works of John Milton*, vii, *1659–60*, 388.

26. Buckroyd, Julia, 1987, *The Life of James Sharp, Archbishop of Saint Andrews, 1618–1679*, Edinburgh, 44–5.

27. Clarke, '1659 and the road to Restoration', 256.

28. Milton, *Readie and Easy Way*, 356–7.

29. For evidence of the groundswell of support for a free Parliament in Ireland before Waller's attempted 'engagement', see E. Viscount Conway to Col. E. Harley, 11 February 1660, *HMC Portland ms*, iii, 217.

30. Hutton lays particular stress on the impact of London street politics, *The Restoration in England and Wales*.

31. Buckroyd, J., 1987, 'Bridging the gap: Scotland 1659–1660', *SHR*, lxvi, 5–6, 13; Davies, *Restoration*, 230–1.

32. Dow, *Cromwellian Scotland*, 231, 261.

33. Monck to Douglas, 14 March 1660; 1842, *The Letters and Journals of Robert Baillie*, The Bannatyne Club, Edinburgh, iii, 585–6.

34. Davies, *Restoration*, 230.

35. Slaughter, Thomas, P., 1984, *Ideology and Politics on the Eve of Restoration: Newcastle's Advice to Charles II*, Philadelphia, 65–6.

36. 1660, *Declaration of the General Convention of Ireland*, Dublin, 4.

37. The phrase 'startling assertion of independence' is Toby Barnard's: 'Planters and policies in Cromwellian Ireland', *P&P*, 61. He has now revised these views, see 'The Protestant interest, 1641–1660' and 'Settling and unsettling Ireland: the Cromwellian and Willliamite revolutions', in Ohlmeyer, Jane (ed.) 1995, *Ireland from Independence to Occupation 1641–1660*, Cambridge, 239, 288.

38. Bridges *et al.*, *Perfect Narrative*, 14; anon., 1660, *A Faithful Representation of the State of Ireland*, London.

[1 8]   39.   *Declaration of the General Convention*, 5.

40.   Ogilvie, J.D. (ed.) 1940, *Diary of Sir Archibald Johnston of Warriston*, iii, *1655–1660*, SHS, Edinburgh, 174.

41.   Charles Stuart to Coote, 16 March 1660, Bodl. Carte Ms 30 f551.

42.   Quoted in Woolrych's introduction to Ayers, *Milton*, 194.

43.   Hutton, *The Restoration in England and Wales*, 107.

44.   Coote to Monck, *HMC Leyborne-Popham*, 179; Broghill to Thurloe, *State Papers of John Thurloe*, vii, 859, 908.

2

THREE KINGDOMS, ONE CHURCH?

Historians do not agree about the longer-term significance of 1660. Did it mark the start of a new era – 'Year One' of the so-called 'long eighteenth century' – or are continuities with the past more important?[1] In at least one respect, however, the demarcating effect of the Restoration is clear: the religious settlement. Before 1642 'puritanism' coexisted uneasily within the bounds of the Church by law established. During the bishop-free deregulation of the later 1640s and 1650s it splintered into a host of Protestant sects. Then between 1660 and 1662 episcopacy was reimposed in each of the three kingdoms. Sectarians and Presbyterians, no longer like their puritan forebears even nominal members of the Church, were now deemed Nonconformists or Dissenters. In the age of the confessional state, refusing to conform to the state Church amounted to an act of civil disobedience, inviting the imposition of civil disabilities and penalties. Dissent was therefore a political problem. Some Dissenters passed from the realm of passive civil disobedience, which their conscience enjoined, into the netherworlds of political disaffection and conspiracy. That is hardly surprising. As we have seen, Baptists and Quakers were deeply implicated in army 'radicalism' in 1659–60. Presbyterians too, their frequent protests to the contrary notwithstanding, were suspected of republican sympathies. 'No bishop, no king' as their critics put it. Yet there can be no doubt that the extent (and fear) of Dissenter involvement in anti-government conspiracies was at the time exaggerated. With the memory of regicide, dispossession, exile and religious 'fanaticism' fresh in their minds, the king's servants were quick to credit the alarmist reports reaching them almost daily from the government's thriving spy network.[2] The close connection that existed in the official imagination between political disaffection and nonconformity is vividly demonstrated by the Dublin administration's response to Colonel Blood's abortive coup in 1663. Although a number of Presbyterian ministers were involved, if only tangentially, in that episode, many who were not were afterwards arrested and imprisoned.

[2 0]   The story of the repression of the Dissenters, and of their resistance, is at times so dramatic, indeed heroic, that it is easy to overestimate their impact on society and politics – to forget that they were everywhere, even in Scotland, a minority. In England, popular Anglican piety, or in Scotland the pragmatism of the conforming clergy, were more representative of the Restoration religious dispensation. However, the persecution and the struggles of the Dissenters had reverberations which belie their numbers. Both central and local government consistently overestimated the strength and misunderstood the intentions of the Dissenters. Their deep distrust of the Quakers was particularly misplaced. But those anxieties, no matter how flimsy their foundation, shaped public policy and kept the issue of nonconformity and toleration near the top of the political agenda. Sometimes minorities make history.

Before Charles Stuart set foot in England the fate of the sects had been sealed along with the republic with which they were inextricably identified. The defeat of Presbyterianism, above all in its Scottish heartland, was less predictable. In fact in the spring of 1660 the prospects for a Presbyterian ecclesiastical settlement looked good. General Monck supposedly favoured a moderate Presbyterian form of Church government and in a closing gesture England's Long Parliament reaffirmed the Solemn League and Covenant. In Ireland the convention appointed a Presbyterian, Samuel Cox, as its chaplain, and nominated Presbyterians, including Cox and the Ulster minister Patrick Adair, to its eight-strong committee on religion, charged to advise it on ecclesiastical matters. That committee in turn was asked to promote a clergy that would be 'pious, orthodox, sober and ordained' – a formula consistent with Presbyterian ambitions because it implicitly repudiated the sectaries and independents on the one hand and omitted prelacy on the other.[3] In Scotland the Resolutioner party had eclipsed its 'radical' Protestor rival, while episcopacy had been so thoroughly rooted out of Scottish soil and the sects were so marginal that a religious settlement based on either did not enter into calculation. But the signs were misleading. Moves to secure the re-establishment of the Church of England were already afoot.

In March 1660 negotiations opened in London between episcopalians and representatives of 'moderate' English Presbyterianism. Later that month Edward Hyde's agent, Dr George Morley, arrived in the hope of winning over the Presbyterian leadership, notably Richard Baxter, Edmund Calamy, Thomas Manton and Edward Reynolds. A compromise, on the model of Archbishop Ussher's 1645 proposals, whereby the national Church would 'comprehend' diverse opinions, by combining presbyters with bishops in its governance, was clearly a realistic objective. Men like Baxter had no strong doctrinal objections to prelacy. Drawing on the traditions of pre-sectarian 'anglo-puritanism' they abhorred the spirit of separatism and adhered to the values of Godly discipline and orthodoxy. From their standpoint comprehension was preferable to toleration or independence. By May Morley reported that Calamy and Reynolds were ready to accept episcopacy but could not, as yet, vouch for the attitudes of their brethren. Reynolds later accepted the bishopric of Norwich.[4]

The trend towards 'moderate' or Ussher-style 'reduced episcopacy' did not go unnoticed. From the sterner perspectives of Resolutioner Edinburgh, the London-based English Presbyterians stood revealed as unreliable allies. And as the Resolutioners well knew, the consequences of such backsliding were potentially disastrous. The danger lay in England's political and military dominance. In short, the London government had the capability, if it chose to exercise it, of imposing episcopacy on a weak, defeated and still garrisoned Scotland. One possible way to prevent this was by coordinating the efforts of the Presbyterian interest in each of the three nations. Broghill, Colonel Georges, the governor of Ulster and, 'in the name of the Presbyterian ministers', John Greig, appear to have had a strategy like this in mind when they wrote to the leading Resolutioner, Robert Douglas, on 12 March, advocating 'a close correspondence with Scotland, and showing their hearty concern for settling religion, and liberty, and uniformity in the three nations, in concert with General Monck' and requesting the dispatch of James Sharp or some other 'trusty friend' to Ireland 'to concert measures for the settlement of all those upon righteous and solid foundations'. On 29 March Douglas clearly set out the reasoning behind this strategy in a position paper which he sent to Sharp in London:

> Concerning the power of settling government, it is in the respective parliaments of England, Scotland and Ireland . . . England is but a part, and their representatives doth only represent that part; now no part can conclude and determine the whole. All three nations have always had their respective parliaments, until the unhappy changes under the late usurpation, which hath overthrown the liberties of all three nations. If anything be determined by a part, which is not agreeable to the mind of the rest, it must be imposed without a free consent, and by force; and this is the continuance of that very bondage upon others, under which both they and we have lien this while bygone. A greater freedom of expression is required in this particular, in so far as concerneth Scotland, which is in a worse case than any of the other two, because the power that is in the other two, by divine providence, puts them in a capacity to act for themselves, whereas Scotland is, by that same power, impeded from acting towards their own liberty.

[2 2]   The Resolutioners could not enforce their demands. A few days earlier Sharp informed Douglas that 'The English are willing Scotland be as free a nation as they are; but the general is for keeping us in subjection, 'till he sees how matters go in parliament.'[5]

If Douglas was right to identify England as the site of an Anglican *revanche* that would end all hope of a Presbyterian settlement in three nations and pose a threat to the Scottish Kirk, the direction that affairs soon took in Ireland can only have deepened his forebodings. Despite its initial open-ended approach to religious policy, and in contrast to the Long Parliament, the Dublin convention refused to reaffirm the Solemn League and Covenant. By late April, as the essentially conservative temper of the Protestant elite became increasingly evident, the titles, though not the jurisdictions, of the surviving bishops of the established Church (which, unlike its English counterpart, had never been formally disestablished) were restored. As Patrick Adair later complained, those few bishops who had been virtually ignored when he arrived in Dublin to lobby the convention had, before he left, 'become high, and much courted'.[6]

In retrospect it is clear that the trend towards re-establishment was gathering force, yet alternative possibilities remained in play. The Declaration of Breda, noting that 'the passion and uncharitableness of the times have produced several opinions in religion', guaranteed 'a liberty to tender consciences, and that no man shall be disquieted or called into question for differences of opinion in matter of religion which do not disturb the peace of the kingdom; and that we shall be ready to consent to such an act of parliament as, upon mature deliberation, shall be offered to us, for the full granting that indulgence'. Of course, in the delicately balanced circumstances of the moment, it made good political sense for Charles to maximise his support by conciliating as many of his subjects as possible. However, everything we know about him suggests that in purely religious matters Charles's instincts were genuinely irenic – subject always to political expedience. Thus his professions of goodwill towards the Scottish Kirk, offered to James Sharp when he travelled to Breda in April, or later to representatives of Ireland's Presbyterians, were probably given in good faith.[7] Nor were Low Church advocates of Ussher-style 'primitive episcopacy with presbytery', such as the future bishop of Exeter, John Gauden, merely pragmatists.[8]

The commitment of Charles and men like Gauden to reconciliation was real and not untypical, but many of the bishops in waiting and some of the king's senior advisers, like Hyde and Ormond, worked to a different agenda. The view of the re-establishment of the Church of England as a sort of

'Laudian' counter-revolution engineered by High Church veterans of the
1630s has not withstood close scrutiny,[9] but the high-flyers did have powerful friends in high places. Thus it is argued that whereas Charles sincerely
sought an accommodation with English Presbyterians, the supervisor of
that policy, Hyde, hoped ultimately that the negotiations would strengthen
the Church position by sowing dissension among its Presbyterian rivals.
Similarly, the speed with which bishops were appointed in Ireland from
June onwards, owed as much to Ormond's influence at court as to the convention's desire for a Church 'resettled in doctrine, discipline and worship'
as it had been in Charles I's reign.[10]

The ecclesiastical settlement:
England and Wales

The High Church faction's room for manoeuvre, if not always its ambitions,
was delimited by the political realities of post-interregnum England. By
April some form of moderate or comprehensive episcopal settlement seemed
likely. By July the well-informed Sharp had ruled out the possibility of the
Presbyterian option in England, though not yet Scotland. The following
month he reported that the 'episcopal party' in London 'are still gaining in
number, as well as confidence. Some think, they fly so high, that they will
undo their own interest.'[11] The architects of the Restoration Church were
unable – and in some cases unwilling – to replicate the Laudian Church.
Neither the Court of High Commission in England nor in Scotland the
prayer-book or Caroline liturgy, was revived. The 'several opinions in
religion' acknowledged by the Declaration of Breda could not be wished
away. The so-called 'Clarendon Code' – a term unknown to seventeenth-
century Englishmen later applied to a batch of anti-Dissenter penal laws,
which Clarendon did not draft – implicitly recognised, albeit negatively,
the more or less permanent existence of religious pluralism.

In the intermediate term, efforts to reach a compromise that would comprehend Presbyterians within a broad-bottomed national Church continued
into 1661. On 10 July 1660 the Presbyterians, meeting at Sion College,
set out their position. Their proposals addressed three areas of contention:
Church government, liturgy and ceremony. Unsurprisingly, they opted for
the Ussher model of Church government, 'without alteration'. Acknowledging that the prayer-book did require alteration, they suggested that

[2 4]   its revision be entrusted to a working party of learned and moderate divines 'of both persuasions'. Finally, they proposed that ceremonial practice, for example kneeling at the sacrament, making the sign of the cross at baptism or use of the surplice, ought to be a matter for the individual minister's conscience.[12] The immediate episcopal response was hostile. Agreement likewise eluded the Convention Parliament which, on 16 July, referred the issue of ecclesiastical settlement to the king. The next attempt to resolve the problem began in early September at a conference, convened at Hyde's London residence, Worcester House. The Sion College proposals were once again put forward by the Presbyterian delegation, led by Baxter, and strongly informed the subsequent Worcester House Declaration. This recommended reduced episcopacy, a commission to revise the prayer-book and a synod to consider liturgy and ceremonial. King Charles helped to secure that formula by dismissing Hyde from the negotiations and replacing him with the Presbyterian politicians Arthur Annesley and Denzil Holles. However, despite the king's clearly signalled endorsement, in the shape of a bill the Worcester House compromise failed to win a majority in the Convention Parliament.

    The king, not parliament, pushed against the current. Despite the fact that Baxter flatly rejected toleration for sectaries at Worcester House, in popular as well as in High Church eyes Presbyterians were tainted by association with regicide, sectarianism and a discredited republican regime. And during the summer of 1660 meeting houses were attacked and Baptists and Quakers were harried on the streets by angry crowds or thrown into gaol by vengeful magistrates.[13] In Wales Vavasor Powell, the most prominent Godly reformer of the hated puritan experiment, was arrested in July. Hundreds of others, especially Quakers, shared his fate. Powell's treatment, however, was unusually severe. He spent just over nine of the next ten years in prison, where he died in October 1670.[14] Clerical initiatives matched popular reaction. Whereas the newly appointed bishops in England were generally 'moderates' (Ireland and Wales had a different experience), the lower clergy generally were keen to reassert the privileges and prerogatives of the Church. With the support of the local county elites, Anglican priests began unilaterally to reoccupy their former livings and the cathedral chapters. In a sense the Act of September 1660, which restored ejected ministers, simply conferred formal legality upon a *fait accompli*. The narrow and intolerant Church that had emerged by 1662 was as much the product of a spontaneous counter-revolution from below as of the machinations of single-minded, politically connected 'Laudians'.

The Savoy Conference held between April and July 1661 represents the last attempt from above to achieve a comprehensive settlement. But like the Worcester House project, it too ran into the wall of episcopal intransigence, erected on this occasion by the Bishop of London, Gilbert Sheldon, and of opposition in parliament. For the Presbyterians, again led by Baxter, the political context could scarcely have been worse. The Convention Parliament was dissolved in late December 1660, to make way for fresh elections. Then, for three days in January, Thomas Venner's Fifth Monarchist insurrection delivered a sharp reminder to the electorate of the consequences of religious licence. Twenty-two people were killed, a royal proclamation forbade meetings of 'Anabaptists, Quakers and Fifth Monarchists' and a second great wave of arrests quickly followed. Four thousand or more Quakers were imprisoned.[15] But perhaps the most significant effect of Venner's rising was its impact on public opinion. Attitudes hardened. The 'Cavalier Parliament' which first met in March had markedly fewer 'Presbyterian' MPs than its predecessor, and a majority more Anglican and more royalist than the king. Baxter and his colleagues could expect little sympathy from that quarter.

On 17 May parliament voted for the Solemn League and Covenant to be burned by the common hangman.[16] The following month it repealed an Act of 1641 excluding bishops from the House of Lords. And as the Savoy House negotiations ground to an inconclusive halt, the bishops, then sitting in convocation, assumed responsibility for revising the prayer-book. By the summer of 1661, in parliament and in the country at large, the Anglican reaction had gained irreversible momentum. Toleration and comprehension were no longer viable options. The High Church party, lay and clerical, had triumphed. All that remained was the drafting and the details of the legislation.

The principal legislative instrument of the ecclesiastical settlement, the Act of Uniformity, received royal assent on 19 May 1662. Under that Act, by St Bartholomew's Day (24 August) all ministers were required to abjure the Solemn League and Covenant, use the revised prayer-book and, in certain cases, submit to episcopal reordination. 'Black Bartholomew's Day' brought to a traumatic climax the ejections of 'Puritan', 'independent' and Presbyterian clergymen from their livings, which had continued haphazardly from the early summer of 1660. The exact figures involved are uncertain, but approximately 1,800 ministers and a further 200 or so lecturers and college fellows were deprived during the two years preceding 24 August 1662. In Wales ninety-five – or 73 per cent – of 130 deprived ministers had already

[2 6] been ousted or 'voted with their feet' before the great ejection.[17] Yet in other respects St Bartholomew's Day did represent a defining moment. It could be argued that the enforcement of the Act of Uniformity unwittingly strengthened nonconformity by purging from its ranks the trimmers and the faint-hearted. Less than 200 of the ejected subsequently conformed. Still, the lines dividing nonconformity from occasional nonconformity and conformity remained remarkably blurred. In that sense the overwhelmingly Anglican allegiance of the English people suggested by the 1676 religious census may be misleading. As Tim Harris shrewdly observes, 'our impression of the religious balance of this society would be very different if, instead of trying to establish how many people were out-and-out nonconformists, we asked how many were out-and-out anglicans'.[18] The predominantly Anglican character of the Cavalier Parliament is not, however, in doubt. The churchmen had a powerful political ally in parliament if not always at court. The Act of Uniformity set the capstone to an Erastian ecclesiastical settlement – the re-establishment of a state Church – which proceeded from essentially political calculations.

Ireland

At the end of March 1661, Clarendon wrote to the Earl of Orrery expressing his hope that the Irish parliament would 'abhor the covenant'. The English House of Commons voted to burn the Solemn League and Covenant on 17 May; the Irish House of Lords on 27 May.[19] But it would be a mistake to conclude that this was simply another instance of the English dog wagging its Irish tail. In fact, the Erastian, political and intolerant ecclesiastical settlement in Ireland outpaced that in England. Orrery had come a long way since the time when, as Lord Broghill, he had sought the cooperation of like-minded Scots in defence of the covenant. From pillar of the Cromwellian establishment to promoter of the Restoration – for which he was rewarded with his earldom – and to the end of his life a staunch defender of the 'Protestant Interest' in Ireland, Orrery's religious principles were nevertheless firmly subordinated to the imperatives of political survival. His silent desertion of the Presbyterian cause during the summer of 1660 clearly signalled its likely fate.

Paradoxically, Irish – or more precisely, Ulster – Presbyterianism suffered rapid eclipse because of its relative strengths: its coherent sense of identity, doctrinal rigour, discipline and regional concentration. Ulster's

Presbyterians, Scottish born or of Scottish extraction, proved less tractable [27]
concerning inessential forms and Church government than their 'moderate'
Baxterite English counterparts. Some at least of the southern Presbyterians,
who were in the English tradition, were open to comprehension schemes on
the Ussher model, but their numerical weakness rendered such willingness
irrelevant. In Ireland the line dividing Presbyterians from Anglicans was
sharper, and easier to identify, than in England. Indeed it is in Ireland that
something approximating to a 'Laudian' counter-revolution did occur.
The key figure here was the first Restoration Archbishop of Armagh, John
Bramhall. An unreconstructed royalist, Bramhall served as chaplain to Lord
Deputy Wentworth and as Bishop of Derry during the 1630s, where he
vigorously implemented the High Anglican policy of 'thorough'. Oliver
Cromwell dubbed him 'Ireland's Laud'. Working closely with Ormond at
court, and in advance of parliamentary sanction, Bramhall fashioned an
Irish episcopate after his own image.

Nine of the twenty-one bishops appointed, reappointed or translated
during 1660 were, like Bramhall, English. Four were Scottish, two Welsh,
the rest Irish born. Five were formerly chaplains to either Ormond or
Wentworth. Only one, Henry Jones, Bishop of Clogher and sometime
Scout-master General of the Cromwellian army, failed to fulfil the criterion
of 'conspicuous loyalty' during the interregnum. But Jones, like Broghill,
had worked his passage into the new regime through his services at the
Restoration. Two of the more interesting appointments were George Wilde
to the see of Derry and Jeremy Taylor to Down and Connor, the dioceses
with the largest concentrations of Presbyterians in the country. In contrast
with the other English appointees, neither Wilde nor Taylor had previous
experience of Ireland. Both were inveterate enemies to nonconformity,
and on the face of it Taylor's intellectual distinction and superior abilities
ought to have secured him a place on the English bench. What ruled him
out, apparently, was his High Churchmanship.[20] What a later admirer termed
Taylor's 'Catholicity',[21] handicapped him at a time when the king hoped to
craft an episcopate hospitable to moderate Presbyterians. It is probable that
the further an appointment was from London, and the sphere of the king's
personal attention, the freer the hand played by the king's servants. Ormond
got his way, Hyde did not. This would also explain why Norwich got the
erstwhile Presbyterian, Edward Reynolds, as bishop, and Exeter, the Low
Church John Gauden, whereas the Welsh bishops of the Restoration period,
who were almost all Englishmen, have been described as 'hand-picked
royalists and Laudians'. Certainly, William Lucy, appointed to the see of
St David in 1660, cannot be accused of fudging his position: '*Schismatis*

et Haeresium averruncator strenuus' reads his epitaph ('Strenuous banisher of schism and heresy').[22]

After the Dublin Convention dissolved without reaching a formal ecclesiastical settlement, there was little that Ireland's Presbyterians could do to shape the future course of events. A self-styled 'synod' which met at Ballymena, County Antrim, drafted an address to the king which it entrusted to two ministers, William Keyes, 'an Englishman', and William Richardson, 'a Scotchman'. Keyes and Richardson travelled to London to present the address. There they met with Sir John Clotworthy, James Sharp and some of the London ministers, but they could not, at first, gain access to the king. Monck refused to help them. Nor did the London ministers, unnerved by the reference in the address to a covenanted king, offer their assistance. Sharp took a deeply pessimistic view of their prospects, estimating that 'the most they can expect will be a forbearance a little in the exercise of their ministry, but they will not be permitted to meet in presbytaries, or a synod'. On balance, however, he thought the presence of the Irish ministers useful. They could counteract the aspersions being cast upon Presbyterian loyalty and help 'obtain some abatement of the rigour and persecution they have cause to fear from the prelates . . . they have need' he concluded 'of our prayers; for the crushing of them will blast the Lords work, in that kingdom, in the bud'.[23] Finally, on 3 August, after two months' delay and after accepting advice to expunge all reference to the covenant, the two ministers were granted an audience with the king. Although Charles's assurances 'satisfied' the delegates at this meeting, they left without binding guarantees. Before the year was out, one of them, Richardson, warned his congregation to 'get the bible by heart, for the time of persecution [is] at hand'. Samuel Cox, the convention chaplain, was suspended from his living in St Catherine's Church, Dublin.[24]

In the end Presbyterian diplomacy counted for nothing. On 27 January 1661, twelve bishops were consecrated in an elaborate service at St Patrick's Cathedral in Dublin. Taylor delivered the sermon while Bramhall, in Edmund Ludlow's words, consecrated the new prelates 'with as many superstitious and idolatrous ceremonyes as if he had received particular directions therein from the pope himselfe'.[25] The new bishops moved swiftly and decisively. Ministers who refused episcopal reordination were expelled from their livings. Taylor ejected thirty-six Presbyterian ministers in a single day from his east Ulster diocese of Down and Connor.[26] The 'yoke of prelacy' had descended upon God's stiff-necked people once more. 'The time of persecution' was at hand.

Scotland

In fact, by early modern European standards the Ulster Presbyterians' 'time of persecution' was mild – certainly, the yoke of prelacy rested more lightly on their shoulders than on their co-religionists across the narrow water in Scotland. The Scottish ecclesiastical settlement was the most nakedly Erastian, the most unpopular and the least successful in any of the three kingdoms. As early as June 1660 it had become clear that the strategy of safeguarding the Kirk by securing a Presbyterian settlement in the three kingdoms was no longer viable. Nevertheless Douglas and the Resolutioner ministers believed that their Church could still be salvaged. Sharp returned to Edinburgh on 31 August bearing a letter, dated 10 August, to Douglas from the king. The letter acknowledged Resolutioner loyalty, commended Sharp for his services, and promised 'to protect and preserve the government of the Church of Scotland as it is settled by law'.[27] This assurance appears to have satisfied the Edinburgh ministers, even though it was merely an earnest of royal grace and favour, lacking statutory force – and what the king granted, the king could at any time take away.

The Scots certainly were not unaware of their subordination to the southern kingdom. The 'Noblemen, Gentlemen and Burgesses' who petitioned Charles that June to recall the Committee of Estates, requested the withdrawal of English troops from Scotland, and their replacement by 'such Scots subjects as you shall think fit for securing of the garrisons, and the peace of the kingdom'. Nine months later Sharp reported to a London correspondent a rumour that 'the English forces must remain upon us till we conforme to your southerne mode: if this be an invention to facilitat designes, I know not: O poor Scotland.' Nor, of course, was the enforcement of a church settlement at musket-point an entirely novel departure. After all, it was not long since the Scots had tried, by force of arms, to make the English conform to their northern mode. Thomas Sydserf of Galloway, the only bishop to survive into the Restoration from the pre-1638 Church, warned that the continuation of Presbyterianism in Scotland would encourage 'the discontented party' in England, and urged the maintenance of a standing army north of the border.[28]

The Committee of Estates convened at Edinburgh on 23 August, and as one of its first acts ordered the arrest of a church elder and ten Protestor ministers, including James Guthrie, who in an address had reminded the king of his covenant oath. Another leading Protestor, Sir James Steward, and the Marquis of Argyll were already in prison and a warrant was issued for the

[3 0] apprehension of Johnston of Warriston. Argyll and Guthrie were executed in 1661; Warriston, lured back from exile in the Netherlands, went to the gallows two years later. Although the crack-down on their old rivals did not affect the 'moderate' Resolutioners directly, the implications were ominous, for the impetus behind the arrests were not only anti-'radical', but anti-clerical as well.[29] The Scottish nobility who now constituted the political nation were determined never to return to the theocratic tyrannies of the recent past. The Scottish clergy, despite the central role often ascribed to Sharp's apostasy, were allowed almost no part in the making of the ecclesiastical settlement. All the key decisions were made in London, or by the Scottish Parliament which sat from January 1661.

The unicameral parliament, which under the procedures of the Lords of the Articles could not initiate legislation, was closely managed by the king's Commissioner, and Clarendon's protégé, the Earl of Middleton. Whereas the London-based Secretary of State for Scotland, the Earl of Lauderdale, favoured conciliating the Presbyterians, Middleton, with whom he was engaged in a struggle for power and for the king's favour, gave no quarter. Indeed, Middleton even outran his patron. On 26 March Clarendon advised that 'deferring this great alteration [in Church government] for some time seems to me to carry a more reasonable hope of execution with more general consent, for besides a good settlement here will facilitate all designs there'.[30] Just two days later, and presumably before Clarendon's letter reached Edinburgh, parliament passed the notorious Act Rescissory. By annulling all the Acts passed by the 'pretended parliaments' between 1640 and 1648, including those concerning Presbytery, the Act Rescissory cleared away all statutory obstacles to the re-establishment of episcopacy.

It is only at this point, in about April or May 1661, when progress towards an Erastian and prelatic settlement became unmistakable, and probably irreversible, that Sharp abandoned his rearguard action. His motives were pragmatic and political. Although as late as March that year he declared himself 'a Scotsman and a Presbyter', objected to English meddling in the Church affairs of Scotland, and predicted that the reimposition of bishops would 'bring on suffering upon many honest men', he also acknowledged that the 'former actings' and 'overreachings' of the Scottish Presbyterians rightly aroused the suspicions of lawful authority. Sharp insisted, however, that those 'just prejudices' against them notwithstanding, the staunchest Presbyterians could now be relied upon 'to yield more in Church matters to the king than before to any of his Royal progenitors since the reformation from poperie'.[31] For Sharp, submission to royal authority clinched all arguments, so when the Clarendon–Middleton view prevailed he had no option, as he saw it, but to cooperate.

On 14 August Lauderdale wrote to the council in Scotland informing them of the king's intention 'to interpose our royall authority for restoring that church to its right government by bishops'. The council met on 5 September and the following day issued a proclamation at the Cross of Edinburgh abolishing Presbytery as unsuitable 'to his Majestie's monarchical estate'[32] – no bishops, no king. As in England attempts were made to ameliorate a starkly espiscopal settlement by recruiting prominent 'moderate' Presbyterians as bishops, but with even less success. Douglas turned down the offer of St Andrews brought to him by Sharp, and the general intractability of the Resolutioner leadership ensured that the Restoration Scottish episcopate more closely resembled its ardently royalist Irish and Welsh counterparts. There was an important difference, however. Since neither the articles of Perth nor the prayer-book were revived, the liturgy remained intact. Thus to the ordinary worshipper at service, major change was not immediately apparent.

Sharp himself was nominated to the archbishopric of St Andrews on 14 November 1661, and consecrated with three other bishops at Westminster Abbey on 15 December. A further six bishops were consecrated in Edinburgh on 7 May 1662, and two more at St Andrews on 3 June. The new parliament which met in May now conformed to the English and Irish pattern. It renounced the Solemn League and Covenant as 'treasonable and seditious' and passed the Collation Act which restored to the bishops the right to confirm presentations to parishes. Collation paralleled the English Act of Uniformity and the practice of episcopal reordination in Ireland and led to broadly similar results. Between September 1662 and June 1663, up to 200 ministers who refused to submit to presentation and collation were expelled from their livings. The figures are smaller than those for England, but the proportion of clerical nonconformists was much greater – perhaps one-third of the ministry.[33] And, as events would soon show, Sharp's misgivings were not unfounded: in Scotland the restoration of the bishops would indeed visit suffering upon many honest men.

Notes

1. Scott, Jonathan, 1988, 'Radicalism and Restoration: the shape of the Stuart experience' (review article), *HJ*, 31: 2, 453–67; Harris, Tim, 'Introduction:

revising the Restoration', in Harris, Seaward P. and Goldie, Mark (eds) 1990, *The Politics of Religion in RestoratFion England*, Oxford, 1–28.

2. The history of anti-government plotting in all three kingdoms is meticulously detailed in R.L. Greaves's trilogy, 1986, *Deliver Us from Evil: The Radical Underground in Britain, 1660–1663*, Oxford; 1990, *Enemies Under his Feet: Radicals and Nonconformists in Britain, 1664–1677*, Stanford; and 1992, *Secrets of the Kingdom: British Radicals from the Popish Plot to the Revolution of 1688–1689*, Stanford.

3. McGuire, J.I., 1983, 'The Dublin Convention, the Protestant community and the emergence of an ecclesiastical settlement in 1660', in Cosgrove, A. and McGuire, J.I. (eds) 1983, *Parliament and Community*, Historical Studies xiv, Belfast, 131–2, 135.

4. Spurr, J., 1991, *The Restoration of the Church of England, 1641–1689*, New Haven and London, 30–1; Lamont, W.M., 1979, *Richard Baxter and the Millennium: Protestant Imperialism and the English Revolution*, London, 210–15.

5. Wodrow, Rev. R., 1828, *The History of the Sufferings of the Church of Scotland, from the Restoration to the Revolution* (Burns, Rev. R. ed.), Glasgow, 4 vols, i, 12–14.

6. McGuire, 'The Dublin Convention', 132–3; Seymour, St John D., 1912, 1969 edn, *The Puritans in Ireland 1647–1661*, Oxford, 183.

7. Hutton, R., 1991, *Charles the Second, King of England, Scotland and Ireland*, Oxford, 131–2; James Sharp to James Wood, 29 May 1660 in Airy, O. (ed.) 1884–5, *The Lauderdale Papers*, Camden Society, 3 vols, 26–8; Sharp to Douglas, 4 August 1660 in Wodrow, *Sufferings of the Church of Scotland*, i, 53.

8. Green, I.M., 1978, *The Re-establishment of the Church of England 1660–1663*, Oxford, 8, 23; Spurr, *Restoration of the Church of England*, 31–3.

9. The Laudian thesis is presented by Robert S. Bosher in 1951, *The Making of the Restoration Settlement 1649–1662: The Influence of the Laudians*, London, and refuted by Green, *Re-establishment*.

10. Green, *Re-establishment*, 208–10; McGuire, J.I., 'Policy and patronage: the appointment of bishops 1660–61' in Ford, A., McGuire, J. and Milne, K. (eds) 1995, *As by Law Established: The Church of Ireland Since the Reformation*, Dublin, 118.

11. Sharp to Douglas, 26 July and 11 August 1660, Wodrow, *Sufferings of the Church of Scotland*, i, 53.

12. This paragraph draws on Spurr, *Restoration of the Church of England*, 29–42.

13. Watts, M.R., 1978, *The Dissenters from the Reformation to the French Revolution*, Oxford, 215.

14. Jenkins, G.H., 1992, *Protestant Dissenters in Wales 1639–1689*, Cardiff, 41.

15. Watts, *Dissenters*, 222–3.

16. Spurr, *Restoration of the Church of England*, 39; Seaward, P., 1989, *The Cavalier Parliament and the Reconstruction of the Old Regime, 1661–1667*, Cambridge, 164.

17. Watts, *Dissenters*, 219; Spurr, *Restoration of the Church of England*, 43; Jenkins, *Protestant Dissenters in Wales*, 43.

18. Harris, T., 1993, *Politics Under the Later Stuarts: Party Conflict in a Divided Society 1660–1715*, London and New York, 11.

19. Seaward, *The Cavalier Parliament*, 164; Seymour, *The Puritans in Ireland*, 201.

20. These observations on the character of the Irish Restoration episcopate are based on McGuire, 'Policy and patronage', *As by Law Established*, 112–19.

21. Bolton, F.R., 1959, *The Caroline Tradition of the Church of Ireland, with Particular Reference to Bishop Jeremy Taylor*, London.

22. Jenkins, *Protestant Dissenters in Wales*, 46–7.

23. Sharp to Douglas, 15 July and 26 July 1660, Wodrow, *Sufferings of the Church of Scotland*, i, 52–3.

24. Seymour, *The Puritans in Ireland*, 184, 196–7; Adair, P., 1866, *A True Narrative of the Rise and Progress of the Presbyterian Church in Ireland, 1623–1670*, Belfast, 243.

25. Worden, A.B. (ed.) 1978, Edmund Ludlow 'A voyce from the watchtower, pt. 5, 1660–1662', *Camden*, 4th ser. (21) 284.

26. Adair, *True Narrative*, 251; Bolton, *The Caroline Tradition*, 33–5.

27. Buckroyd, Julia, 1987, *The Life of James Sharp, Archbishop of St Andrews, 1618–1679*, Edinburgh, 62.

28. Petition of the 'Noblemen, Gentlemen and Burgesses of your Majesties Antient Kingdome', June 1660; Sharp to Drummond, 19 March 1661, Airy, *Lauderdale Papers*, i, 32–3, 83–90; Davies, D. and Hardacre, P.H., 1962, 'The Restoration of the Scottish episcopacy, 1660–1661', *Journal of British Studies*, i (2), 39.

29. The anti-clericalism of the Scots nobility in 1660–62 is strongly argued by Julia Buckroyd, 1980, *Church and State in Scotland 1660–1681*, Edinburgh, and 1987, 'Bridging the gap: Scotland 1659–1660', *SHR*, lxvi.

30. Cited by Davies and Hardacre, 'The Restoration of the Scottish Episcopacy', 44.

31. Sharp to Drummond, 19 March 1661, *Lauderdale Papers*, i, 83–9.

32. Gowan, I.B., 1976, *The Scottish Covenanters 1660–1688*, London, 45.

33. Buckroyd, *Sharp*, 74–80.

3

DISAFFECTION AND DISSENT: THE HEROIC AGE

In legal terms, though not always in practice, the English Act of Uniformity in 1662 (and the prayer-book which accompanied it) drew a clear line between the Church by law established and nonconformity. The penal legislation that followed, subsequently labelled 'the Clarendon Code', proceeded from that fundamental and, as it proved, irreversible separation. Moderate Presbyterians like Baxter continued to pursue the chimera of comprehension, the king favoured toleration or 'indulgence', but the Anglican-Cavalier-dominated parliament worked to a different agenda. The purposes of the Five Mile Act, the Conventicle Acts and so on, were coercive. Religious Dissenters who refused to conform to the state Church would not be permitted to worship outside it, at least not publicly. However, the effectiveness of the penal laws depended on at least three variables: the ability of the authorities to enforce the laws, the political will to do so, and the resilience of the Dissenters. All three variables conspired to ensure the survival of dissent. First, the early modern state simply did not possess the coercive machinery needed to suppress persistent, widespread, organised civil disobedience. In the absence of a police force the state had to rely upon local unpaid magistrates, who could call on the army in support of the civil power, and upon the often dubious information generated by paid spies and busybodies. Second, the will to enforce the law remained contingent upon the temperament and sympathies of individual law officers and upon the changing national political context. Finally, motivated by the deepest religious convictions, many Dissenters, especially Quakers and Scots covenanters, stood their ground. They could do no other. In 1683 all three problems of enforcement – ability, will and resistance – were neatly summed up by the Irish Lord Lieutenant, the first Duke of Ormond. Closing down Dissenter meeting houses, he remarked, 'is no better than scattering a flock of crows that will soon assemble again, and possibly it were better to leave them alone than to let them see the impotence of government upon which they may presume'.[1]

Quakers

Unfortunately for the Dissenters not all the king's servants took so relaxed a view as Ormond. An episode that occurred at Horsleydown in Sussex on 25 July 1670 illustrates dramatically just how Draconian the penal laws could be. A group of Quakers had gathered for a 'meeting' when

> There came in some musketeers, and haled them forth into the street, where the troopers came, and rod in amongst them in a violent manner, beating and abusing both men and women, and punching them on the feet with the but-ends of their pikes and muskets, till they broke several of them, also running the muzzle of their muskets with violence against the bodies of many, and then a party of horse came and desperately, and sought to ride over them; but the horses being more merciful than their riders, and not going forward, they turned their horses, and by curbing and reining them backward, strove to do what mischief they could. The number of those that were wounded, and sorely bruised, and had their blood spilt that day were above twenty persons.

Nor was that the end of it. The soldiers, 'horse and foot', returned to the meeting house on 2, 9 and 16 August, 'striking and knocking down, without respect to age or sect'. To the Quakers who published this account in a pamphlet, *The Cry of Innocent Blood*, the implications were unavoidable. If they could be thus physically assaulted 'before we are brought to a trial, or condemned by law; then farewel good government, and the fundamental laws of England'.[2] This was an unusually brutal incident, but it does highlight the manner in which the Quakers were singled out among the various sects for especially severe treatment.

On the face of it the pacifism and political quietism of the post-1660 Quakers should have rendered them an unlikely target for such severity. But to contemporaries they retained a reputation for fanaticism which their obdurate behaviour did nothing to dispel. Unlike some other Dissenters the Quakers always bore witness to the truth. The Welsh stalwart, Richard Davies, explained that imperative by citing Luke (xiv, 27): 'Whosoever doth not bear his cross, and come after me, cannot be my Disciple.'[3] Quakers never paid tithes nor swore oaths, regardless of the consequences; they never doffed their hats to their social 'superiors' and they never conformed, or pretended to, no matter what the price. Not surprisingly, such behaviour was often construed as provocative. For example, on 31 January 1676 (the anniversary of the execution of King Charles the 'martyr') Samuel Fox, a Quaker shopkeeper in Rochester, refused, as required by law, to close his shop for the day. The town constable did so. Fox reopened. In June 1690,

[3 6]   shortly after King William had landed at Carrickfergus, George Gregson of Lisburn, 'the most eminent preaching Quaker in the province of Ulster', refused to celebrate his 'deliverance' from Catholic tyranny by lighting a bonfire in the manner of his neighbours. The local soldiery were so incensed that they emptied his stores of wheelbarrows, shovels, axes, pitch and tar barrels 'and piled them up before his own door in a stately bonfire'.[4]

Quaker doctrines and attitudes placed them on the outer limits of nonconformity. Even their fellow Dissenters distrusted them. Baptists and Presbyterians readily concurred with churchmen in identifying the wholly subjective 'inner light' as subversive of the scriptural and sacramental bases of traditional Christian beliefs. When Richard Davies stood before the magistrates in 1660, one of the Justices of the Peace declared him to be 'mad'. He refused to take the oaths of allegiance and supremacy, and when quizzed by an Anglican priest, 'which was first, reason or scripture?', Davies replied 'reason was before scripture; God made man a reasonable creature, in his own image'.[5] Quaker men and women paid a heavy price for their consistent defiance. At least five of Davies' co-religionists died in Welsh prisons in the 1660s and 1670s.[6] These persecutions are uncommonly well documented. One of the few ways in which the victimised could respond, since they would not resist physically, was to record and compile their sufferings carefully, which they could then publish or use to petition the authorities. For instance, the Irish Quaker William Stockdale published a pamphlet in Dublin in 1683, entitled *The Great Cry of Oppression 1671–81*, in which he records the imprisonment of 780 Friends during the reign of Charles II.[7] The other main option available was emigration to America, particularly after 1681 when William Penn received his charter. Thus, between 1682 and 1700, the already small numbers of Welsh Friends were seriously depleted by the departure of around 2,000 of them for the New World.[8]

Quakers were a special case. Other Dissenters generally attracted less attention from the magistrates and were regarded with less suspicion by their neighbours. Strategies of evasion, subterfuge and occasional conformity were open to them. Often their experience of the penal laws hinged on the sympathies of their local magistrates, on the temper of the parish priest, or on the political complexion of the county's gentry elite. In some places these contingencies led to *de facto* toleration (as a rule, towns were safer for Dissenters than rural areas), in other places Dissenters could expect little but harassment and hostility. Baptists and Independents (literally) rubbed shoulders with Quakers in the overcrowded gaols of Restoration England – these sects were insignificant enough in the other two kingdoms to be largely

ignored – but as noted earlier, in the case of Vavasor Powell, John Bunyan's
twelve-year sojourn in Bedford prison was exceptional.

'The Lord's people' and 'the Good Old Cause'

The rigour of the penal laws and their sometimes Draconian application can appear wildly disproportionate to the 'threat' posed by nonconformists, especially when their tiny numbers are taken into account. Because of the blurring effect caused by the practice of occasional conformity and in the absence of accurate census data, precise numbers cannot be calculated, but Dissenters probably amounted to only 5 per cent of the English population and as little as 2 per cent of the Welsh. Outside the Presbyterian community in Ulster, Irish dissent barely reached five figures.[9] In Scotland too, radical Protestantism flowed along different channels. The reasons that the government wielded a sledge-hammer to crack such a puny nut were essentially political. The Dissenters could not distance themselves in the eyes of officialdom from their regicide-republican past. Reporting to Whitehall 'a conventicle held in York every Sabbath . . . frequented by a great many of the town', an informant reflects that 'these unlawful assemblies look like a fore-runner of the late sad rebellion; therefore I hope they may be suppressed'.[10] Furthermore, that aura of disaffection was enhanced by the perceived social composition of nonconformity as largely urban and poor. That perception over-simplified a more various reality, but Bunyan, for example, did speak to the poor, and his congregation consisted of 'shopkeepers and craftsmen, hatters, cobblers [and] heelmakers'.[11]

If the blanket conflation of dissent with disaffection was undeserved, it was not groundless. Dissenters *were* prominent in the conspiracies that punctuated Restoration politics, and the literature of political opposition was saturated by the language of radical Protestantism. Readers of the notoriously seditious pamphlet, *Mene Tekel*, were left in no doubt about the vital intersection of religion and politics. Published in 1663 under the *nom de plume* 'Laophilus Misotyrannus', it appears to have been written by the former Cromwellian officer Captain Roger Jones, although government sources also attributed it to others, including the seemingly ubiquitous Colonel Thomas Blood. The government believed that publication was connected with the northern rising of Cromwellians and Dissenters that year and received a report of 1,000 copies being printed in Holland – the refuge of English republican and Scottish covenanting exiles – for shipment to Scotland and Ireland. In 1664 the printer John Twyn was convicted of treason and hanged.[12]

The government's strong reaction to this pamphlet is understandable. *Mene Tekel* is a stridently anti-monarchical tract, which repudiates the doctrine of hereditary succession and defends the right of resistance to tyranny. It denounces magistrates as 'publick thieves who cheat the whole nation of their liberties, estates, birth-rights and *Gospel privileges*' and it anticipates the rhetoric of Thomas Paine 130 years later, by deriding the 'empty titles of knights, lords, dukes and the like'. The bishops are likewise condemned, revealed in the fierce parlance of the Scottish covenanters as 'wicked antichristian prelates'. And all this is justified on the grounds of the birthright (of free-born Englishmen), the 'law of God and nature' and scripture. One need only look to scripture to see that 'tyrants and oppressors have been often resisted by *the Lords people*'.[13] The 'Good Old Cause' of the republican remnant and Godly reformation were, it appeared, one and the same.

There is no evidence that *Mene Tekel* circulated in either Scotland or Ireland, certainly not in any great numbers, but the report that copies were destined for the two kingdoms, the alleged imbrication of the pamphlet in the northern rising and the attribution of authorship to the Irish Cromwellian plotter Colonel Blood, underline government fears that it faced a coordinated British Isles-wide conspiracy. In fact, after the Venner uprising in 1661, the next serious challenge to constituted authority came from Ireland. In terms of personnel – army veterans – the core of the 'Blood plot' paralleled its English counterparts. The plot was hatched, however, in circumstances peculiar to Ireland. Whereas the army had in large part supported the restoration of the monarchy in order to secure the Cromwellian land settlement, the king had other debts to pay. Thus a court of claims established after the 1662 Act of Settlement held out the prospect of recovering confiscated land to royalists and to 'innocent papists', at the expense, inevitably, of Cromwellian grantees and, the losers argued, of the Protestant Interest in general. For that reason the Blood plot reached deep into the Irish Protestant elite, involving up to ten Members of Parliament. Seven MPs were subsequently expelled from the house and one, Alexander Jephson, was executed.[14]

The conspiracy, which included a plan to seize Dublin Castle and was uncovered in May, had a strong Ulster dimension. Blood travelled north in the early spring in the hope of winning Presbyterian support. There he met with a number of ministers in County Down whom he acquainted with his plans. They agreed to report the matter to the rest of their brethren, but declined 'to certify . . . their adherence to the designe' by signing a note for Blood's Dublin committee. Soon after the colonel returned to east Ulster with his chief Presbyterian ally, the Rev. William Leckey, and they provided another minister, Andrew McCormack, with a horse, to facilitate communication between Dublin and the northerners.[15] Because these transactions were secret it is impossible to establish the true extent of the Presbyterians' involvement, but their canniness in dealing with Blood suggests caution. The wholesale arrest of ministers who were held at gaols in Carrickfergus, Carlingford, Lifford and Derry, as well as in the Munster garrison towns of Limerick, Cork, Youghall and Waterford, seems to have been an overreaction, albeit an overreaction that reflected official attitudes. On the other hand, the 'authorised' Presbyterian account in Patrick Adair's *True Narrative*, which singles out only a few misguided mavericks, understates the case.[16]

The Blood manifesto invoked the Solemn League and Covenant, and R.L. Greaves identifies six dissenting ministers who were implicated in the plot: a Congregationalist, Edward Baines, and five Presbyterians, Leckey, McCormack, Robert Chambers (a Dublin-based 'Independent'), John Crookshanks and Stephen Chranock. To this list might be added Thomas Boyd and William Jacque, both of Dublin, and Michael Bruce, who was born in Scotland and ejected from his living in Killinchy, County Down, in 1661.[17] Three of these, Crookshank, McCormack and Bruce, fled to Scotland and were soon active preaching in illegal field conventicles. In 1664 Crookshank produced a translation of George Buchanan's classic – and outlawed – sixteenth-century defence of tyrannicide *De juri regni apud Scotos* and alongside McCormack played a leading role in the covenanter uprising in 1666. Both of them were killed at the battle of Rullian Green in the Pentland Hills just outside Edinburgh.[18] Bruce continued to slip back and forth between Scotland and Ulster, eluding the law and specialising in inflammatory sermons. Captured in Stirlingshire in 1668 and sentenced to banishment, after a period of imprisonment in London he was allowed to return to Killinchy. Unchastened by the experience of incarceration Bruce delivered his most famous sermon, 'The Rattling of Dry Bones', at Carluke, Scotland, in 1672.[19]

The government imagined a trilateral knot of conspirators linking Ulster Presbyterians and Irish Cromwellians with English radicals and Dissenters and Scottish covenanters. For example, the (English) northern rising in October 1663 was seen as somehow a ramification of the Blood plot six months earlier. In a similar way the Archbishop of Glasgow discerned covert

[40]   collusion in the circulation of Crookshank's translation of *De juri regni* and
the intended publication of 'treasonable pamphlets' in England.[20] But if the
disaffected ever did coordinate their activities across the three kingdoms –
and that is unlikely – they certainly did not do so in any sustained way or to
any notable effect. A better way of conceiving of these linkages is as a set
of 'horizontal' relationships, between English radicals and (southern)
Irish radicals, and between Presbyterians in the north of Ireland and their
covenanting brethren in Scotland, particularly the south-west.

The southern axis proved less dynamic than the Ulster–Scotland one.
Irish army veterans continued to plot and channels to their English counterparts remained open. They may even have planned to assassinate Ormond.[21]
Blood fled from Ireland and entered with ease into the English radical
underground. But the seditious activities of Irish radicals had already peaked
by the spring of 1663. Ormond had succeeded in reducing the size and
purging the ranks of the army, and outside the army the 'Good Old Cause'
had little natural constituency in the essentially conservative milieu of Irish
Protestant society. Outside Presbyterian Ulster Irish dissent was equally
feeble. Moreover, during the Restoration period it was also in decline. Except
for Dublin the English Presbyterian tradition in the south of Ireland quietly
melted into the established Church after 1660.[22] The numbers of Baptists,
Quakers and 'Protestant strangers' – refugees from continental Europe –
were negligible. At least two causes may be ascribed for such enfeeblement:
the comparative absence of urban concentrations, and the pressure of the
native Catholic majority. For example, in 1682 the old Cromwellian, Colonel
Richard Lawrence, a 'Baptist' and a former sectarian controversialist, argued
that, confronted by the Catholic threat, Irish Protestants could not afford the
luxury of division.[23]

Covenanters

The Ulster–Scotland connection continued to trouble the civil authorities, in
London as much as in Dublin or Edinburgh. Unlike the small and scattered
nonconformist congregations of the south of Ireland, the more numerous
Presbyterian community in the north-east boasted well-organised ecclesiastical structures, social cohesion and a strong sense of collective identity.
These characteristics in themselves rendered the Presbyterians of Ulster
among the most formidable groups of Dissenters in the three kingdoms.

Church and state could view them as rivals or as potential rivals in ways that did not apply to the smaller denominations. But the decisive difference lay in the Scottish connection. The Ulster Presbyterians were all Scots by birth or descent, most of the ministers were trained in Scotland and often ordained there; above all, Scotland was close. Indeed, on a clear day the Scottish coast is visible from County Antrim, and that proximity facilitated a constant exchange of goods, people and ideas. Ulster even imported Scottish controversies, irrespective of their relevance under local conditions. As A.T.Q. Stewart notes, 'the divisions of the Kirk of Scotland tended, like fault lines in the geological structure, to reappear on the Ulster side of the North Channel'.[24] Thus during the late seventeenth century the covenanting-conventicling movement secured a foothold in Ulster, despite the fact that because of their status as a permanent minority within Protestant Ireland the Presbyterians could not, in contrast with their Scottish co-religionists, aspire to be the national Church.

The Edinburgh and Dublin administrations, sometimes unilaterally, sometimes in cooperation, and at other times upon instructions from London, tried repeatedly, and failed repeatedly, to control the movement of people between Ulster and Scotland. In February 1661 the Scottish parliament passed an Act requiring persons arriving from Ireland to provide documents signed by magistrates attesting to their 'good behaviour', while in the wake of the Blood plot two years later, Ormond received instructions from the English secretary of state to restrain released prisoners 'from coming over into England, or passing over into Scotland'. In 1666 when the Covenanters in Galloway rose in armed rebellion, frigates patrolled the northern channel.[25] But these efforts were undermined by the absence of sustained coordination between Edinburgh and Dublin, and by the personal hostility of Lauderdale and Ormond towards each other. This occasionally led to their working at cross-purposes. Ormond sought to transport Presbyterian ministers to Scotland at a time when the Scottish Privy Council issued instructions to return suspect Irishmen to Ireland.[26] In any event, attempting to control the movement of people (or of contraband literature) across frontiers, on land or sea, was a hopeless exercise. The policing capabilities of the early modern state were simply not up to the task.

By 1665 Archbishop Burnet of Glasgow attributed the continuing resistance to the reimposition of episcopacy as due in part to 'ane intercourse between the Scots in the north of Ireland and our male-contents in the west', an opinion confirmed by his counterpart, the Bishop of Derry. Jeremy Tayor, the Bishop of Down and Connor, believed that the 'the Scotch rebellion [in

[4 2] 1666] was either borne in Ireland or put to nurse there'.[27] It is true that two Ulster ministers, Crookshank and McCormack, played a leading role in the Galloway–Pentland uprising, and Taylor may have had in mind the peripatetic Michael Bruce, whom he had expelled from his living in 1661. But undoubtedly the bishops exaggerated. The Scots covenanters needed no outside encouragement. Ulster's true importance lay in its convenience as a bolthole for fugitives.

The covenanting-conventicling movement mounted the most sustained and the most formidable opposition to the Restoration ecclesiastical settlement anywhere in the three kingdoms. It is easy to forget that the Covenanters composed a minority within Scotland and within the Scottish Church. Many ministers conformed, especially in the east, and north of the Tay. Aberdeen remained a bastion of episcopalian sentiment and in the Highlands there survived pockets of Gaelic-speaking Catholics. Nevertheless, the Covenanters were a sizeable, determined, organised and geographically concentrated minority, and as one of their modern historians observes, this conflict was not 'fought on the strength of percentages and majorities, but in terms of commitment'.[28] The commitment of Church and state to facing down the challenge to law and constituted authority represented by conventicling is not in question. However, the civil and ecclesiastical powers were divided over tactics: Lauderdale and Sharp inclined towards a pragmatic compromise, Burnet advocated repression. Burnet's position had been weakened by the dismissal of the equally hardline Middleton in 1663, and vitiated by the less than full-blooded resolve of some of the magistrates at local level. Then the case for a quasi-military clampdown on the south-west Lowlands assumed sudden urgency with the outbreak of the second Dutch war in 1665.

Fifth columnists are a concern in any war. In 1665 the presence of exiled Covenanter ministers in the Netherlands made that concern unusually acute. Several of these ministers continued throughout the Restoration years to intervene in Scottish affairs from their base in Holland. Whereas English radical pamphlets tended to be printed in England, covenanting propaganda was usually written and printed in Holland. John Brown's *Apologetical Relation of the Particular Sufferings of the Faithful Ministers and Professors of the Church of Scotland since August 1660* appeared in 1665. Brown had been imprisoned three years previously and banished in 1663. At Rotterdam he worked with fellow exile and pamphleteer Robert MacWard, and subsequently, also in Rotterdam, he ordained Richard Cameron (who gave his name to the most militant covenanters in the 1680s). The *Apologetical*

Relation invoked the rhetoric of 1640s Presbyterian 'imperialism' by calling [4 3]
for uniformity of religion and the 'extirpation of Popery, Prelacy, superstition, heresy [and] schism' in the *three* kingdoms, and for 'all places of trust . . .
[to] be filled with such as have taken the covenant'. That 'damned book', as
Archbishop Sharp denounced it, also condemned the civil magistrates and
defended conventicles.[29] Thus in time of war the Dutch dimension elevated
the challenge to law and authority into probable treason.

During the winter of 1665/6 state coercion tightened. This consisted
mainly in the exaction of fines, usually in kind, for non-attendance at
officially sanctioned church services or for refusing to take oaths of allegiance (because, according to the Presbyterian doctrine of 'two kingdoms',
one spiritual, one temporal, oaths of allegiance amounted, in effect, to oaths
of supremacy).[30] More provocatively, troops were quartered on the properties of the recalcitrant. Together with the spread of armed field conventicles,
free quarters militarised the south-west, raising tensions and creating conditions under which conflict became almost inevitable. On 13 November
1666 a local fracas at Dalry involving soldiers under the command of
Sir James Turner, stationed at nearby Dumfries, suddenly flared into a major
confrontation. The following day some 200 insurgents entered Dumfries,
capturing Turner and his military retinue. They then headed north through
Ayrshire before turning eastward towards Edinburgh where, it seems, they
wished to petition the council. Rebel numbers probably never exceeded
1,000; they were poorly armed, poorly led and ill-prepared for the cold
winter weather. Driven back from the southern outskirts of the city, on
28 November fifty of the insurgents were killed at Rullion Green and a further eighty taken prisoner. Twenty-one of the prisoners were executed in
Edinburgh that December, along with seventeen others in Glasgow,
Dumfries and elsewhere. Many of those who escaped the rope were transported to Barbados, Virginia or Tangier. The 'chiefe commander', James
Wallace, escaped to Carrickfergus in a fishing boat.[31]

Although the 'Pentland uprising' had not, in itself, constituted a serious
threat to national security, the episode did concentrate the official mind
on the apparent intractability of the Covenanter problem. In its wake
Lauderdale began to look to conciliation as a solution. That approach
reached its culmination in the Indulgences of 1669 and 1672, which
extended limited toleration under licence to ministers outside the established
Church. Forty-two ministers availed themselves of the first Indulgence and
ninety of the second. This policy thus succeeded in siphoning off some of the
opposition and sowing division among the Covenanters, but the persistence

[44]   of conventicles during these years and the resumption of repressive tactics from the mid-1670s demonstrate its ultimate failure.

Why were the Covenanters so militant? The mobilising power of the covenanting cause drew on 'class' and national(ist) as well as on purely religious sources. The theocratic excesses of the 1640s and 1650s had alienated most of the landed classes, who were now confirmed in their distrust of 'fanaticism' by the lawlessness and violence of the adherents of the Solemn League and Covenant. The majority of conventiclers were of the 'meaner sort', the working poor of the countryside and tenant farmers. The Earl of Rothes described the Pentland prisoners as 'all of them being only mean beggerlie fellowes, bot stuborne in their wicked and rebellious way, the most of them declaring ther willingness to dye for the covenant'.[32] If anything the laity were even more irreconcilable than their ministers. As those who accepted the Indulgence soon discovered, 'the peasantry were more than their equals in debates on the nature of ecclesiastical government'. Likewise in Ulster the local ministers disapproved of the itinerant field preachers from Scotland, because they were fearful of drawing down the attention of the civil power. Nevertheless, they muted their objection because of the enthusiasm for the Scottish visitors among their congregations.[33] Another aspect of this popular movement was the prominence of women. In Rothes' opinion they were worse than devils. When Michael Bruce was taken to Edinburgh as a prisoner it was the women who planned to rescue him. And of course one of the most notorious episodes of the 'Killing Times' of the 1680s was the execution of two women Covenanters by drowning.[34]

The Covenanters objected to a prelatic and Erastian Church primarily on doctrinal grounds, but there was a sense in which the Restoration Church appeared particularly noxious because of its perceived English forms and inspiration. Put another way, the Covenanters defended not only the true reformed religion but the true Scottish Kirk. According to that view in the days of the covenants 'as to publick profession of the truth, and almost as to the number of persons, the Church of Scotland was of equal extent with the nation'. Burnet is 'that fiery zealot for the height of English hierarchy and ceremonies', while in 1680 the Sanquhar Declaration appealed to 'the covenanted nation of Scotland'. And that invocation of nation resonated with an heroic past and a present of suffering and election. 'The lot,' wrote the authors of *Napthali*, 'seemeth to have fallen upon Scotland, to assert and wrestle more eminently than many others, for the crown and kingdom of Jesus Christ.' Nor must the elect people flinch. After all, their 'fathers for far less matters, contested with the powers of the earth'.[35]

Perhaps the best route into the Covenanter *mentalité* is through the rhetoric of the tracts; that 'canon of radical covenanting political theory substantial enough', in Colin Kidd's phrase, 'not to be an aberration'.[36] One of the most striking features of this literature is the repetition of certain key words: 'overturning', 'usurpations', 'corruptions', 'apostacy', 'defection' and, above all, 'backsliding'. There is no room for compromise here between God's faithful and the foul 'hirelings' of the unchristian, state-controlled Church. Thus the special venom reserved for the indulged ministers who had cast such shame upon the true Kirk. David Houstan, who was, admittedly, volatile and extreme, even by Cameronian standards, considered 'the indulged party' more anti-christian than 'the popish or prelatick', indeed he preached 'generally nothing but against the indulgence, very litle against any other sin'.[37] What this language reveals is the Covenanter's absolute faith in his righteousness, and that sense of righteousness was further stiffened by the scale of the issue at stake, by his (and her) apocalyptic belief that he was living in the last times.

Other key words in the literature include 'whore', 'Babylon' and 'Antichrist'. Early modern Protestants generally identified the Pope as either *the* Antichrist or as *an* Antichrist (the Turk, or Infidel, was another favoured candidate) and the Protestant–Catholic conflict must always be understood in its millenarian as well as in its European context. Viewed from that vantage-point the mass hysteria generated by the bogus 'popish plot' in England in 1678–79 no longer appears so 'irrational'. In Europe Protestantism was on the defensive, and England, an 'elect' nation in the long struggle with the Antichrist, stood as a prime target of Jesuit intrigue. Scotland, another elect nation, was likewise another target. The threat emanated from the alleged increasing numbers of 'professed papists' but, much more dangerously, from 'the great affinity betwixt papacy and prelacy'.[38] In the pages of *Napthali* that affinity is enumerated as

> the already authorised and practiced conformity of the one to the other, not only in government and discipline, whereby they have for the most part, the same ecclesiastical courts and officers; but also in worship, whereby they have the same liturgy . . . the same ceremonies of rising, standing to the east, bowing, kneeling, crossing etc. the same superstitions and fool like vestments, the same observations of many days, the same adoring of churches and chappels, with altars, books, candles, candlesticks, basings, images and crucifixes or windows.

And all that 'backsliding . . . Leadeth into the great whore'. In that 'damned book', complained Sir Robert Moray, might be found 'all that a toung set on fire by hell can say'.[39]

[4 6]   In fact, that apocalyptic rhetoric had yet to achieve its fullest, most force-ful (and perhaps coherent) formulation. That prize must go to Alexander Shields's *A Hind Let Loose, or a Historical Representation of the Testimonies of the Church of Scotland*, published in 1687, during the long and bloody aftermath – the 'Killing Times' – of the battle of Bothwell Brig. Shields locates the per-secution of the Covenanters firmly in its millenarian and (thus) international context:

> now the Devil is come down in great wrath as knowing his time is but short, and therefore exerting all the energy of the venom and violence, craft and cruelty of the Dragon; And AntiChrist, alias Pope, his Captain General, is now universally prevailing and plying all his hellish engines, to batter down, and bury under the rubbish of everlasting darkness, what is left to be destroyed of the work of Reformation: and the crowned heads or horns of the Beast, the tyrants, alias Kings, of Europe, his council of war, are advancing their prerogatives upon the ruines of Nations and Churches priviledges.

Protestants were everywhere under attack, in France, Hungary, Piedmont. . . . Naturally therefore, Scotland's 'Ancient and sometimes famous Reformed Church' was now 'enrolled in the catalogue of [the] suffering'. Indeed, 'the deformation of the Church of Scotland . . . which in a retrograde motion hath gradually been growing these 27 years, going back through all the steps by which the Reformation ascended' had 'returned [it] to the very border of Babylon'.[40]

The violence of Shields's language mirrors the intensified physical vio-lence that began with the assassination of Archbishop Sharp (a member of the Scottish Privy Council) on 3 May 1679, and was soon followed, on 1 June, by the defeat inflicted by Covenanters at Drumclog upon goverment forces under John Graham of Claverhouse. The Covenanters then encamped, their numbers steadily growing, at Bothwell Brig near Hamilton, where they were routed on 22 July. Sixteen were subsequently executed and over 250 transported. From this episode, particularly from the debates among the Covenanters which preceded the actual battle, emerged the 'Cameronians', who took their name from the field conventicler, Richard Cameron. The Cameronians have been dismissed as 'an insignificant remnant', yet their activities were met with 'an unprecedented volume of repression'.[41] Cameron himself was killed almost exactly one year later, and up to the revolution of 1689–90 almost 200 more died, either in the field or by execution.

As with the over-reaction to Quakerism in England, the levels of state violence in Scotland in the 1680s were disproportionate to the scale of the threat at which it was directed. There are at least three reasons for the ferocity of the government-sponsored 'Killing Times': the presence in Scotland of James, Duke of York, Cameronian extremism, and once again, the three kingdom ramifications, real and imagined, of Cameronian resistance.

James had been diplomatically 'exiled' to the northern kingdom in 1680, as his elder brother negotiated the Exclusion Parliaments' attempt to debar the duke, as a Catholic, from the succession. As a Catholic, and as a Stuart with a high sense of royal prerogative, James showed no mercy – at this stage – to the enemies of Church and state. The third Indulgence of June 1679 was withdrawn and in the parliament of 1681 James secured an oath of loyalty to the royal supremacy in all eccesiastical and temporal affairs. A succession Act, acknowledging 'the inviolability of divine hereditary right', gave answer to the Exclusion Parliaments south of the border. James, buttressed by a 'flourishing circle of episcopalians, led by the lord advocate Sir George Mackenzie' – and untrammelled by the steadying influence of Lauderdale, after his departure in October 1680 – may even have contemplated dissolving the dynastic union and setting up in Scotland (and, presumably, Ireland) alone. As Shields remarked sourly, 'tho' the parliament of England, for his poperie and villanie, and his plotting and pursuing the destruction of the nation, did vote his exclusion; yet degenerate Scotland did receive him in great pompe and pride'.[42]

The extremism of Cameronian rhetoric and action, exemplified by the 1680 Sanquhar Declaration's blunt invocation of armed resistance, simply could not be ignored, especially if there did, in fact, exist a 'close correspondence' between the English Whig exclusionists and the Scots rebels. In addition to declaring the 'tyrant' and 'usurper' Charles's crown 'forfeit', the Sanquhar Declaration protested the succession of the 'profest papist', James, Duke of York. *The Declaration of the Oppressed Protestants Now in Arms in Scotland* similarly aligned itself with the English opposition by denouncing the 'universal plot carried on, for subversion of the Protestant religion, and for subjecting these lands under the antichristian bondage of popery, as by secret undermining and murderous practices in England, so by the open introduction of slavery and tyrannical government in Scotland'.[43] However, the political affinities – at that moment – of Scottish and English antipopery did not add up to covert collusion. Active connections tended to be with Dublin and Ulster.

Throughout the Scottish troubles the authorities in Edinburgh and London had kept a watchful eye on Ireland. Twice during the 1670s, and again in 1685 at the time of the Argyll rebellion, east Ulster was garrisoned with troops, ready to suppress local insurgency or to reinforce crown

[4 8] forces across the narrow water.[44] Many Bothwell rebels fled to Ireland where, despite the protestations of loyalty to the government by the Ulster Presbyterian 'General Committee', they found refuge. And, as earlier, Scots officials continued, into the 1680s, to complain about Dublin's tardiness in apprehending and returning fugitives.[45] A number of the most prominent Cameronians, incuding James Renwick and the legendary Alexander Peden, surfaced in Ireland at this time. After his ordination in Holland in 1683, Renwick, who became the leader of the so-called 'United Societies' before his execution in 1688, made his way to Scotland by way of Dublin. Later that year the United Societies wrote to fellow nonconformists in Newcastle and to 'those who desire to joine with [us in] the cause of God' in the Irish capital.[46]

The turbulent career of Renwick's closest associate in Ireland, David Houstan, straddled the three kingdoms. Born in Scotland, a graduate of Glasgow University, he came to Ulster in the 1660s. In 1671 Houstan received a reprimand from his County Antrim meeting for his 'irregular carriage', 'scandalous behaviour' and for 'fixing tent against tent', that is for unsanctioned preaching. Despite his promise to behave in future, Houstan was suspended the following year and again in 1686. He then went to Scotland and joined the United Societies. Two years later he was captured back in Ulster, but freed upon his enforced return to Scotland when his rescuers killed four and wounded ten of the guard escorting him. Undaunted, Houstan immediately resumed his inflammatory preaching, drawing 'complaints and accusations' about his 'offensive expressions and practices' even from his colleagues and from as far afield as Newcastle.[47]

The primary – his detractors insisted the sole – target of Houstan's invective was the 'indulged ministers'. Of course steadfast Covenanters had railed against the backslidings of those who had accepted the terms of the various Indulgences since the 1660s; but the royal Indulgences of 1687 were viewed as of an altogether more sinister character. At the end of 1662, when Charles's comprehension project had been thwarted irrevocably, he resorted to prerogative, issuing a non-statutory 'declaration' of Indulgence extending limited toleration to (English) nonconformists. Another declaration was issued in 1672 and the same year Ulster's Presbyterians had a type of legitimacy bestowed by the grant of a yearly royal stipend, the *regium donum* (denounced, predictably, by Houstan). Both declarations were soon overturned by parliaments hostile to dissent, on the grounds that they were arbitrary and unconstitutional. Another, and probably more important, reason for parliamentary opposition was what many perceived as the

'Catholic design' of Charles's policies. Always the shrewd politician, the king could not offer toleration to his Catholic subjects alone; he did, however, smuggle them into the broad category of nonconformity. This, together with a foreign policy directed against the Protestant Dutch, pursued – so Andrew Marvell alleged in his 1677 *Account of the Growth of Popery and Arbitrary Government in England* – in cahoots with Catholic France, fed fears of popish conspiracy in the highest places in the land. And for many these dark suspicions were confirmed when the Test Act came into force in 1673. Several prominent Catholics, including the heir to the throne, were flushed out of public office. In Marvell's words, 'There has now for diverse years, a design been carried on, to change the lawful government of England into an Absolute Tyranny, and to convert the established religion into downright popery.'[48] At least in Scotland in Charles's reign the Indulgence strategy was not burdened with a Catholic dimension. Rather it was a tactical manoeuvre, appropriate to highly specific Scottish conditions, designed to placate and/or divide the covenanting movement. But when the Catholic James succeeded to the throne in 1685 all that, as irreconcilables like Houstan and Alexander Shields clearly understood, changed.

Protestant dissent in the reign of James II and VII

The first challenge to James's tenure came just three months into his reign in the shape of the Monmouth–Argyll rebellion. Conceived, planned and launched by English Whig and Scottish Presbyterian exiles in Holland, many of the forces arrayed against the Stuart regime since 1660 were concentrated in this episode. The ninth Earl of Argyll, chieftain of the powerful Highland Campbell clan, and son of the martyred Covenanter, landed on the west coast of Scotland at the beginning of May. He failed, however, to rally either his own kinsmen or the Cameronians, who refused to fight alongside the non-covenanting rebels in his ranks. Argyll's attempt was savagely put down and on 30 June 1685 he followed his father to the gallows. Monmouth's more formidable enterprise proved equally doomed. Landing at Lyme Regis in Dorset on 11 June, Charles II's bastard son and claimant to the throne, James Scott, the Duke of Monmouth's 82-man 'expeditionary force' contained in microcosm the elements of Restoration era disaffection and dissent. This cadre included the Scottish republican Andrew Fletcher,

[5 0] Samuel Venner, whose brother Thomas had led the Fifth Monarchist uprising in 1661, and the Baptist and former Cromwellian officer Abraham Holmes. Their destination made political and military sense; as a bastion of Protestant dissent the west country, and in particular the town of Taunton, promised – and delivered – an enthusiastic reception. Indeed, it would not be stretching it too far to describe this, the last rebellion on English soil, as a Dissenter insurrection. The Presbyterians, Baptists, Independents and, remarkably, the handful of Quakers who marched with Monmouth, or fought at the battle of Sedgemoor, were driven more by religious conviction and fear of popery than by any dynastic consideration. As one of their historians frames it, these men chose their leader 'because he was available as a leader and not because he was the Duke of Monmouth'.[49]

The Monmouth–Argyll rebellion is emblematic of opposition to the Stuart regime in a further sense: it was crushed. Even James's incorrigible Catholicism could not, at that point, weaken his hold on power. James's most dangerous enemy was himself. Only he proved capable of sapping the ideological foundations of kingship; of undermining the Tory–Anglican consensus based on the doctrines of divine right, hereditary succession and non-resistance. The reasons for King James's ultimate political failure and, what is much the same thing, the origins of the revolution, are complex and various, but clearly the 'Catholic Question' – and the ways that it was linked to the problem of Protestant dissent – must occupy centre-stage of any explanation of the events of 1688. James's Catholic design was probably much more modest than his frightened subjects believed. At the minimum he sought toleration for Catholicism. Insofar as he sought to reconvert England (and Scotland) he favoured proselytising over coercion.[50] To achieve his ends – whatever they were – James amplified the strategy earlier pursued by Charles, not simply comprehending Catholics within a broader toleration, but hoping thereby to forge a political alliance with all those excluded from the Anglican monopoly on public office.

James's objectives may have been limited, even realistic; his tactics were disastrous. In retrospect many of his decisions appear to have been contrived to alienate and enrage his Protestant subjects without obtaining any compensating political advantage. The admission of a Jesuit to the Privy Council, the attempt to impose a Catholic president on Magdalen College, Oxford, or the refurbishing of the chapel in Holyrood Castle in Edinburgh for Catholic liturgy were all panic-inducing measures which increased hostility to the king, but which did not advance his agenda in any significant way. Events beyond James's control also contributed to the spreading sense of alarm. The revocation of the Edict of Nantes in 1685, the very year of his accession, and the flight of French Huguenots to England, confirmed British Protestant images of an aggressive, Catholic, French absolutist tyranny. Even more worrying was the apparent shape of things to come in Ireland. Under the lord deputyship of James's old confidant, Richard Talbot, Earl of Tyrconnell, the Irish kingdom experienced a process of re-'Catholicisation', the rapidness and thoroughness of which may even have outstripped the king's wishes.[51] In despair Irish Protestants began making their way to Wales, England and Scotland, bringing with them tales of popish persecution.

The cumulative effect of these developments increased the reluctance of the Dissenters to cooperate with James, even when he offered to suspend their legal disabilities.[52] Aside from the Quakers, who now enjoyed a special relationship with the crown through the close personal friendship of William Penn and the king, the majority of nonconformists did not subscribe to addresses of thanks for the 1687 Indulgence. James's hoped-for Dissenter–Catholic alliance never materialised. He did succeed, however, in reintroducing the Dissenters as a key player in the political arena by prompting the Tory–Anglican 'party' to outbid him for their support. Thus as the crisis unfolded, Anglicans and Dissenters began to forge a loveless, pan-Protestant, anti-Catholic front. When the seven bishops petitioned the king against reading the reissued Declaration of Indulgence from the pulpits of the established Church, they did not do so, they claimed, from 'any want of due tenderness towards the Dissenters'. The growth of 'arbitrary power' and, especially from William of Orange's Dutch perspective, James's subservience to Louis XIV's France, both prepared the way for the 'Glorious Revolution', and from that angle the overthrow of the king entered the Whig annals as the triumph of liberty over tyranny. But to contemporaries the events of November–December 1688 appeared above all to be a Protestant revolution.

Although nowadays it is fashionable to stress continuity over change at the time of the revolution, in 1689 one phase in the history of English nonconformity came to an end and another began. The possibility of 'comprehension' was once more canvassed in both Houses of Parliament, once again referred to convocation of the Church of England, and once more baffled, as in 1660–62, by the guardians of Anglican orthodoxy. But this time parliament did opt for the other alternative which had been available to the makers of the Restoration ecclesiastical settlement – toleration. Under the terms of the Toleration Act, Trinitarian Protestant Dissenters were granted freedom of worship, although the Test and Corporation Acts

[5 2] debarring them from public office stayed in place. The revolution settlement had defused the problem of nonconformity without resolving it.

In Scotland the revolution came near to fulfilling the 'second-best' aspiration of Robert Douglas and the resolutioners in 1660: the establishment of Presbyterianism in at least one kingdom. The new dispensation fell short of that aspiration, though, and of Cameronian ambitions, because it did not include the covenants. Yet in sharp contrast with the Restoration settlement, which had been imposed from Whitehall, the revolution settlement was made by entirely Scottish hands. At another level, of course, the Scots merely responded – quickly and decisively – to a situation created by the temporary lapsing of political authority in England. Within days of King James's flight in December 1688, armed gangs of nonconforming Presbyterians began a campaign of 'rabbling' episcopal clergymen, ransacking their houses and expelling them from their livings. Up to 300 ministers were forcibly removed in this manner and this at a time 'when episcopacy was yet the established government of the national church'.[53] There was a sense, therefore, that in terms of the ecclesiastical settlement, the convention of estates which met in March 1689 dealt with a *fait accompli*, particularly after James's episcopal supporters unilaterally withdrew from its proceedings. The Claim of Right presented to King William did not fudge the matter. 'Prelacy,' it declared, 'and the superiority of any office in the church above Presbyters, is, and hath been a great and insupportable grievance and trouble to this nation, and contrary to the inclinations of the generality of the people, ever since the reformation (they having been reformed from popery by Presbyters), and therefore ought to be abolished.'[54]

In England the revolution moderated the position of the Church by permitting limited toleration; in Scotland the revolution reversed the Restoration settlement, and by 7 June 1690 Presbyterianism became the Church by law established. But there is a paradox here. If the extent of change in England sometimes requires restatement, the undoubted alteration in the legal status, respectively, of episcopacy and Presbyterianism in Scotland masks real continuities. At first the new General Assembly of the Kirk comprised ministers expelled in 1660–62, men who were, not surprisingly, reluctant to comply with King William's wish to restore episcopalians now prepared to accept the new dispensation (Houstan, predictably, even opposed cooperation with formerly indulged ministers),[55] but a combination of political pressure and practical imperatives left them little alternative. Many ministers were restored with the result that many parishes far removed from the episcopal heartlands north of the Tay were run by the same people before and after the revolution. More importantly, just as the laity would generally have noticed little or no change in the liturgy of pre- and post-Restoration services, so in the 1690s Low Church Presbyterian moderates coalesced imperceptibly with Low Church episcopal moderates.

Appearances can mislead. The long shadows cast by the rabbling of previously conforming ministers, the part played by the Cameronians in the defeat of the Scottish Jacobites at the battle of Dunkeld in August 1689 and, above all perhaps, the bitter legacies of physical and rhetorical violence, of persecution and armed resistance, disguised a working compromise. North and south of the border episcopal apologists were quick to castigate the Presbyterian *revanche*, to recall covenanting's recent unsavoury past and to warn of the dangers of its proven expansionist tendencies and ambitions. These pamphleteers highlighted the role of the Cameronians in the revolution, denouncing them as 'republicans', 'fanatics', 'Fifth Monarchists', 'malignants' and 'mountaineers'. Typically they insisted that the men driving the revolution in Church and state were an unrepresentative faction; that episcopacy had been endorsed by twenty-seven Scottish parliaments; that it was the preferred form of Church government among the respectable classes and that, conversely, Presbyterianism was the preserve of the 'commonalty, the rude, illiterate *Vulgas*.'[56]

For the most part this propagandist literature was printed in London and directed at an English audience. Outnumbered and outflanked on their home turf the Scottish episcopalians turned south for support. Moreover, they argued, the king could ill afford *two* established Churches in his realms; Churches that were not simply different but historically and doctrinally antithetical. How, ran one of the pamphlets, could the king expect that

> the English, who so justly love and reverence episcopacy will unite with
> Scotland, if subjected to Presbytery, especially since the Presbyterians, who
> generally own the covenant, are sworn to extirpate episcopacy . . . which
> oath will certainly bind them to overthrow episcopacy in England more
> industriously, when England by the union becomes a part of their native
> country.[57]

English Tories at least were a receptive audience. In May 1690 one Suffolk squire welcomed the turn of events in Scotland 'if it will make that nation quiet', 'but,' he continued,

> I perceive many wise men are of opinions that the consequences are of such a
> restless temper, that if they want work at home they will come and help their
> dear brethren in England (as they once did before) to pull down our popish

establishment and erect their superfine Protestant discipline in the room of it . . . their new notions and discoveries, which undoubtedly are all made of republican mettal, and when they have once ruined the church I am afraid will undermine the monarchy.[58]

The animosity between the Kirk and High Anglicanism persisted and would later complicate the negotiation of the Anglo-Scottish union. But in the early 1690s the fears – real, or feigned for polemical purposes – of a revived Presbyterianism ready to resume its challenge to episcopacy beyond its jurisdiction, were wide off the mark. The problem of dissent continued, in different and less virulent forms long after the revolution, but only in Ireland did the classic Presbyterian–Anglican rivalry have a serious political future. The Ulster Presbyterians had always been distinguished from other dissenting groups in the three kingdoms by their geographic concentration and strong ethnic-based sense of identity. In that they resembled their covenanting kinfolk, but unlike the Scots Presbyterians, and like, say, English Baptists, they were consigned to permanent minority status. Nevertheless, there was nothing feigned about the fears of Presbyterian expansionism entertained by Church of Ireland divines after 1690. In an echo of the Cameronians at Dunkeld, the Presbyterians played a crucial, if hotly disputed, role in the Williamite victory by holding out at the siege of Derry. And, again emulating their Scottish brethren, they took decisive advantage of the hiatus in political authority by establishing the Synod of Ulster – described by one historian as 'the first Protestant Dissenting synod in the British Isles'.[59] King William doubled the *regium donum* and when he arrived in Ireland the ministers 'and others of that perswasion' at Belfast assured him that his 'royal bounty' and the prospect of religious liberty would entice 'those of our number now in Scotland to return, which will prove a special means of more fully planting this province with such Protestants as will be endeared to your majesty's government, and a bulwark against the Irish papists'.[60] A bulwark against the papists, yes, but a threat as well to the privileged position of the established Church.

With William secure on the throne the heroic age of Protestant dissent – the age of John Bunyan, the age of the 'Killing Times' – came to a close. In England and Ireland legal disabilities against nonconformists remained on the statute books, and so for them the revolution was incomplete. But they now enjoyed a measure of legal toleration, and throughout the eighteenth century Dissenters were generally ranked among the most reliable supporters of the revolution settlement and of its subsequent constitutional guarantor, the 1714 Hanoverian succession. However, the compromise of 1688–90

was an uneasy one in all three kingdoms. There were many like the Suffolk [55]
Tory William Glover, who feared that crypto-republican Dissenters were
determined upon 'completing' the revolution and bringing down the established Church. Political alignments still ran along religious grooves. Tories
and crypto-Jacobites now rallied behind a new slogan: 'Church in Danger!'

Notes

1. Quoted by Raymond Gillespie in 'Dissenters and Nonconformists' in Herlihy,
   K. (ed.) 1995, *The Irish Dissenting Tradition 1650–1750*, Dublin, 14.

2. Anon., 1670, *The Cry of Innocent Blood, Sounding to the Ear of Each Member in
   Parliament being a Short Relation of the Barbarous Cruelties Inflicted Lately upon the
   Peaceable People of God called Quakers, at their Meeting in Horselydown in the County
   of Sussex*, 3–6.

3. [Davies, Richard] 1765, *An Account of the Convincement, Exercises, Services and
   Travels, of that Ancient Servant of the Lord, Richard Davies, with Some Relations of
   Ancient Friends, and the Spreading of Truth in North Wales*, London, 28.

4. John Commy to Joseph Williamson, *Cal. S.P. (dom) 1675–76*, 536; anonymous
   account of landing of William III at Carrickfergus PRONI: T 1062/49/12
   (typescript).

5. Davies, *Account*, 58–9.

6. Rees, T.M., 1925, *A History of the Quakers in Wales and their Emigration to North
   America*, Carmarthen, 61.

7. Stockdale is cited by Harrison, R.S., '"As a garden enclosed": The emergence
   of Irish Quakers: 1650–1750' in Herlihy, K. (ed.) *The Irish Dissenting Tradition
   1650–1750*, Dublin, 85n; for a statistical analysis of the numbers of Quakers
   imprisoned in the English counties, based on Joseph Besse's 1753 *A Collection
   of the Sufferings of the People called Quakers*, see Butler, David M., 1988, 'Friends'
   sufferings 1650–88: a comparative survey' in *The Journal of the Friends
   Historical Society*, 55: 6, 180–4. And for an example of a contemporary com-
   pilation drawn up by Quakers for the purpose of petitioning see 'The present
   state of the oppressed prisoners called Quakers in some gaols for their
   religious peaceable meetings', *Cal. S.P. (dom) 1683*, 132–3.

8. Jenkins, G.H., 1992, *Protestant Dissenters in Wales 1639–1689*, Cardiff, 66–7.

9. These estimates are taken from Harris, T., 1993, *Politics under the Later Stuarts:
   Party Conflict in a Divided Society 1660–1715*, London and New York, 9–11;

[5 6]   Jenkins, *Protestant Dissenters in Wales*, 71; Herlihy, K. (ed.) 1995, *The Irish Dissenting Tradition 1650–1750*, Dublin.

10.   T. Aslaby to J. Williamson 4 October 1669, *Cal. S.P. (dom) 1669*, 516.

11.   Hill, Christopher, 1988, *A Tinker and a Poor Man: John Bunyan and his Church, 1628–1688*, New York, 87, 92.

12.   The Dutch report is contained in a letter, dated 2 June 1664 in *Cal. S.P. (dom) 1663–4*; the execution of Twyn and the connection with the northern rising are referred to by Lois Schwoerer, 'Liberty of the press' in Jones, J.R. (ed.) 1992, *Liberty Secured? Britain Before and After 1688*, Stanford, 207–8; for attributions of authorship see the letter cited above (Nathan Strange), Leonard Williams to Bennet, 9 September 1664 (Roger Jones), and Information of A.W. (March?) 1665 (John Goodwin) *Cal. S.P. (dom) 1663–4*, 6, 234. See also Bennet to Ormond, 25 August 1666 (Thomas Blood) in [Brown, T.] 1702, *Miscellanea Aulica: or a Collection of State-treatises*, London, 414–15. *Mene Tekel* is listed under [Roger Jones] in Greaves, R.L., 1986, *Secrets of the Kingdom: British Radicals from the Popish Plot to the Revolution of 1688–1689*, Stanford.

13.   [Roger Jones] 1663, *Mene Tekel; or, the downfall of tyranny. A treatise, wherein liberty and equality are vindicated, and tyranny condemned, by the law of God and right reason: and the peoples power, and duty, to execute justice, without, and upon, wicked governors asserted*, 3, 5, 8–10, 16, 27, 72 (italics in quotations added).

14.   Connolly, S.J., 1992, *Religion, Law and Power: The Making of Protestant Ireland, 1660–1760*, Oxford, 24.

15.   'Intelligence', Bodl. Carte Ms 52 f244.

16.   Mountalexander to Ormond, 7 August 1663, Bodl. Carte Ms 33 f28; Instructions to garrison commanders in Munster, 5 August 1663, Carte Ms 144 ff39–40; Adair, Patrick, 1866, *A True Narrative of the Rise and Progress of the Presbyterian Church in Ireland*, Belfast. Kilroy, Phil, 1994, *Protestant Dissent and Controversy in Ireland*, Cork, 229.

17.   Greaves, R.L., 'That's no good religion that disturbs government' in Ford, A., McGuire, J. and Milne, K. (eds) 1995, *As by Law Established: The Church of Ireland since the Reformation*, Dublin, 124; Greaves, R.L., 1990, *Enemies Under his Feet: Radicals and Nonconformists in Britain, 1664–1677*, Stanford, 57; Kilroy, *Protestant Dissent*, 118–24; Col. Vernon to [Joseph Williamson] 1 July 1663, *Cal. S.P. (Ire.) 1663–5*, 157–8; for an account of Bruce see Porter, Classon, 1885, *The Seven Bruces: Presbyterian Ministers in Ireland in Six Successive Generations*, Belfast, 5–12.

18.   Crookshank, William, 1749, *The History of the State and Sufferings of the Church of Scotland from the Restoration to the Revolution*, i, 184, 202–3; Archbishop Burnet to Archbishop Sheldon, 2 March 1664, *Lauderdale Papers*, ii, app. iv.

19. See Porter, *The Seven Bruces*, n. 17. Westerkamp, Marlyn, 1988, *Triumph of the Laity: Scots–Irish Piety and the Great Awakening 1625–1760*, Oxford, 61.

20. Bennet to Ormond, 3 November 1663, in *Miscellanea Aulica*, 319–20; Archbishop Burnet to Archbishop Sheldon, 2 March 1664, *Lauderdale Papers*, ii, app. iv.

21. E[dward] Bagot to Ormond, 2 August 1663, Bodl. Carte Ms 33 f18.

22. See for example the case of the 'English' Presbyterians in Cork: Kilroy, *Protestant Dissent*, 39.

23. Connolly, *Religion, Law and Power*, 159–61; Herlihy, *Irish Dissenting Tradition, passim*; Lawrence cited by Smyth, J., 'The communities of Ireland and the British State, 1660–1707' in Bradshaw, B. and Morrill, J. (eds) 1996, *The British Problem, c. 1534–1707: State Formation in the Atlantic Archipelago*, Houndsmills, 246.

24. Stewart, A.T.Q., 1989, *The Narrow Ground: The Roots of Conflict in Ulster*, London, 96.

25. Greaves, *Enemies Under his Feet*, 56, 71; Bennet to Ormond, 16 June and 4 August 1663, *Miscellanea Aulica*, 286–7, 297.

26. Barnard, T.C., 'Scotland and Ireland in the later Stewart monarchy' in Ellis, S. and Barber, S. (eds) 1995, *Conquest and Union: Fashioning a British State 1485–1725*, 252, 262; Greaves, *Enemies Under his Feet*, 56–7; Greaves, 'That's no good religion', 124.

27. Burnet to Sheldon, 18 April 1665, *Lauderdale Papers*, ii, app. xviii–xx; Greaves, *Enemies Under his Feet*, 65.

28. Gowan, I.B., 1976, *The Scottish Covenanters, 1660–1688*, London, 54.

29. Brown, John, 1845 edn, *An Apologetical Relation of the Particular Sufferings of the Faithful Ministers and Professors of the Church of Scotland since August 1660*, Edinburgh, 49 and section xvi. Gowan, *Scottish Covenanters*, 61.

30. The old Ulster hand the Rev. John Livingstone's equation of allegiance with supremacy led to his expulsion from Scotland in 1663: *A letter written by that famous and faithful minister of Christ, Mr John Livingstone unto his parishioners at Ancrum in Scotland, dated Rotterdam October 7 1671* in Tweedie, Rev. W.K. (ed.) 1845, *Select Biographies*, Edinburgh, Wodrow Soc., 235.

31. Gowan, *Scottish Covenanters*, 62–73. For Wallace see Greaves, *Enemies Under his Feet*, 58, and Rothes to Lauderdale, 6 December 1666, *Lauderdale Papers*, i, 253–5.

32. Rothes to Lauderdale, 6 December 1666, *Lauderdale Papers*, i, 253–5.

[5 8]   33. Gowan, *Scottish Covenanters*, 79; Adair, *True Narrative*, 258–60.

34. Rothes to Lauderdale, *c.* 1665, and Tweeddale to Lauderdale, 18 June 1668, *Lauderdale Papers*, i, 233–4, ii, 106–7; Gowan, *Scottish Covenanters*, 126–7.

35. Stewart, Sir James and Stirling, Rev. James, 1721 edn, *Napthali, or the Wrestlings of the Church of Scotland for the Kingdom of Christ*, Glasgow, ii–iii, xix, 243; *A letter written by . . . John Livingstone*, 284; the Sanquhar Declaration is reprinted Mackenzie, George, 1691, *A Vindication of the Government in Scotland during the Reign of King Charles II against Misrepresentations made in Several Scandalous Pamphlets*, 54–6; for arguments about the importance of nationalism and the Kirk see Buckroyd, Julia, 1987, *The Life of James Sharp, Archbishop of St Andrews, 1618–1679*, Edinburgh, 106, and Westerkamp, *Triumph of the Laity*, 60.

36. Kidd, Colin, 1993, *Subverting Scotland's Past: Scottish Whig Historians and the Creation of an Anglo-British Identity, 1689–c. 1830*, Cambridge, 54.

37. *A letter by . . . John Livingstone*, 284; 1842–3, 'Out of Mr Alexander Shields' *Memoirs* for the year M.D.C.lxxxviii', *Wodrow's Analecta*, Edinburgh Maitland Club, i, 184–5.

38. Since the Jesuits were everywhere and behind everything that went awry, including the great fire of London and the emergence of the sects, they were also, of course, the artful originators of anti-prelatic propaganda. According to the English churchman, Robert Ware, Jesuits were active among the Scottish Covenanters, hoping thereby to weaken Protestantism by sowing divisions within, and one of their most effective stratagems had been to mislead the people 'into a hatred of the governors of the church, by telling them of their near approaches to popery'.

39. Stewart and Stirling, *Napthali*, viii–ix; Moray to Lauderdale, 10 December 1667, *Lauderdale Papers*, ii, 86–7.

40. Shields, Alexander, 1687, *A Hind Let Loose, or a Historical Representation of the Testimonies of the Church of Scotland*, n.p., 2–3, 93.

41. Lynch, Michael, 1992, *Scotland: A New History*, London, 295.

42. Goldie, Mark, 'Scotland and England 1660–1707' in Bradshaw, B. and Morrill, J. (eds) 1996, *The British problem, c. 1534–1707: State Formation in the Atlantic Archipelago*, Houndsmills, 226–7; Shields, *A Hind Let Loose*, 131.

43. Cited by Clark, J.C.D., 1994, *The Language of Liberty 1660–1832: Political Discourse and Social Dynamics in the Anglo-American World*, Cambridge, 228–9. For reference to the text of the Sanquhar Declaration, see note 35 above.

44. Lauderdale to Danby, 8 November 1677, Danby to Lauderdale, 15 November [59]
    1677, *Lauderdale Papers*, iii, 89–92; Smyth, 'The communities of Ireland and
    the British State', 252; Beckett, J.C. 'Irish–Scottish relations in the seventeenth
    century', 1972, *Confrontations: Studies in Irish History*, London, 34–43; *HMC
    Buccleuch & Queensberry Ms*, ii, 68.

45. 1679, *News from Ireland. Being the examination and confession of William Kelso, a
    Scotch rebel taken in Ireland, whiter he fled, after the defeat of the rebels in Scotland*;
    Kilroy, *Protestant Dissent*, 237; Moray to Queensberry, 26 July 1684, 4 April,
    18 April and 30 April 1685, *HMC Buccleuch & Queensberry Ms*, ii, 30, 47–8,
    53, 61.

46. Kilroy, *Protestant Dissent*, 116–17, 125–6; Greaves, *Secrets of the Kingdom*, 265.

47. Reprimand of David Houstan, 23 August 1671, Wodrow Ms (copies)
    PRONI T 525/17/1–2; Kilroy, *Protestant Dissent*, 114–15; 'Out of Mr
    Alexander Shields' *Memoirs* for the year M.D.C. lxxxviii', *Wodrow's Analecta*,
    i, 178, 184. Loughridge, Adam, 1984, *The Covenanters in Ireland*, Belfast, 11–
    13.

48. Marvell, Andrew, 1677, *An Account of the Growth of Popery and Arbitrary
    Government in England*, Amsterdam, 3.

49. Earle, Peter, 1977, *Monmouth's Rebels: The Road to Sedgemoor 1685*, New York,
    ix, ch. 1 and appendix; see also McDonald, Wigfield W., 1980, *The Monmouth
    Rebellion: A Social History*, New Jersey, 24–31.

50. I find John Miller's 1978, *James II: A Study in Kingship*, Hove, particularly
    persuasive.

51. Miller, J., 1977, 'The Earl of Tyrconnel and James II's Irish policy,
    1685–1688', *HJ*, 20: 803–23.

52. This paragraph draws on Speck, W.A., 1989, *Reluctant Revolutionaries:
    Englishmen and the Revolution of 1688*, Oxford, 175–87, and Watts, M.R., 1978,
    The Dissenters, Oxford, 257–62.

53. *The Case of the Episcopal Clergy of Scotland Truly Represented* in *Somer Tracts*, xii,
    358–61.

54. There is a lucid account of these important years in Scottish politics by
    Cowan, I.B., 'Church and state reformed? The revolution of 1688–9 in
    Scotland' in Israel, J. (ed.) 1991, *The Anglo-Dutch Moment: Essays on the Glorious
    Revolution and its World Impact*, Cambridge, 163–83.

55. *Wodrow Analecta*, i, 196.

[6 0]   56.   1689, *A Memorial for his Highness the Prince of Orange in Relation to the Affairs of Scotland . . . by Two Persons of Quality*, London; 1690, *An Account of the Present Persecution of the Church in Scotland in Several Letters*, London.

57.   *Memorial . . . in Relation to the Affairs of Scotland*, 7–8.

58.   W. Glover to Edmund Bohun, 16 May 1690, CUL Sel. 3.237 (f143). A number of Glover's letters are bound in this (Sel. 3.237) volume of pamphlets.

59.   Brooke, Peter, 1987, *Ulster Presbyterianism: The Historical Perspective 1610–1970*, New York, 59.

60.   *The Address Presented to the King at Belfast in Ireland, on June 16th 1690*.

4

THE CATHOLIC PROBLEM

Religion and politics meshed inextricably in the late Stuart kingdoms. Often that tight relationship manifested itself in the real and imagined, fertilising interactions of Protestant nonconformity and political radicalism. To some churchmen the Dissenter-radicals represented the greatest threat to Church and state. To others it seemed popery posed the real danger. Both types shared a conviction of the existence of deep-laid conspiracy against Church and state; only the alleged conspirators differed. Conspiracy theories were a staple of the seventeenth- and eighteenth-century mind and to consign them to mere credulity or 'paranoia' is to misunderstand their widespread appeal.[1] In the absence of modes of explanation for political or social change which stress 'impersonal forces', pre-modern men and women turned to divine providence or to individual human agency, to account for the otherwise inexplicable. And if the 'causes' of events were not immediately apparent, that suggested that they were hidden. Plots and plotters – usually Jesuits – were conscripted to explain everything from the civil wars, to the rise of the sects, to the great fire of London. Yet even by the seventeenth century's generous standards the uncovering of conspiracies could descend to ludicrous levels. One churchman claimed that nonconformity was the outcome of a 'Jesuitical division' designed to weaken the reformed religion from within; that Jesuits were active among the Scottish Covenanters; and that Peter Talbot (a future Catholic Archbishop of Dublin) had attended Cromwell's funeral and soldiered in General Lambert's army![2] Of course, to the nonconformists and Covenanters the affinity between the episcopal and Roman Catholic Churches, between 'our high-flown hierachicks, and their brethren the papists',[3] was obvious, sinister, and not coincidental.

[62] Anti-popery and the Popish Plot

English fears of, and contempt for, Catholicism were as old as the Reformation. Catholics were stereotyped as superstitious, idolatrous, devious and servile. Catholicism became a synonym for poverty and tyranny. Catholic monarchies, such as the Spanish, the French, and indeed the English during the reign of Queen Mary in the 1550s, persecuted Protestants as heretics. In those fortunate lands where the reformed religion had secured a footing, eternal vigilance had to be exercised against an international Catholic conspiracy to extirpate it. The Catholic powers of Europe presented a clear military threat; Catholics within a Protestant kingdom, owing allegiance to a 'foreign prince' – the Pope – represented a fifth column. The conflict, moreover, transcended politics. Many seventeenth-century Protestants interpreted the struggle with Rome in millenarian terms, identifying the Pope as Antichrist, and England as an 'elect nation'. Richard Baxter described Rome as 'the whore of Babylon' and Henry Jones, Bishop of Meath, characterised the Pope as 'the man of sin'.[4] And for Protestants in all three kingdoms, who shared in some version of that world-view (Scotland had its own claim to 'election'), reprobate Ireland, with its majority Catholic population, stood out as a special problem.

The anti-popery of the Irish – or 'New English' – Protestant minority is easily explicable. Irish Catholics constituted an inveterately hostile majority, which by the 1641 massacres had demonstrated, beyond all reasonable doubt, its fundamental irreconcilability to a Protestant polity. English, Welsh and Scottish anti-popery is, on the surface, less readily understandable. Catholics on the island of Britain constituted a tiny minority. Estimates of the Catholic population of England are as low as 1.1 per cent, or about 60,000 of a total population of 5 to 5.5 million. In Scotland a figure of 2 per cent has been suggested.[5] The patently unthreatening character of that minority in retrospect has prompted some historians to dismiss anti-popery, and in particular the Popish Plot episode of 1678–81, as 'irrational'.[6] From a seventeenth-century standpoint, however, suspicions about a Catholic 'design' could appear entirely sane. First, the geographic concentration of Catholics, in Northumbria and Lancashire, along the Welsh borders in Herefordshire and Monmouthshire, in the Scottish Highlands and in and around Aberdeen, created a sort of optical illusion of numerical strength. In addition, the disproportionate Catholic representation in the ranks of the gentry and nobility – still small in absolute terms, but like the Duke of Norfolk, or his Scottish son-in-law, the Marquis of Huntley, highly visible

– enhanced that misperception.[7] Then there was the incontestable matter of record. 'Bloody Mary's' 'fires of Smithfield' burned brightly in the Protestant imagination, and only the Bible outsold the Protestant martyrologist John Foxe's *Acts and Monuments* in this period. There was also the matter of Catholicism's international character. Viewed from the European angle, the English saw themselves as an 'island people' holding out against aggressively expansionist Catholic power, and Louis XIV's ambitions for 'universal monarchy'. In Shaftesbury's formulation 'the foreign Protestants are a wall; the only wall and defence to England ... the protection of the Protestants abroad is the greatest power and security the crown of England can attain to, and which can only help us to give check to the growing greatness of France'.[8]

'Classic' conspiracy theories, a variant of the king's 'evil councillors' school of political analysis, customarily pinpointed highly placed, and malevolent, courtiers as the source of secret intrigues. Thus in 1673 a House of Commons address demanded that Richard Talbot – Peter's brother, and a friend of James, Duke of York – 'who hath notoriously assumed to himself the title of agent of the Roman Catholics in Ireland', be forbidden access to the royal court.[9] Indeed the events of 1673 confirmed the worst suspicions of Protestant Englishmen, lifting parliamentary and popular anti-popery into a higher, sharper, register. The Lord Treasurer Sir Thomas Clifford's carriage overturned on the Strand in London, discharging him and a Catholic priest, in full robes, on their way to mass.[10] But it was the fall-out from the first Test Act which aroused most concern. The Test Act reversed Charles II's Declaration of Indulgence in 1672 by instituting a test denying the doctrine of transubstantiation for all holders of public office. The result was as shocking as the implication was devastating: the Lord High Admiral, and heir presumptive to the throne, James, Duke of York, resigned his post. The king to be had identified himself publicly as a papist.

Anti-popery thrived on a rich diet of fear and prejudice, fact and fable; it took James's 'coming out', however, and the issue of the succession, to thrust it into the centre of Restoration politics. The mid-1670s witnessed a shift in political alignments, with the construction by the Earl of Danby of a church-and-court 'party', the nucleus of the 'Tories' as they would be called in 1679; and the emergence, under the leadership of Shaftesbury, of a country opposition, or Whig 'party' as it would be named, also in 1679. Tories and Whigs differed on the role of parliament, the nature of sovereignty, and toleration; but it was the succession that mattered most. Tories accepted the doctrines of hereditary succession, divine right and non-resistance, although in 1677

[64] Danby, a firm Protestant, and no doubt with an eye to the future, brokered the marriage of the sonless James's daughter, Mary, to the Protestant, William Prince of Orange. Whigs hoped to prevent, or at the very least 'limit', a Catholic monarch. Shaftesbury, for example, suggested that Charles should secure the Protestant succession by divorcing his Catholic wife, Catherine of Braganza, and remarrying to a Protestant princess. By late 1678 proposals surfaced to oblige a future Catholic king to raise his heir as a Protestant, and to divest him of the right to appoint bishops to the Church of England. Yet the repugnance of James's religion to the majority of Englishmen notwithstanding, the sheer weight of legitimist ideology, the force of tradition, the Stuarts' jealous guardianship of royal prerogative – of which hereditary succession was the supreme instance – and the horror of innovation, so recently demonstrated by civil wars, republicanism and military rule, all militated against the likelihood of any dilution of regalian rights.[11] The prospects for constitutional restraints, and even of the Duke of York's exclusion from the throne, were abruptly boosted, however, in September 1678, by Isaac Tonge's and Titus Oates's 'revelations' of a Popish Plot.[12]

Tonge's, Oates's and subsequently William Bedloe's allegations concerning a wide-ranging and elaborate Catholic plan to assassinate the king, the Irish Lord Lieutenant, Ormond and even James if he did not fall into step with the plotters' designs, were a gigantic fabrication. But that did not prevent them persuading a majority of Privy Councillors and the 'public' of their veracity. The precision and detail of the claims lent credence to the plot,[13] while for many its existence was confirmed by the discovery of incriminating letters written by the Duke of York's former secretary, Edward Coleman, to Louis XIV's confessor, and by the mysterious murder of Sir Edmund Berry Godfrey, the magistrate to whom Oates had sworn his original deposition. On 20 October Catholics were ordered out of London. In the provinces magistrates raided houses to search for priests and Jesuits – always thought of as a separate and more deadly category – to disarm papists and to arrest supposed plotters. As always with the decentralised system of law enforcement, the intensity of religious persecution was a function of local politics, and along the Welsh borders – Bedloe's home ground – and in south Wales, the site of confessionally based gentry rivalry, the campaign against the Catholic priesthood 'was conducted with a vicious obstinacy unique even at the time'.[14]

Although the executions, which claimed nine Jesuits, four other priests and over twenty Catholic laymen, continued into 1681, as a popular

phenomenon the plot scare had virtually run its course by the end of 1679.
Anti-popery found expression through many media in these years. An
avalanche of pamphlets, scurrilous woodcuts and broadsheets, triggered by
rumour, fear and political animus, and enabled by the lapsing of the
Licensing Act, were disseminated through the land by post and by an
'underground network' of Whig activists. The Whigs of the Green Ribbon
Club also stage-managed some spectacular street theatre with the great
Pope-burning processions in London on 17 November (the anniversary of
Queen Elizabeth's accession in 1558) 1679, 1680 and 1681.[15] But by 1680
the plot, as such, was less the issue than the pretext for the real Whig
business of exclusion.

The Cavalier Parliament which sat for eighteen years was followed by
three parliaments in only three years. Each election returned a 'Whig' majority and the first two Parliaments carried bills to exclude James from the succession. Charles prorogued the first parliament before the bill could proceed
from the House of Commons to the House of Lords; in the second parliament the second bill failed to clear the upper house, while in the third
Parliament, which met briefly in royalist – and garrisoned – Oxford, a third
exclusion bill was read but not voted on before dissolution. The Whigs
mobilised public opinion on an unprecedented scale, orchestrated mass petitioning in support of exclusion, and in the process applied enormous pressure on the king. Both the royal dukes, York and the 'alternative candidate'
for the throne, Monmouth, were effectively exiled for the duration of the
crisis, and for a time Charles seemed prepared to concede 'limitations'.
However, the Tories fought back with pamphlets and petitions of their own.
The exclusionists were beaten in the end by the resilience of the legitimist
doctrines which they sought to circumvent, by the frank exercise of prerogative to neutralise their parliamentary victories, and by their own success
in raising the 'mob'. The spectre of 'the people', especially in London, rallied
'the men of property . . . to the crown'. The 'fear of civil war', it has
been observed, 'is the essential if usually unspoken background to late
seventeenth-century politics'.[16]

Catholic Ireland: *revanche* and defeat

A paradox of the Popish Plot is its failure to take hold in Ireland. After all,
as Henry Jones, Bishop of Meath, pointed out in 1676, Ireland 'is above all

[6 6]   other nations in Europe influenced by the power of Rome', a fact that Irish
Catholics themselves 'acknowledged and gloried in'.[17] Ireland, it is true, did
provide the plot's most illustrious victims, the Archbishop of Armagh, Oliver
Plunkett, executed in 1681, and the aged Archbishop of Dublin, Peter Talbot,
who died in prison the previous year, but, in a comparative sense, the country escaped the worst excesses of persecution. That 'escape' cannot, however,
be attributed to any lack of zeal on the part of the plot-mongers. The
'insolence' of the Irish papists was broadcast in the English House of Lords
as early as October 1678, and the arrests of the Talbot brothers and disarming proclamations did not satisfy the Lord Lieutenant Ormond's hardline
Protestant critics within Ireland.[18] In March 1680 Shaftesbury, in cahoots
with Henry Jones, presented 'evidence' of the plot's Irish dimension to the
English Privy Council.[19] Yet the plot refused to boil, not least because
Ormond refused to allow it. Writing to his old rival and long-time advocate
of repressive measures, Orrery, he remarked dryly that the scare in Orrery's
province of Munster 'seem[s] to be greater than in any other part of the
kingdom, from whence I do not hear but that Protestants that live out of
garrisons lie down quietly and rise safely'.[20]

    It is significant that Sir John Temple's lurid catalogue of popish perfidy in
1641, *A History of the Irish Rebellion*, was twice reprinted in London during
1679, but not at all in Dublin.[21] No friend to the Catholics, during his time
at the Castle, between 1661 and 1669, 1677 and 1685, Ormond adopted a
minimal coercion approach. Above all else a royalist and a churchman, in the
1660s he presided over a land settlement which attempted, hopelessly, to
reconcile the king's promise to restore confiscated property to Catholics
(innocent papists) who had never been in rebellion, *and* to confirm the titles
of the adventurers and soldiers who had benefited from the confiscations.
The Acts of Settlement and Explanation in 1662 and 1665, and the court of
claims which adjudicated between conflicting entitlements, thus signified
the dilemma so memorably summed up by Ormond: 'there must be discoveries made of a new Ireland, for the old will not serve to satisfy these engage-
ments'. It proved an impossible task. Catholic ownership of land rose from
under 10 to over 20 per cent in the decade after the Restoration, fuelling
Protestant anxieties while leaving a sense of Catholic grievance intact.[22]

    In the political realm it was the Catholics themselves who attempted
to reconcile contradictory positions. In answer to the standard Protestant
charges of disloyalty, and of compliance to the foreign jurisdiction of Rome,
in December 1661 a number of Catholic laymen, some clergy and one
bishop drafted a 'remonstrance', conceding the authority of the king in

temporal affairs. This formulary caused the Catholic community to split. One [6 7] group, the 'remonstrants', were represented by the 'Ormondite' Dominican friar Peter Walsh; the other, the 'anti-remonstrants', were unprepared to abandon Church teaching, and were heavily endorsed by the hierarchy. The Irish propositions were also condemned by Rome, and by the theological faculty of the University of Louvain. In June 1666 the leading Catholics, including the exiled Archbishop of Armagh, Edmund O'Reilly, were permitted by Ormond to assemble in Dublin to settle the matter. Rejecting the original remonstrance, the assembly offered instead the first three of the six 'Sorbonne propositions', one of which did indeed deny the Pope's right to depose princes. But this did not go far enough for the government. Ormond, who had probably predicted some such outcome,[23] seized on the rejection of the remonstrance as evidence of Catholic disaffection and moved swiftly to arrest O'Reilly and the anti-remonstrant priests. For the Catholics the whole episode amounted to a self-inflicted political disaster.[24]

In Ireland, like England, the rhythms of anti-Catholic coercion were dictated by the national and local political contexts. For example, Irish Catholics enjoyed a very relaxed regime during the lord lieutenancy of the Earl of Berkeley in the early 1670s, although less so in Munster where they came under the ever-vigilant purview of Orrery.[25] In addition the fate of the Irish Catholics also depended upon the course of events in England. The sharp reversal of Berkeleyan licence in 1673 owed everything to the anti-popery offensive in the English Parliament. Yet on balance, compared with their experience during the 1650s or of Williamite Ireland, Catholics fared moderately well during the Restoration era. Certainly that is how they themselves saw it in retrospect. The first civil article of the Treaty of Limerick in 1691 stated that 'The Roman Catholics of this kingdom, shall enjoy such privileges in the exercise of their religion, as are consistent with the laws of Ireland, or as they did enjoy in the reign of King Charles II.'[26]

The accession of a Catholic king in 1685 represents the most dramatic instance of how changing circumstances in England could alter the Irish situation. James embarked upon a 'Catholicising' policy in all three kingdoms. Catholics were admitted to the English Privy Council, and appointed as Justices of the Peace. Declarations of Indulgence in 1687 and 1688 extended toleration to Catholics and Protestant Dissenters in England and Scotland. The political cost was, of course, enormous, and with hindsight appears predictable. James's objects and motives are open to debate, but one thing at least is clear: if his Catholic policy stood any chance of success anywhere, it was in Ireland.

[6 8]   The re-Catholicising of the Irish polity did not commence immediately, or follow inevitably, upon the succession of a Catholic king.[27] James at first appointed an impeccable churchman, the second Earl of Clarendon, as Irish Lord Lieutenant, and had good reason to maintain the *status quo*. An aggressive Catholic policy in Ireland ran the risk of alienating his Protestant subjects in England. James also retained a conventional view of Anglo-Irish relations. During the 1689 Irish Parliament, for example, at a time when his fate rested largely in the hands of his Irish Catholic supporters, he stubbornly refused to countenance their demand for the repeal of Poynings Law, which lodged ultimate control of Irish legislation in the English Privy Council.[28] At court in 1685 the advocates of a cautious and traditional reliance of the English and Protestant Interest in Ireland predominated. But it was the counsel of Richard Talbot, now ennobled as the Earl of Tyrconnell, that prevailed. This has been attributed to the force of his personality and to his skilful appeals to the king's prejudices.[29] It can also be attributed to the dynamics of Irish society.

After Tyrconnell replaced Clarendon – in a concession to his rivals at court as Lord Deputy, not Lord Lieutenant – in early 1687, the process of Catholicisation began to gather a virtually self-sustaining momentum. In fact the process was already well under way. As commander of the army in 1685, he seized upon the failed Argyll rebellion in Scotland as an opportunity for disarming the distrusted Ulster Scots. He next instigated a purge of 'Cromwellian' officers, while simultaneously recruiting ever increasing numbers of Catholic rank and file. By 1688 the army had an almost entirely Catholic personnel. Catholics were appointed as judges and Justices of the Peace, and admitted to town corporations under the terms of remodelled charters. Preparations were laid for a new Parliament which, Catholics hoped, and Protestants feared, would overturn the Act of Settlement. What were Tyrconnell's objectives?

First, it should be stressed that the Lord Deputy always saw himself as the champion of the Old English. His native Irish co-religionists stood to gain from his policies, but neither he, nor his master, were overly concerned for the welfare of the 'O's' and the 'Macs'. And second, John Miller raises the interesting theory that Tyrconnell may have contemplated the idea of Ireland going its own way upon the death of James and the succession of a Protestant to the throne of England. With the army, corporations, local government and judicial bench securely under Catholic control, the Irish could look forward to a 'king of their own . . . under the protection of France'.[30] But whatever his objectives might have been, the effects of his policies are unmistakable. For the Protestant community the Tyrconnell era, instantly memorialised by Bishop William King's *State of the Protestants of Ireland under the Late King James's Government,* constituted a collective trauma not soon forgotten.

'James', King asserted, 'designed to destroy and utterly ruin the Protestant religion, the liberty and property of the subjects in general, the English Interest in Ireland in particular, and alter the very frame and constitution of the government.' As a bishop of the established Church, King wished to exonerate the Protestants for departing from their obligation of passive obedience to their sovereign. The Protestants, he argued, faced the threat of extirpation, and 'by endeavouring to destroy us he [James] . . . in that very act abdicated the government'.[31] This was a starkly sectarian analysis. Everyone knew, he insisted, that the cause of the popish Irish could only be advanced at the expense of the 'English Protestants': 'either they or we must be ruined'.[32] But King also spoke for the men of property. The new officer corps and soldiery, the sheriffs and the deputy lord lieutenants of the counties, were characterised as 'the sons or descendants of rebels in 1641', as 'tories' or robbers, 'poor' 'servants', 'cowherds, horseboys or footmen', as 'men of little or no fortune' and 'the scum and rascality of the world'.[33] The Catholic *revanche*, lethal enough on religious grounds, thus represented a terrifying social revolution as well.

There is a sense in which King's book is as much about what *might* have happened as it is about what actually happened. The depredations of tory bands, or the repeal – despite James's opposition – of the Act of Settlement, with the provision for future forfeitures, by the Irish Jacobite Parliament, do not stand comparison with the 1641 massacres. Many Protestants nevertheless deciphered their sudden, steep reversals of fortune as a portent of massacre. King's argument that the Protestant community was *about to be* exterminated is not merely to justify its armed self-defence; rather it catches the essence of the Protestant experience in these years. The siege of Derry, the Jacobite Parliament's Act of Attainder against Williamite Protestants in rebellion or in exile in England, and the battles of the Boyne and Aughrim in 1690 and 1691, were very real and had a profound emblematic impact on that community (or communities); yet the full extent of its trauma can only be grasped by registering the chilling effects of fear and rumour, myth and panic.

Tyrconnell's regime caused many Protestants to flee the country, in comparatively small numbers at first; by December 1688 they were reportedly leaving Dublin by the shipload.[34] In Ulster the circulation of an anonymous

[7 0]   warning – the famous 'Comber letter' – of a general massacre planned for 9 December sparked off an exodus to Scotland and England, and stiffened the resolve of the Protestants who had crowded into the walled city of Derry and shut the gates on 7 December. The panic spread even to England, where some county militia companies turned out in response to bogus reports that 'the Irish' were coming to slit Protestant throats.[35] The sense of catastrophe narrowly averted lies behind King's understanding of the Williamite 'deliverance' as providential. It also goes a long way towards explaining Protestant attitudes – which might be summed up as 'never again' – underpinning the subsequent penal laws.

The civil articles of the Treaty of Limerick signed in October 1691, which brought the war to an end, offered the vanquished Catholics generous terms. It was, however, a treaty made by military commanders in the field for military reasons. Fatally, for the Catholics, it also lacked statutory force. The Irish Protestants, who believed that they had won the war only to lose the peace, were never prepared to honour the spirit of the treaty, and in the chambers of the exclusively Protestant Parliament succeeded in weaving into the Williamite settlement a formidable fabric of anti-Catholic legislation. Nor in England did the triumph of Parliament, 'liberty' and religious toleration, celebrated by eighteenth-century Whig politicians and nineteenth-century Whig historians, extend to Catholics. Indeed the later emphases on Parliament's struggle against arbitrary power under-represents the contemporary stress on the struggle against popery.

The 'interim government' of 'the Lords spiritual and temporal', which assumed control in London after James's flight and before William's arrival in December 1688, ordered all Catholics from the city and issued instructions for the arrest of Jesuits at all ports in Sussex and Kent.[36] Catholics were formally excluded from the provisions of the 1689 Toleration Act, as John Locke argued they ought to be in *A Letter Concerning Toleration*.[37] The Test Act of 1673 was now applied to the monarch. From 1692 Catholics were subject to double taxation, and by the Act for further preventing the growth of popery in 1700 (the Scottish Parliament passed an equally severe law the same year) Catholic schools were outlawed and bishops and priests caught in the exercise of their functions were liable to life imprisonment. Nevertheless the premier historian of English Catholics, John Bossy, maintains that 'statutes, beneficial or penal, have on the whole had a limited effect' and that 'English Catholics during the century after 1688 were not on any reasonable judgement an oppressed minority'.[38] In contrast, Edmund Burke described the Irish penal laws as 'well fitted for the oppression, impoverishment, and degradation of a people, and the debasement in them of human nature itself, as ever proceeded from the perverted ingenuity of man'.[39]

Any assessment of the penal laws, based purely on an examination of the statute books, would surely confirm Burke's opinion. Beginning in 1695 the Dublin Parliament enacted a series of anti-Catholic measures which became known, collectively, as the 'penal code'.[40] Under this 'code' Catholics could not bear arms or own a horse worth more than five pounds; bishops and regular clergy were banished and diocesan clergy had to register and to abjure the Pretender, James III and VIII; no new churches could be built; Catholics were restricted to 31-year leases while their estates were subject to partible subdivision or gavelkind, rather than primogeniture, unless a son converted to the established Church, in which case he stood to inherit all the land while the father's status became that of tenant-for-life; Catholics were not permitted to serve in the army or the navy or attend the university and they were excluded from every area of public life including the Parliament, the Bar, the Bench and the corporations; in 1727 they were disenfranchised outright.

Moving from the legal theory to an examination of the laws in practice, Burke's uniformly bleak picture needs to be complicated. Almost 400 regular clergy and a number of bishops left Ireland as a result of the Banishment Act of 1697,[41] and, according to Arthur Young, by 1775 only 5 per cent of Irish land remained in Catholic ownership. On the other hand, purely religious persecution fell largely into disfavour among Protestants themselves within the first two decades of the eighteenth century, while the figure of 5 per cent 'ownership' does not take leasehold tenancies into account, and masks the subtle ways in which some converts remained, at least for the first generation, part of the 'Catholic interest'.[42] Echoing Bossy on the English Catholic experience, one historian has written recently that 'the penal laws resulted in a life which was rarely, if ever, uncomfortable, but it was one which could never be completely settled'.[43] Irish Catholic gentry families devised numerous survival strategies, such as exporting 'surplus' sons to Catholic Europe, or going into trade, to an extent that the eighteenth century witnessed the rise of a Catholic mercantile middle class.[44] And if the impact of the penal laws has been downgraded by modern scholarship, the motives behind them have likewise been reassessed. In place of a purposive, coherent 'code', we are now presented with 'a ragbag of measures, enacted piecemeal'. Instead of a Protestant elite with a vested interest in maintaining a monopoly of power by continuing to exclude the papists from public life, historians now detect an authentic conversionist impulse behind the laws.[45]

[7 2]   Undoubtedly interpretation of the nature and significance of the penal laws will continue to be contentious, and the current revisionist approach runs the risk of understating the extent to which discriminatory laws, even when they did not impinge directly on most people's lives, were nonetheless felt as grievances, or the extent to which these laws succeeded in subduing Catholic Ireland. There can be no question, for instance, that the 'natural leadership' of the Catholic community, the gentry, was the prime target of the laws; or that this was indeed the group hardest hit. Nor does Jonathan Swift's high estimate of the effects of anti-Catholic legislation sit comfortably with the new understanding. 'We look upon' the papists, he wrote in 1708,

> to be altogether as inconsiderable as the women and children. Their lands are almost entirely taken from them, and they are rendered uncapable of purchasing any more; and for the little that remains, provision is made by the late Act against Popery, that it will daily crumble away: to prevent which, some of the most considerable among them are already turned Protestants, and so, in all probability, will many more. Then, the popish priests are all registered, and without permission (which, I hope, will not be granted) they can have no successors; so that the Protestant clergy will find it, perhaps, no difficult matter to bring great numbers over to the church; and, in the mean time, the common people without leaders, without discipline, or natural courage, being little better than *Hewers of Wood, and Drawers of Water*, are out of all capacity of doing any mischief.[46]

Of course the polemical context is crucial here. The pamphlet from which this passage comes is directed against the Irish Presbyterians and Swift's purpose in downplaying the 'Catholic threat' is to counteract calls for pan-Protestant unity and, as a corollary, the proposition that Dissenters ought to be exempt from civil disabilities. The previous shining exemplar of Protestant solidarity had supposedly occurred at the siege of Derry in 1688–89,[47] so Swift was equally anxious to belittle the dangers of Jacobitism. The Catholics were not, he asserted, 'likely to join in any considerable numbers with an *Invader*, having found so ill success when they were much more numerous and powerful; when they had a prince of their own religion to head them, had been trained for some years under a *Popish Deputy*, and received such mighty aids from the *French King*'.[48] Perhaps he was right. One of the more striking features of the Jacobite rebellions in 1715 and 1745 is Catholic Ireland's inaction. This can be accounted for by Ireland's low priority in Jacobite strategy. But it was also due, surely, to the effectiveness of the penal laws.

Notes

1. Wood, Gordon, 1982, 'Conspiracy and the paranoid style: causality and deceit in the eighteenth century', *William and Mary Quarterly*, xxxix: 401–41.

2. Ware, Robert, 1682, *Foxes and Firebrands or, a specimen of the danger and harmony of popery and separation wherein is proved from undeniable matter of fact and reason, that separation from the Church of England is, in the judgement of papists, and by sad experience, found the most compendious way to introduce popery, and to ruine the Protestant religion*, Dublin, A3 Book One, 61–3, Book Two, 96–7.

3. The phrase is taken from a slightly later period, Ridpath, George, 1702, *A Discourse upon the Union of Scotland and England*, Edinburgh, 124–5.

4. Baxter, Richard, 1663, *Fair Warning: or, xxv. Reasons Against Toleration and Indulgence of Popery*, London, 1; Jones, Henry, 1676, *A Sermon Preached at Christ-Church, Dublin, Novemb. 12. 1676*, Dublin, 1.

5. Miller, John, 1973, *Popery and Politics in England 1660–1688*, Cambridge, 11; Macinnes, Allan I., 1996, *Clanship, Commerce and the House of Stuart, 1603–1788*, East Lothian, 175.

6. Haley, K.H.D., 1985, *Politics in the Reign of Charles II*, Oxford, 1.

7. The numbers, distribution and character of English Catholics in this period are detailed in John Bossy, 1976, *The English Catholic Community, 1570–1850*, Oxford. See too DesBrisay, Gordon, 1996, 'Catholics, Quakers and religious persecution in Restoration Aberdeen', *The Innes Review*, 47:2, 136–68, and Jenkins, Philip, 1980, 'Anti-Popery on the Welsh Marches in the seventeenth century', *HJ*, 213:2, 275–93.

8. *The Parliamentary History of England*, iv, *1660–1688*, 1116–18; Scott, Jonathan, 'England's troubles: exhuming the Popish Plot' in Harris, T., Seward, P. and Goldie, M. (eds) 1990, *The Politics of Religion in Restoration England*, Oxford, 107–31. A good contemporary example of treating the Catholic 'threat' as a European phenomenon is Edmund Everard, 1679, *Discourses on the Present State of the Protestant Princes of Europe: Exhorting These to an Union and League amongst Themselves, Against all Opposite Interests*, London.

9. *The Parliamentary History of England*, iv, *1660–1688*, 579–81.

10. Haley, *Politics in the Reign of Charles II*, 58.

11. Ronald Hutton argues that Charles II's position was so strong, and the possibility of the Whigs altering the succession so weak, that there was in fact no exclusion 'crisis' at all: 1991, *Charles II, King of England, Scotland and Ireland*, Oxford, 357.

[7 4]

12. The best narrative account of the plot is still John Keynon, 1972, *The Popish Plot*, London. For a rigorous, high-definition, scholarly examination see Knights, Mark, 1994, *Politics and Opinion in Crisis, 1678–81*, Cambridge.

13. Sir Cyril Wyche's reaction illustrates how plausible Oates could seem. Oates's 'discovery', he wrote, was 'of that nature that is equally difficult to believe it and not to believe it . . . The accuser is so positive in his charge, so exact in all circumstances, so agreeing with himself in the whole, and each particular, and swears it with such assurance, that it seems impossible to be a fiction': Wyche to Ormond, 26 October 1678, *HMC Ormond Ms*, iv, 221.

14. Keynon, *Popish Plot*, 244–5. Jenkins, 'Anti-Popery on the Welsh Marches'.

15. See Knights' section on the press, *Politics and Opinion in Crisis*, 153–92; Harris, Tim, 'The parties and the people: the press, the crowd and politics "out-of-doors" in Restoration England' in Glassey, L.K.J., 1997, *The Reign of Charles II and James VII & II*, Manchester, 125–51.

16. The last point is stressed by Christopher Hill in 1980, *The Century of Revolution 1603–1714*, Nelson, 200.

17. Jones, *A Sermon Preached at Christ-Church, Dublin, Novemb. 12. 1676*, 'Epistle Dedicatory' to the Lord Lieutenant, the Earl of Essex.

18. Ossory to Ormond, 23 October 1678, Orrery to Ormond, 39 November 1678, Ormond to Orrery, 7 December 1698, Ranelagh to Conway, 5 December 1679, 'Anonymous accusations against Ormond', *HMC Ormond Ms*, iv, 219–20, 246–51, 265–8, 299–300, 361–4. The 'Anonymous accusations' are also printed in *Cal. S.P. (dom) 1679–1680*, 71–3.

19. *Cal. S.P. (dom) 1679–1680*, 424, 426; Barnard, T.C., 1990, 'Crises of identity among Irish Protestants 1641–1685', *P&P*, 127:58.

20. Ormond to Orrery, 7 December 1678, *HMC Ormond Ms*, iv, 265–8.

21. Barnard, 'Crises of identity among Irish Protestants', 55.

22. Sean Connolly provides a succinct analysis of the Restoration land settlement in his section on 'settlement and explanation': 1992, *Religion, Law and Power: The Making of Protestant Ireland 1660–1760*, Oxford, 12–17. Ormond's phrase cited on p. 14.

23. Long after the event Ormond claimed to have anticipated the subsequent divisions of the Catholics 'to the greater security of the government and Protestants': Lady Burghclere, 1912, *The Life of James, First Duke of Ormonde*, London, ii: 51.

24. Connolly, *Religion, Law and Power*, 17–21; Corish, Patrick J., 1981, *The Catholic Community in the Seventeenth and Eighteenth Centuries*, Dublin, 52–3.

25. Connolly, *Religion, Law and Power*, 21.

26. The Treaty of Limerick is extracted in Curtis, Edmund and McDowell, R.B. (eds) 1943, *Irish Historical Documents*, London, 171–5.

27. My account is indebted to Miller, John, 1977, 'The Earl of Tyrconnel and James II's Irish policy, 1685–1688', *HJ*, 20:4, 803–23.

28. Simms, J.G., 1969, *Jacobite Ireland, 1685–91*, London, 78–80.

29. Miller, 'The Earl of Tyrconnell and James II's Irish policy', *passim*.

30. Miller, 'The Earl of Tyrconnell and James II's Irish policy', 807–8, 821–2.

31. King, William, 1692 edn, *The State of the Protestants of Ireland under the Late King James's Goverment*, London, 5, 11. The duties of passive obedience and non-resistance were restated in a reply to King by his fellow Trinity College Dublin alumnus, the non-juror Charles Leslie, in 1692, *An Answer to a Book Intituled The State of the Protestants in Ireland under the Late King James Government*, London. Another Irish Protestant, on the other hand, simply dismissed these doctrines as 'impracticable notions': 1690, *An Account of the Transactions of the Late King James in Ireland*, London.

32. King, *State of the Protestants*, 61, 270.

33. King, *State of the Protestants*, 24–5, 62.

34. King James to Tyrconnel, 17 October 1687, *Cal. S.P. (dom) 1687–88*, 84–2; Sunderland to Tyrconnel, 14 July 1688, *HMC Ormond*, viii, 235; 'Diary of Events from 1685 to 1690', *HMC Ormond*, viii, 347, 365.

35. Jones, G.H., 1982, 'The Irish fright of 1688', *Bulletin of the Institute of Historical Research*, 55: 148–57.

36. 'Minutes of the Lords Spiritual and Temporal assembled Guildhall, Dec. 11' and 'An order of the Lords Spiritual and Temporal, assembled at Westminster, Dec. 22', *Cal. S.P. (dom) 1687–1688*, 378–80, 382.

37. Horton, John and Mendus, Susan (eds) 1991, *John Locke: A Letter Concerning Toleration in Focus*, London, 45–7, 53–4.

38. Bossy, John, 'English Catholics after 1688' in Grell, O.P., Israel, J.I. and Tyacke, N. (eds) 1991, *From Persecution to Toleration: The Glorious Revolution and Religion in England*, Oxford, 370, 374.

39. Burke, Edmund, 1792, *A Letter to Sir Hercules Langrishe*, Dublin.

40. This legislation is conveniently summarised by Wall, Maureen, 1961, *The Penal Laws, 1691–1760*, Dundalk, reprinted in O'Brien, Gerard (ed.) 1989, *Catholic Ireland in the Eighteenth Century: Collected Essays of Maureen Wall*, Dublin, 1–60.

[76]   41. O'Brien, *Collected Essays of Maureen Wall*, 9–12.

42. Cullen, L.M., 1986, 'Catholics under the penal laws', *Eighteenth-Century Ireland*, 1: 23–36.

43. Harvey, Karen J., 'The family experience: the Bellews of Mount Bellew', in Power, T.P. and Whelan, K. (eds) 1990, *Endurance and Emergence: Catholics in Ireland in the Eighteenth Century*, Dublin, 192.

44. Wall, Maureen, 'The rise of a Catholic middle class in eighteenth century Ireland' in O'Brien, Gerard (ed.) 1989, *Catholic Ireland in the Eighteenth Century: Collected Essays of Maureen Wall*, Dublin, 73–84; Dickson, D.J., 'Catholics and trade in eighteenth-century Ireland: an old debate revisited' in Power, T.P. and Whelan, K. (eds), *Endurance and Emergence*, 85–100.

45. Connolly, *Religion, Law and Power*, 263–313; Connolly, Sean, 1983, 'Religion and history', *Irish Social and Economic History*, x: 73–9; Bartlett, Thomas, 1992, *The Fall and Rise of the Irish Nation: The Catholic Question 1690–1830*, Dublin, 17–29.

46. Swift, Jonathan, *A Letter from a Member of the House of Commons in Ireland to a Member of the House of Commons in England, Concerning the Sacramental Test* in McMinn, Joseph (ed.) 1991, *Swift's Irish Pamphlets: An Introductory Selection*, Dublin, 41.

47. The Presbyterian–episcopalian unity which the siege was believed to have exemplified was in fact something of a myth: see MacBride, Ian, 1997, *The Siege of Derry in Ulster Protestant Mythology*, Dublin, 21–32.

48. Swift, *A Letter from a Member of the House of Commons*, 41.

5

CONSTITUTIONAL RELATIONS, NATIONAL IDENTITIES, UNION

Two of the more important motives behind the decision to impose epis-copacy on Scotland in 1661 were first, that Presbytery was deemed unsuitable 'to his Majestie's monarchical estate', and second, the assumption that if complete uniformity of Church government and liturgy in the three kingdoms was unobtainable, there should at least be greater congruence between all of the Churches in the king's realms.[1] The already defunct Cromwellian union had not been revived at the time of the Restoration because, in Clarendon's words, the king had no desire to 'build according to Cromwell's models'.[2] But nor could he, however much Clarendon might have wanted it, build according to Laudian models of imposed uniformity either. The continuation of a Low Church liturgy and the non-introduction of the revised prayer-book in Scotland after 1662 stemmed from a recogni-tion of Scottish distinctiveness. On which models, then, could Charles II build? Or to pose a different and more pertinent question: why should he have chosen to build on any? In 1660 there were no compelling military, political or commercial reasons pressing the English crown, court or Parlia-ment towards closer integration with Scotland or Ireland, or towards a reordering of Anglo-Scottish or Anglo-Irish constitutional relationships. Nor, of course, was there anything exotic in early modern Europe about the kind of 'composite monarchy' that Charles had inherited.

Charles succeeded to three kingdoms, but to two, not three crowns. The title of *Ard Rí* (High King) notwithstanding, Gaelic Ireland never 'developed' into a unified kingdom. Shortly after the Norman intervention in the twelfth century, King Henry II granted 'Ireland', which in practice meant the territory under Norman control, as a lordship to his son John. When, by the accident of Richard I's death, John became king, the lordship of Ireland was subsumed under the crown of England, which status Ireland retained until the Act for Kingly Title in 1541. By that Act Ireland became a kingdom, but a kingdom annexed to the crown of England. There was no separate Irish crown, and throughout the seventeenth century Englishmen routinely

[7 8] described Ireland as a 'subordinate' or 'dependent' kingdom. In addition, that status was underlined and complicated by the disputed contention that it was moreover a conquered country – an English colony, governed by English settlers and subject to English common law. On the other hand, Scotland at the time of the regnal union in 1603 was indisputably an 'ancient kingdom', boasting all the attributes of sovereignty, including its own Parliament, constitution and a distinctive legal system. The Act of Union united the separate crowns of Scotland and England in the person of James VI and I, and, despite the fact that the English Parliament declared him to be in possession of '*one* Imperial Crown', separate they remained.[3] Crucially, as it would turn out, each kingdom retained its own law of succession. The union of crowns, in other words, could be dissolved.

It is worth noting that, physically, the British monarchs of the seventeenth century possessed two crowns; that the two crowns were never melted down and merged into a single British one; and that both Charles I and Charles II – under widely different circumstances – had Scottish, in addition to English, coronation ceremonies. Physically, as well as in constitutional theory, no separate Irish crown existed. The dissimilarity in the status of the Scottish and Irish kingdoms becomes evident when we look at the great constitutional upheavals of the time. In 1649 the English Parliament treated the crown as in one sense indivisible by its Act for 'abolishing the kingly office of England and Ireland' but in another sense, and by default, as divisible, by leaving the Scottish succession intact.[4] The 'third civil war' resulted from the presumption of the Scots in crowning Charles II king not simply of Scotland, but of Britain. Again, in 1689 the English Convention Parliament deemed itself competent to offer the crown of England and Ireland to William and Mary. The Scots made their own offer, slightly later, and on their own conditions. Finally, the root cause of the crisis that produced the Anglo-Scottish legislative union in 1707 was the real possibility that the Scots, who were not bound by the English Act of Settlement in 1701, would, upon Queen Anne's death, opt out of the Hanoverian succession. In sharp contrast, and even though the 'Scottish option' was not even theoretically available, in 1703 the Irish Parliament nonetheless formally endorsed the Act of Settlement.[5]

John Bull's other kingdoms during the Restoration

The *status quo* in 1660 afforded the English court real political and, many believed, commercial advantages. 'John Bull's other kingdoms' were both, in their different ways, subordinate. Take, for example, the comparative strengths of the Parliaments. English Restoration Parliaments demonstrated repeatedly their ability to thwart, or at the very least to trouble, royal policies. Most notably Charles II never got his way on the issue of religious toleration. Just as importantly, Parliament began to assume the character of a permanent fixture in the political landscape. And if the king, as the 'country' and later the Whig opposition led by Shaftesbury came to suspect, did indeed have 'absolutist' ambitions, he never realised them. Parliament set limits to the exercise of prerogative. Only in the final four years of his reign did Charles dare dispense with it.

In Scotland and Ireland the king's ministers enjoyed a freer hand. The Irish Parliament sat only from 1661 to 1666 in this period. In Scotland, the 'Lords of the Articles' entrusted control of the Parliament's legislative agenda to the royally appointed Scottish Privy Council. In fact, the extent of *English* royal control was underlined by the operation between 1660 and 1667 of a Whitehall-based Scottish Council dominated by prominent English politicians including Clarendon. At one end of the political spectrum, Lauderdale boasted to Charles that 'never was a king so absolute as you are in poor old Scotland'; at the other end Shaftesbury complained bitterly at the time of the Popish Plot that 'in England popery was to have brought in slavery; in Scotland, slavery went before, and popery was to follow'. Whigs argued that arbitrary government in Scotland (and Ireland) was not merely deplorable in itself, but a clear and present danger to English liberties as well. And nothing illustrated that danger more vividly than the Act of Succession which James, Duke of York, pushed through a Scottish Parliament at the precise moment when an English Parliament sought to exclude him.[6]

The capacity of the Irish polity for independent action lay under three critical restraints: the chief executive officer, the Lord Lieutenant, was, of course, a royal appointee; laws enacted by the English Parliament which named Ireland were binding on Ireland – this did not apply to Scotland – and, most notoriously, under the procedures of Poynings Law, all legislation made in the Irish Parliament was subject to amendment by the English Privy Council. The Duke of Ormond, the Lord Lieutenant who stamped his character on Restoration Ireland, serving between 1662 and 1669, and again between 1677 and 1685, happened to be Irish-born; all the other holders of that office, with the dramatic exception of the Old English Catholic Tyrconnell, were English. But Ormond, a Cavalier to his fingertips, considered himself 'a perfect Englishman' anyway, and never allowed his mere place of origin to interfere with his impeccable royalism. In practice then, tenure of the highest office in the land was intimately tied to English court

[8 0] politics. Thus, for example, when Ormond's patron, Clarendon, fell from
office in 1667, Ormond's position soon, and perhaps inevitably, became
untenable.[7]

The issue of Poynings' Law arose at the outset of the Irish Restoration
Parliament. In June 1661 the manner of drafting a bill concerning the right
of outlawed (i.e. Catholic) lords to sit in the upper house caused sufficient
doubts for it to be submitted to judicial review. The judges were required to
rule 'as it involved the royal prerogative and the privileges of the commons'
and the political gloss that the king's ministers placed on this episode is
instructive. One of the three Lords Justice, who served in the absence of the
Lord Lieutenant, informed Whitehall that the vote was deliberately 'directed
against Poynings Act', and was urged in return to prevent anything being
'done or imagined against' that Act, because that would prove of 'unimagin-
able inconvenience'.[8] The Act was not contravened on this occasion, but
the brief contretemps highlighted a major theme, and continuing source of
friction, in Anglo-Irish relations: Irish resentment at legislative restraint, and
England's determination to maintain her grip.

Protestant Irish resentment had commercial, in addition to political,
sources. The 'English Interest' in Ireland objected to being bound by laws
made at Westminster to which they had not given their consent. More prac-
tically, they bristled at the consequences of English commercial legislation
which curtailed Irish trade. Here the parallel with Scotland was clear-cut.
Scottish and Irish opinion divided over the desirability of continuing the
Cromwellian union in 1659–60. Everyone wished to be rid of high and
disproportionate taxation; but the advantages of trading freely in the rich
English markets were compelling for merchants in both countries.[9] Daniel
Defoe would much later claim that during the 1650s 'Scotland flourished . . .
trade increas'd, money plentifully flowed'.[10] Over-generous as that retro-
spective assessment undoubtedly was, from 1660 to 1707 and beyond,
economic self-interest lay behind much pro-unionist sentiment in Ireland
and Scotland.

In this age of mercantilism, however, and of fierce maritime commercial
rivalries, particularly with the Dutch, English farmers and manufacturers
stoutly resisted allowing open competition from the neighbouring low-cost,
cheap-labour economies. Perceived economic self-interest, in other words,
fuelled English parliamentary opposition to schemes for union. The reimposition by England of customs duties in 1660, and the Navigation Act which
regulated the overseas trade of her *soi-disant* sister kingdoms with her
colonies, set the pattern of future commercial relations. Further restrictive

acts followed, in 1663, 1667, 1671 and 1699. Moreover the 1667 Act, which prohibited the export of Irish cattle to England, was quickly reinforced by a similar Scottish Act. A reordering of commercial relations formed the basis of Anglo-Scottish union discussions in 1668, and featured prominently in unionist discourse thereafter. 'Trade,' observed Andrew Fletcher in 1703, 'is now become the golden ball, for which all nations of the world are contending.'[11]

Another factor, more subtle, less tangible, but just as important as economic protectionism and the maintenance of political control, militated against a unionist disposition in England: chauvinism. This was a more complex matter than simple xenophobia or racism, although elements of both were ever present, and impacted differently on the different historical experiences and constitutional realities of Scotland and Ireland. The English possessed an innate, unshakable sense of cultural superiority: why should they enter into a new partnership on a more equal footing with either Scotland or Ireland? The ingrained assumption of superiority is evident, for instance, in an English pamphlet published in 1664 whose author argued for a 'union of laws'. By this he meant not 'a mixture, and composition to extract a new form out of the laws of both kingdoms' but the 'incorporating of Scotland into England, under the laws of England, and with the same privileges which the people of England do enjoy under the same prince'.[12] And if Scotland's status as a sovereign kingdom with its own regalia, courts, judicatures and Parliaments could not be denied, there was a sense in which the English almost *had* to deny it. Ingenious antiquarian-polemicists duly resolved this unnatural and inconvenient conundrum, at least to their own satisfaction. Scotland, it turned out, was an inferior kingdom after all. Scots kings had, since the eleventh century, owed *homage* to the 'Imperial' English crown.[13]

In the real world Scotland was indeed a subordinate, but also a distinct and no petty kingdom. Only by conquest could it be unilaterally 'united'. Otherwise union would have to be achieved, if England sought it, through bilateral agreement. In turn that hard political fact rested upon separate and densely textured senses of national identity. An incorporating union, such as that canvassed by the anonymous pamphleteer in 1664, would result in effect in a 'Greater England'. But it was never likely that Scottish pride, Scottish tradition or Scottish uniqueness could be absorbed with ease, or without resistance. For any union to succeed it would need first to preserve certain Scottish institutions and second to be predicated upon a new supranational identity: Britishness. Herein lay one of the crucial divergences

[8 2]   in the Scottish and Irish experience. The Anglo-Scottish unionist agenda
had always adopted a self-consciously and explicitly British rhetoric.
Pre-1707 Anglo-Irish unionist advocacy – over 90 per cent of which
emanated from Ireland – usually, though not always, ignored, and sometimes
eschewed, the concept of a common Britishness as a bridge to closer political integration.

Apart from the Scots Presbyterians in Ulster, the settler community
in Ireland tended not to think of itself as British, but rather as English.
Although full membership of the state depended upon membership of the
established Church, and conversion was open to all regardless of ethnic
background; although, therefore, a number of Anglicans were of Gaelic
origin or even, like Archbishop William King who was born in Ulster, of
Scots extraction, the great majority of Protestants who comprised the political nation were in fact of English provenance. These 'English' had good
reason for stressing their Englishness: it distinguished them from the Scots
in Ulster, whose Presbyterianism and Scottish connections constituted a
rivalry and a barrier; it distinguished them from the native Irish, a despised,
conquered and popish people; and it entitled them, they argued, to the
rights and privileges of 'free born Englishmen'. The word 'British', used as
a self-description, does flit in and out of Anglo-Ireland's vocabulary in this
period, but only enjoyed real purchase in times of pan-Protestant solidarity
against the common Catholic enemy, such as the years 1688–91. When the
threat receded the old English–Scots, Church–presbytery antipathies soon
reasserted themselves.[14] Typically, the term 'British' was used by spokesmen
for the English Interest to denote the Ulster Scots. This is what Bishop
Dopping meant in 1695 when he warned that 'the British are already
possessed of one fourth of this kingdom, that they have spread themselves
into other provinces and that there are frequent colonies coming out of
Scotland to carry on the plantation of the party'. It is also what Attorney
General Cox had in mind in 1704 when he argued that one benefit of a
union between England and Ireland would be that 'all the British would
be[come] good Englishmen'.[15]

Clearly Protestant senses of identity were profoundly complicated,
ambivalent and unstable.[16] Just as they occasionally assumed the name
British, so they sometimes called themselves Irish. The later eighteenth-
century future lay with the Protestant-patriot appropriation of the 'Irish
nation', and this has lured some historians into the whiggish sport of
tracking down an embryonic Protestant Irish identity shared by their
seventeenth-century forebears.[17] Yet while there is no doubt that the 'natural'

processes of settler identification with an adopted homeland were already under way in Restoration Ireland, Protestants were simultaneously anxious to distance themselves from the slur of Irishness. During the debates in Richard Cromwell's 1659 Parliament on whether or not the Scottish and Irish members should be allowed to sit, the MPs for Ireland stressed repeatedly their English credentials. They were 'not Irish Teagues, but faithful persons'. In the 1690s Sir Francis Brewster complained that Englishmen who lived in Ireland 'some few years . . . must rest satisfied with the odious character of Irishman', and another member of the Protestant community rebuked the English habit of looking 'upon [all] the people [in Ireland] in gross'.[18]

At its simplest this was prejudice. The colonists shared in the metropolitan racial and religious stereotyping of the backward and benighted bog Irish. At another level there were serious political implications. The native Irish were excluded from the political nation on two counts, because they were Catholic, and were therefore not merely unfit for liberty, but a danger to it, and because they were conquered. Conquered territories in contemporary political theory were reduced to the status of 'provinces' or 'colonies', wholly dependent for their laws and administration upon the metropolitan power. Thus when seventeenth-century Englishmen argued that 'Ireland' was a conquered nation and conflated all the inhabitants of the island – considered them 'in gross' – Protestants were being reminded of their subservience. Thus if they were to secure political equality, either by legislative autonomy or through union, they had somehow to circumvent the charge of conquest and to establish their (legal) entitlement to equal treatment on the basis of a common Englishness.

Obviously the fact of conquest could not be easily disputed. But who precisely, or what, had been conquered, and by whom? According to the Earl of Orrery, Ireland had been conquered by the ancestors of the present Protestant settlers: 'under the commission of royal authority'. In 1667, lodging a protest over the Cattle Act, Arthur Annesley, Earl of Anglesey, made a similar claim: 'Ireland is a conquered nation' he stated, but it 'must not be so treated, for the conquerors inhabit there'.[19] But it was William Molyneux, in his 1698 *The Case of Ireland being Bound by Acts of Parliament in England, Stated*, who provided the most elegant, though pseudo-historical, solution to the problem. Ireland had not been conquered, he maintained. Rather the Gaelic chieftains had willingly submitted to Henry II in 1171, effectively entering into a contract whereby Henry had in return granted them English common law and the right to hold Parliaments. It followed, therefore, that

[8 4]   Ireland was neither a province nor a colony but, like Scotland, a distinct kingdom.

For the Protestants in Ireland the sometimes elaborate arguments about constitutional status were freighted with immense practical significance. The high-flying rhetoric of the Dublin convention in 1660, about ancient constitutions and the right of holding Parliaments, manifested not only a burgeoning sense of 'colonial identity', but the pressing necessity to legitimate and entrench recent land confiscations. Constitutional discourse centred on three related problems in restoration Ireland: the right to be governed by laws to which the political nation had given its consent; economic prosperity and equality with England; and the containment and ultimately conversion of the 'popish natives'. Legislative independence and union should be seen as alternative means to those ends, not as ends in themselves, predicated upon some need to frame a satisfyingly symmetrical fit between 'identity' and 'state'.

During the Restoration era Ireland as a whole experienced steady recovery from the economic decimation of the 1640s and dislocation of the 1650s. Within the context of that broad trend, however, Protestant or Anglo-Ireland, while it retained its political dominance, suffered a number of setbacks. These included the imposition by England of commercial restrictions and, above all, the partial reversal of the Cromwellian land confiscations through the Acts of Settlement (1662) and Explanation (1665) and the operation of the Court of Claims. Unnervingly, the lands ceded thereby to 'innocent papists' signalled a limited, yet unmistakable, Catholic revival. And by May 1663, the anxieties generated by this drift in government policy fuelled Colonel's Blood's plot as much as did republican nostalgia or Presbyterian alienation. In the late 1660s *A Proposal of Several Officers and Other Gentlemen of English Extraction in Ireland, for a Union of that Kingdom with England* addressed many of these concerns.

Among the grievances arising 'for the want of union' were, first, that 'judges are not agreed whether laws made in England do bind Ireland, though it be named in them'. Second, the people of England living in Ireland 'are accounted foreigners and aliens' particularly in respect of trade with the colonies. Goods imported from the West Indies, for example, had to be shipped via English ports, leading to the payment of double customs duties. Third, the legality of the Acts of Settlement and Explanation was uncertain, and finally, and perhaps most unwelcome of all, in consequence of these grievances, 'the colonies sent from England, are therefore the more disposed in a generation or two to turn Irish'. Union, on the other hand, offered numerous advantages. It would stabilise Irish politics. A new sense of security would reduce the need for an expensive standing army and render the English there 'quiet in their possessions'. Moreover, 'the Irish, being put from their hopes of having any more Irish parliaments, will be the easier disposed to English habit, language . . . living' and to religious conformity. A more anglicised and Protestant Ireland would then attract more English tenants. Finally, in a pointed allusion to the negotiations for commercial union then taking place between English and Scottish commissioners, the authors argue that in the case of Ireland there is 'greater facility [for union] from the general use of the same laws in both kingdoms'.[20]

The other main union proposal in this period came from a transplanted Englishman with wide Irish experience, Sir William Petty. Petty – who, incidentally, sometimes employed the term 'British Protestants' – on at least one occasion envisaged a union of England, Ireland and Scotland.[21] His main concern, however, was Ireland and its seemingly intractable Catholic problem. His solution was dramatic, imaginative and unrealistic. Enumerating the 'inconveniencies' and 'absurdities' of 'non-union', Petty rehearsed the usual litany: that Englishmen in Ireland were treated as aliens, the expense of extra customs, the uncertainty about the location of sovereignty, which 'may be made a pretense for . . . disobedience', the injustice of laws made without representation, and so on. To him the benefits of union were clear. He deplored 'cantonisation' and considered the union between England and Wales an unqualified success. But he went further, advocating what he called 'transmutation'. Quite simply (and maybe only someone who had played a leading role in the Cromwellian experiment of social engineeering in Ireland was capable thinking on this scale), Petty proposed that 20,000 Irish Catholic women of marriageable age be transplanted over two years to England, in exchange for the same number of English settlers transplanted to Ireland. In addition, 'if the Irish must have priests', then they should be provided with *English* priests. Such policies, he believed fondly, would result in the rapid anglicisation, assimilation and neutralising of that hitherto refractory and rebellious kingdom.[22] Written in about 1672, Petty's grand scheme was not published until 1691 at a time when the Catholic problem had been resolved by different, though equally drastic, means: military subjugation.

One of the most striking features of Anglo-Irish constitutional discourse in the Restoration period is its one-sidedness. The English were not interested. They could choose to ignore Ireland's claims without political cost,

[8 6] and they did. This is less true in the case of Anglo-Scottish relations, although English motives for engaging with the Scots are at times hard to pin down. The initiative for the commercial union negotiations of 1688–89 and the political union negotiations of 1670 came from the king himself. William Ferguson speculates that the reason for Charles's new departure may have had to do with foreign policy. The Scots felt victimised by commercial restraints and the king, the Pentland uprising fresh in his mind, worried that the Dutch might attempt to exploit the discontents of his northern subjects.[23] P.W.J. Riley, with characteristic Namierite dispatch, dismisses the commercial agenda as a 'subterfuge'. The reason behind the proposal, he asserts, was a Lauderdalian scheme to draft a 'disciplined corps' of Scottish MPs into Westminster where they could be 'unleashed' upon the country opposition.[24] Talks between the two sides opened in January 1668, dragging inconclusively into the following year, when Lauderdale raised the ante in June by presenting proposals for legislative union to the English Privy Council. Two things stand out about this curious episode: the gener-ally negative response of the Scots to the various schemes on offer and Lauderdale's contradictory behaviour.

Blaming England for their national misfortune, many Scots failed to draw the conclusion that union would remedy their dire situation, indulging instead in anglophobic recrimination, and rewriting the history of the recent Cromwellian coupling. 'The indeavor to have made us slaves by garrisons' wrote Lauderdale, and 'the ruine of our trade by severe lawes in England frights all ranks of men from having to doe with England.'[25] The English, particularly the coal and salt industrial interests who feared free competition, were in any event themselves either lukewarm in their enthusiasm for, or openly hostile to, any new arrangement.[26] Lauderdale pursued a stop–go strategy, promoting fuller union while in London in June 1669 and stalling in Edinburgh in November; proposing at the outset thirty Scottish seats in the new parliament and – surely deliberately – delivering the *coup de grâce* to the negotiations in November 1670 by insisting on behalf of the Scottish delegation that all Scottish MPs be represented at Westminster. It is extremely unlikely that Lauderdale would have willingly jeopardised his northern power-base by entering into a new set of Anglo-Scottish relation-ships, his future role in which had yet to be defined. He followed the king's instructions. It must be assumed too that he also sabotaged the whole enter-prise with his master's blessing. Once again we can only speculate about Charles's hidden agenda and in that regard Ferguson's suggestion that the king was never serious about a closer union, that he wished only to divert

the 'Protestant bigot' Lauderdale's attention while he conducted his secret
diplomacy with Catholic France, is as plausible a theory as any.[27]

Anglo-Irish and Anglo-Scottish relations and the revolution settlement

Upon his death in 1685, Charles left the tripartite structure of his kingdoms much as he had inherited it. One result of his brother and successor James VII and II's policies was to destabilise relationships between the three kingdoms radically. Under the lord deputyship of Richard Talbot, Earl of Tyrconnell, Ireland between 1686 and 1689 experienced what amounted to a Catholic 'counter-revolution'. Ireland's Catholic majority facilitated the re-Catholicisation of the state, although the pace set by Tyrconnell may have alarmed even the king himself. What is certain is that the rate of change in Ireland far outstripped anything that James attempted (or could realistically hope to attempt) in either of his Protestant kingdoms. The varying rates and dynamics of change highlighted Ireland's exceptional character within the composite monarchy, and fuelled fears about James's 'popish design'. In Ireland Scots and English Protestants caught a glimpse of the shape of things to come and they did not like it. What is more, they suspected that James, like his father before him, planned to mobilise an Irish Catholic army to coerce his British subjects. The king, after all, commanded not one but three armies. The legendary Irish Catholic general, Patrick Sarsfield, earned his spurs against Monmouth in 1685, and on the eve of William of Orange's landing Irish Catholic troops were stationed at the Portsmouth garrison.[28]

The logic of the dis-synchronisation, in the three kingdoms, of the royally sponsored Catholic 'counter-reformation' was that Ireland might eventually go its own way. There is evidence that Tyrconnell contemplated placing Ireland under the protection of Louis XIV's France in the event of James dying without heir, and England reverting to its full-fledged Protestant constitution. James may even have agreed, although he remained extremely wary of further alienating English opinion.[29] As in the case of the Protestant Convention in 1660 the Irish Catholic impulse towards greater independence is best understood as a means to an end rather than as an end in itself. And also, as in the case of the Protestants in 1660, the primary issue for the Catholics in the 1689 Jacobite Parliament was land ownership. The Acts of Settlement and Explanation were overturned. Significantly, however, that

[8 8] parliament did not succeed in repealing Poynings' Law. Afterwards James, a Stuart and an English king as well as a Catholic, referred disparagingly to the 'O's' and the 'Mac's', although the majority of MPs were actually Old English. With one eye on English opinion and the other on his prerogative, James refused to relinquish the control that Poynings' Law gave him. But because he was now dependent upon his Irish supporters he did assent to a Declaratory Act which stated that the 'parliament of England cannot bind Ireland'.[30]

Of course the right, or more accurately the ability, of the English parliament to bind Ireland would be decided not by parliaments or politicians or constitutional lawyers in either country but by the sword. From the perspective of 'these islands'' history the revolution of 1688 turned out to be anything but 'bloodless'; as from the standpoint of Irish Catholics and Scottish episcopalians it proved not very 'glorious'. The revolution transformed Anglo-Irish and Anglo-Scottish relations. During William's reign the English parliament, more for reasons to do with war and foreign policy than with any whiggish march of liberty, strengthened its position relative to the crown. Between 1660 and 1688 parliament began to assume a near permanent role in the English polity. After 1688 it sat continuously. William was every inch as jealous of his prerogative as any Stuart, he simply had less room to manoeuvre. In both theory and practice sovereignty started to shift from the crown to the crown-in-parliament, and the consequences for Ireland and Scotland were momentous.

Those historians who see the years 1688–91 as 'a critical moment in the expansion of English control over other parts of the British Isles; a step towards empire', are right.[31] The traditional Irish stance that Ireland was a sister kingdom of England, with the same king, but with its own autonomous parliament, rested upon a crucial distinction between crown and parliament. If, as the Protestants freely acknowledged, the king's authority extended to all his dominions and if – as they were less likely to concede – sovereignty now resided in the crown-in-(the Westminster) parliament, then it followed that that parliament's authority also extended to all the king's dominions, including Ireland. The realignment of English politics cast a long shadow over Scottish affairs too. As Andrew Fletcher remarked in 1703, ''Tis not the prerogative of a king of Scotland I would diminish, but the prerogative of English ministers over this nation.'[32]

Canonised by Scottish nationalist hagiography for his opposition to the 1707 union, ultimately Fletcher's politics were defined by sound Whig principles. As we shall see, he never rejected the idea of union. What he objected to was 'incorporating' union which threatened, in his view, to increase arbitrary power.[33] Briefly in 1689 Fletcher was among those who advocated union as a way of counteracting Scottish Jacobite resistance and locking Scotland into the revolution. On 23 April the convention of estates nominated commissioners to negotiate for union, to which William was not adverse, but in this instance the project went nowhere. This failed unionist scheme did, however, like the 1668–70 bilateral discussions, have the effect of keeping Anglo-Scottish union on the political agenda. The resurfacing of unionist advocacy in Ireland at this time, though more marginal to political discourse than in Scotland, is also worth noting.

Although in retrospect the articles of Limerick, signed in October 1691, and the subsequent departure of the Jacobite soldiers for France – the 'flight of the wild geese' – marks a decisive defeat for Catholic Ireland, a defeat from which it took a century or more to recover, that was not at all clear to either victor or vanquished at the time. The ink on the articles, or treaty as they are usually called, had scarcely dried, when the accountant general James Bonnell wrote to Robert Harley that ''tis clear the Irish are in a much better condition than we hoped they would be in the end of this war'. In other words, the Catholic menace remained, and nothing could secure the Protestant Interest against it, Bonnell averred, 'but increasing the number and power of the English . . . [and] the uniting of this kingdom to England, as it was in Cromwell's time'.[34] In this view a more thorough-going anglicisation – 'increasing the power and number of the English' – offered the best means of finally 'securing' Ireland. And the best way of promoting anglicisation, according to the anonymous author of *Considerations Concerning Ireland in Relation to England and Particularly in Respect of an Union*, published in the early 1690s,[35] was a fuller integration of the two kingdoms. More much-needed English planters would only be attracted, he insisted, if, once settled in Ireland, they continued to have access to English markets, were safe from being overrun by the Irish, did 'not wholly lose their privileges in England, as Englishmen, by removing hither' and were not subject to the 'arbitrary impositions of England without their consent'. Moreover, experience had demonstrated amply the disastrous consequences of the present arrangement. It took roughly seven years for the typical English settler to degenerate into a sort of Irishman, and he was helped along that path by the metropolitan habit of looking 'upon all here [Protestant and Catholic, settler and native] in effect to be Irish'.

Yet metropolitan suspicions of a nascent Protestant patriotism, while misplaced and premature, were not unreasonable. Surprisingly, on the face of

[9 0]   it, there were marked continuities in the behaviour of the mostly Catholic Jacobite or 'pretended parliament' as the victorious Williamites called it, and the exclusively Protestant parliament which met in October 1692 – surprising because so shortly after their deliverance by English (and Dutch) arms, the Lord Lieutenant, Viscount Henry Sidney, for one, believed 'it impossible that people who lay under the greatest obligation to his majesty should have any other thoughts than of gratitude and obedience'.[36] In the event the session of 1692 proved so difficult that Sidney prorogued it after only four weeks. Like King James among the fractious O's and Mac's, he had found himself in the 'company of madmen'. The major dispute concerned the procedure for introducing money or supply bills. The opposition objected to the drafting of such bills in the English Privy Council, insisting, on the contrary, upon parliament's 'sole right' to do so. Revealingly, Sidney worried that the loss of the right to propose money bills was less important 'in itself as in the effects it will have by lessening the dependency of this kingdom upon the crown of England', as earlier he had warned his superiors in London about 'talk of freeing themselves from the yoke of England [and] of taking away Poynings' Law'.[37] Sidney's over-reaction to this constitutional wrangle typifies official English perceptions. English ministers almost always assumed ulterior motives. The Protestants of Ireland, in their view, 'had a mind', as Queen Anne remarked in 1706, 'to be independent, if they could'.[38]

    Sidney's railing notwithstanding, the reality of English control had been underlined in 1692 by the imposition of oaths denying the doctrine of transubstantiation, by enactment of the English parliament, on all who took their seats in the Irish parliament. The Protestants did not balk at being bound by English laws made without their consent whenever it suited them. The unsatisfactory conclusion of that tempestuous session, in which the Lord Lieutenant had failed to carry all the king's business, did, however, point up the paradox of a post-revolution dispensation which had both strengthened the position of the English ministry in relation to the other kingdoms, and at the same time destabilised it. That was particularly true of Scotland, where the repeal of the Lords of the Articles, and the jettisoning of the royalist ballast represented by the bishops, loosened control from above, and enabled the realignment of parliamentary politics along 'party' and competing magnate-factional lines. From the perspective of the court the primary problem soon revealed itself, in Ireland, as in Scotland, as one of 'management'. This might be achieved through the contracting-out of patronage to local magnates or, as they came to be called in Ireland, parliamentary undertakers, responsible in turn for securing government majorities.

Alternatively, it could be achieved through the tightening Poynings'-style legislative restraints, although that alternative ran the clear risk of stirring up 'national' opposition. Viewed in this light, and from London, as David Hayton usefully reminds us, the Anglo-Scottish union appears as a wilful consolidation of English state power. For all its bilateral trappings the union only came about when the English political elite came to see its necessity.[39]

By the mid-1690s, under the skilful management of Lord Henry Capel in Ireland and of Secretary James Johnson in Scotland, a deceptive political equilibrium obtained. Anglo-Irish and Anglo-Scottish relations were soon strained, however, and in the Scottish case strained to breaking-point, by discords too intractable to be soothed by the ministrations of mere patronage-brokers. The causes were economic. In 1695 the Scots decided to 'go it alone'. An Act setting up the 'Company of Scotland trading to Affrica and the Indies' signalled their intention of competing in the European colonial market. The Company targeted Darien in Panama as the site for its colony – 'New Caledonia' – but the difficulties involved in the enterprise proved as fatal as the political consequences were enormous. The East India Company discouraged English investment. Sufficient capital was raised within Scotland, but the settlers of the first expedition in 1698 were decimated by fever and by attacks from the natives. The second expedition, in 1700, surrendered to the Spanish. Crucially, the refusal of provisions or aid from the English West Indies left a legacy of bitterness and recrimination. Equally important, this sorry episode dramatised the seeming 'failure' of the Scottish economy. Part of the context for the Darien scheme had been the subsistence crises of 1695–99, when a sequence of bad harvests had led to mass hunger, starvation and emigration. And if the Darien disaster had demonstrated that Scotland could not 'go it alone', where could it go? While it undoubtedly reinvigorated Scottish anglophobia, the Darien experience also gave new urgency to the economic arguments for union.

The nineteenth-century historian J.A. Froude attributed the English refusal to countenance union with Ireland in the early eighteenth century to 'the meanest and basest spirit of commercial jealousy', while at the time Fletcher detected the same spirit at work in England's treatment of her Irish 'colony'. Noting 'the ill usage of the Scots nation in their late attempt to settle in Darien', he saw the commercial restrictions placed on Ireland, and in particular the 1699 prohibition on the export of wool, as a warning to his countrymen of what they should expect if they allowed themselves to be subordinated into an 'incorporating', and therefore unequal, as opposed to a federal union.[40] Fletcher also alluded to 'some late writers' in Ireland who had countered English claims to dominion on the basis of conquest. This referred to the pamphlet literature generated by the Westminster Woollen Act controversy, and above all to William Molyneux's *The Case of Ireland*.

The Woollen Act, first mooted in 1697, reached the statute books two years later. Rooted in mercantilist assumptions of commerce-as-rivalry, and prompted by the lobbying of the West Country-based woollen interest, the legislation effectively eliminated Irish woollen manufacture.[41] This raised serious political and constitutional as well as economic issues. While a number of Anglo-Irish (if that problematic term can be slipped in at this point) writers argued that a robust Irish economy and freedom of trade redounded to England's advantage, *all* of the polemics from their side focused upon the injustice and inequity of the proposed restriction. Molyneux, for example, does not address the economic issues at all. The loudest refrain of these protests is familiar. Since the woollen trade was concentrated in the hands of the English Interest in Ireland, the Woollen Act was thus directed, by the English parliament, at its own people. Ireland, asserted one of the pamphleteers, 'is an English Protestant country':

> is it because there is a little channel that runs between Wales and Wexford,
> that when any English dare cross the stream they must be divested of English
> privileges, as if they had transgrest some law of nature . . . [yet] we are the same
> people, parents and children, brothers and sisters, sometimes dwelling here,
> sometimes there . . . we are of one religion . . . we are a province of their
> empire, and have neither laws, nor governors, but of their sending.

We 'are Englishmen', declared Francis Annesley, 'sent over to conquer Ireland, your countrymen, your brothers, your sons, your relations, your acquaintance; governed by the same king, the same laws; the same religion, and in the same interest'.[42]

Moreover English policies were not simply and manifestly unjust: they were myopic and foolhardy too. The English Interest in Ireland, according to this argument, acted as a first line of defence against any future Catholic insurgency, and by undermining that interest the metropolitan country dangerously weakened its own power in Ireland. Like the claim to English liberties as the entitlement of transplanted Englishmen, the Protestants-as-indispensable bulwark trope had, by the 1690s, long been part of Anglo-Ireland's rhetorical repertoire. What was new to the polemical exchanges triggered by the Woollen Act was the Scottish dimension to that by then conventional argument. Several pamphleteers predicted – accurately as it turned out – that the main beneficiary of the elimination of the woollen trades would be the linen producers, and in Ireland linen production was concentrated in Scots Presbyterian-dominated east Ulster. Nor, for the churchmen, could such a shift in the centre of economic gravity occur at a worse moment. Since 1696 the Presbyterians, who had already strengthened their organisational structures at the time of the revolution, had boosted their numerical strength by the influx of tens of thousands of emigrants fleeing the collapse of the Scottish rural economy.[43] Sometimes the Church party seem more preoccupied with, and fearful of, resurgent dissent than with the Catholics, and over the next decade the anti-Scottish, anti-Presbyterian animus evident during the Woollen Act controversy would resurface in the discursive context of the union debates.

The outstanding contribution to that controversy, one that moved from the history of day-to-day politics into the history of political thought, came, of course, from the pen of William Molyneux.[44] Molyneux's *Case* recycled the theses put forward in his father-in-law Sir William Domville's 'disquisition' on the constitutional status of the kingdom of Ireland, which he had prepared for the Dublin Convention in 1660. Domville, whose papers were in Molyneux's possession, had in turn drawn freely on the Old English Catholic lawyer Patrick Darcy's 1643 *Argument*, and Molyneux's English critics gleefully drew attention to the Catholic lineage of his position. The greater part of the *Case* then consists of lengthy examinations of parliamentary enactments from the medieval period forward, meant to demonstrate that Ireland was and had ever been a distinct kingdom. That kingdom had the same king as England, but enjoyed its own ancient constitution, with its own, autonomous, parliament and courts. The crown's jurisdiction extended to the kingdom of Ireland; the English parliament's did not. In more than one respect, however, Molyneux's book marked an intellectual advance on the writings of Domville and Darcy. As a friend, correspondent and student of John Locke, the Anglo-Irishman invoked the principle of natural rights. The Protestants of Ireland were entitled, as were all men (except the Irish Catholics!), to be bound only by those laws to which they had consented. Significantly, for Molyneux, whose book would become a foundation text for eighteenth-century Protestant nationalism, government by consent was the end; an independent Irish legislature or representation at a united Westminster parliament were alternative, and equally valid, means to that end.

Another striking innovation in the *Case* is the author's ingenious solution to the problem of conquest. The Earl of Orrery in 1662, the Earl of Anglesey in 1667 and Francis Annesley in 1698 (and Andrew Fletcher in 1703) all acknowledged that Ireland was a conquered country, but insisted that as the conquerors themselves, or as the progeny of the conquerors, they, as English

[9 4] Protestants, were not subject to the law of conquest. Molyneux, in contrast, would not concede that there had been a conquest. Henry II, he asserted, had granted the native Irish English law and the right to hold parliaments, thereby establishing a contract still in force. Finally, it should be noted that Molyneux rejected explicitly the appellation 'colony'. Ireland, as he pointed out, was, after all, *styled* a 'kingdom'.

For all its intellectual agility the *Case*, which rapidly drew fire from English controversialists and condemnation from the English parliament, was logically and empirically flawed. Ireland had been conquered, and reconquered as recently as 1691 – a truism belaboured at Molyneuxesque length by William Atwood,[45] who soon afterwards would champion the 'imperial' attributes of the English crown against the upstart Scots. Yes, Ireland was styled a kingdom, but so too, observed another of Molyneux's adversaries, Simon Clement, were the Spanish colonies of Mexico and Peru. Clement scored another direct hit by turning the 'one people, indivisible' rhetoric back on the English in Ireland. If they were as English as their kin in the mother country, then surely they owed primary allegiance to the whole community of which they were a part. Viewed in that way the well-being of the English woollen industry ought to be more important to them than the pursuit of narrow sectional interests.[46]

At base Molyneux's position rested on a critical distinction between crown and parliament which, in the wake of the revolution settlement, had become increasingly anachronistic and untenable. It is no coincidence, although it is ironic, that both Clement and Atwood were good Whigs. In an English context that cast them in the role of defenders of parliamentary sovereignty – extending to England's 'dependencies'. In an Irish context Whig libertarian principles – government by consent – compelled Molyneux to refute Westminster's claims. In the meantime, however, besides reconfirming perennial English suspicions about Irish Protestant ambitions to 'shake off their dependency', the *Case* caused nothing to happen. English self-interest, and the English parliament's ability to enforce it, settled the argument. A few years later the Irish Whig Henry Maxwell refused to dodge that brute reality, opening his *Essay Towards an Union of Ireland and England* (1703) by affirming that it was not his intention 'to examine whether laws made in England ought to bind Ireland, it being sufficient for those of that nation [Ireland] to know that this is a power which England claims, and is able to vindicate'.[47]

Maxwell's closely reasoned *Essay* caused nothing to happen either. The Protestants may have garrisoned Ireland but in the final resort they

depended for their security upon the English connection. As in the case of
the Woollen Act and the Resumption Act (1700), the English government
showed how it could intervene unilaterally in Irish affairs, or, as with
Maxwell and the 1703 parliament, ignore Irish wishes with impunity. The
Scots were not so easily ignored. The death of the Duke of Gloucester in
1700, and the Act of Settlement in 1701, devolving the succession on the
Protestant House of Hanover, immediately raised fundamental questions
about the position of Scotland. And the mind of the English ministry was
soon concentrated wonderfully by the election to the Scots parliament of a
phalanx of 'Cavalier' (or crypto-Jacobite) MPs in 1703, and by the passing
of the Act of Security, which set down limitations on the prerogative of
Queen Anne's successor. The prospect that these developments opened up,
of a Stuart on the Scottish throne – of two kings on the island of Britain in
time of war with France – was simply unacceptable to the English political
nation. Coupled with the need to manage Scottish politics better, the
impending crisis quickly reduced the ministry's options to two stark altern-
atives: union or conquest.

The making of the union

Of course it could be argued, as P.W.J. Riley did, that the public debate on
the union, in parliament, on the streets, in the kirk and, above all, in the print
media, caused nothing to happen. According to that thesis – a more theoretically sophisticated (and, it must be said, thoroughly documented) version of
Robert Burns' old 'parcel of rogues' jibe – the union was a high political
manoeuvre, or 'job', carried, in contempt of Scottish public opinion, by a
self-serving clique of Junto Whigs and its craven Caledonian clients. True to
Namierite dogma, ideology, or 'principle', and 'public opinion' function as a
sort of optical illusion, blurring the real business of scrambling for the spoils
of office. Riley, for instance, writes off the debate on the economic consequences of union, a debate in which Fletcher and others invested great
significance, as 'irrelevant'.[48] Undoubtedly jobbery, bribery and cynical
political calculation did lubricate the union negotiations; equally clearly,
however, a one-dimensional focus on backstairs fixing is reductionist. Even
some of the high political fixers at the time recognised the importance of
out-of-doors argument and agitation. Reporting to London in 1706 on the
anti-union activity of the Kirk, the Earl of Mar, though confident 'as ever

of succeeding in parl[iament]', warned that 'we go on in our business and are not frightened with their threats, yet those things are not to be despised or neglected'.[49] Robert Harley's decision to recruit Daniel Defoe as a spy and unionist propagandist likewise testifies to the seriousness that the government attached to the public debate.

The long history of unionist and anti-unionist discourse provided one of the vital contexts for the sometimes 'squalid' and 'short-term' dealings delineated in such detail by Riley. 'In drafting the treaty', observed Brian Levack,

> the commissioners had to take into consideration the attitudes towards union that had developed in both countries over the previous century. These attitudes defined the limits within which compromises could be made and helped to determine many of the features of the united kingdom they constructed. The treaty, therefore, was as much a product of the century-old union debate as it was of the immediate needs and relative bargaining strength of both parties.[50]

More recently, John Robertson has insisted upon the intellectual, as distinct from the political and economic, aspects of the union, and argued that the Anglo-Scottish controversy 'generated a significant body of political thought'.[51]

In addition to the practical gain to the court in terms of management and extra votes, the arguments for the union revolved around the claim of English suzerainty over Scotland; the attainment of internal British peace and stability, and of security against external enemies; and the benefits of free trade. The suzerainty claim, advanced by Atwood, marshalled historical 'precedent' to demonstrate the inferiority of the Scottish crown to the 'imperial' crown of England, and succeeded only in arousing Scottish resentment and mobilising counter-arguments from the likes of George Ridpath and John Anderson. The stability and security arguments were more effective, particularly in time of war. A union would eliminate the possibility of another 'civil war' between the kingdoms, and create a 'bulwark of the Protestant Interest' in Europe at a critical juncture when 'the boundless ambition of France makes' union 'more needful in our time, than . . . in the ages of our forefathers'.[52]

Internal peace, political stability and security against the threat of French Catholic 'universal monarchy' would be mutually advantageous to Scotland and England. However, free trade, 'the bait that cover[ed] the hook'[53] dangled by the union's proponents, was presented as mainly, if not solely, to Scotland's benefit. English pamphleteers, such as Defoe, and Scottish unionists, like William Seton of Pitmedden and the Earl of Cromarty, invoked the economic prosperity of Wales since its union with England and, in Defoe's case, of Scotland's positive experience under Cromwell also. Union, they claimed, would open up vast commercial opportunities for Scots merchants in English and English colonial markets. Moreover, as the Darien disaster has so painfully demonstrated, the alternative was bleak indeed. The matter was sometimes resolved into a false, but compelling, binary opposition. 'It's better to increase our trade, manufacture, and riches', declared an advocate of union, 'than to boast of our sovereignty and starve.'[54]

In addition to Jacobite legitimism, the arguments against the union focused on national sovereignty, free trade and the religious settlement. Appeals from sovereignty were either couched, as in Lord Belhaven's celebrated speech, in the rhetoric of sentimental nationalism – 'our ancient mother, Caledonia' – or drew on 'real Whig' resistance to the over-concentration of power. The first style of rhetoric addressed a ready audience. In the winter of 1706 Defoe witnessed ugly outbursts of popular anglophobia on the streets of Edinburgh where the 'rabble' cried out 'no union', 'no union' and 'English dogs', 'they were Scots Men, and they would be Scots Men still; they condemned the name of Britains, fit for Welsh Men, who were made the scoff of the English after they reduc'd them'.[55] Whig polemicists, although they raised the argument onto a more abstract, theoretical, plane, also stressed the threat to freedom, religion and laws which would result from the surrender of the *Scottish* ancient constitution. By every conceivable measure, the Scots would be junior partners in the new dispensation, under-represented and consigned to a permanent minority position at Westminster. And in that situation Scotland's interest could not be other than – and always – subsidiary to England's. Nor did the anti-unionists accept the proposition that a bilateral treaty, which guaranteed Scottish rights, would be fundamental law, unalterable by any future united parliament. On the contrary, the Scots, in their view, were being invited to throw themselves defenceless onto the mercy of their more powerful neighbour.[56]

Most of the anti-unionists did not oppose union in principle. Their quarrel was with an incorporating union. To counteract arbitrary power they proposed either limitations on royal prerogative or federal union. And, while their understanding of federalism usually lacked precision, the numerous references to the Swiss cantons, Poland–Lithuania and the Dutch republic gives some idea of what they had in mind. In his *Account of a Conversation Concerning the Right Regulation of Governments*, Andrew Fletcher posited a correlation between geography and ecology ('God and nature') and political

[9 8] organisation. 'The island of Britain and that of Ireland', like Spain and Portugal, or the Scandinavian countries, constituted a natural unit, and 'seem conveniently situated for one government'. But by 'one government' he meant a decentralised 'union or league' composed, in the case of the British Isles, of up to twelve 'city states'. Such a league would be strong enough to repel invasion, yet too weak to attempt conquest. Even more importantly perhaps, for the republican Fletcher, 'in small governments laws may be duly executed, and the manners of men in great measure preserved from corruption'.[57] All of this was preferable to the 'unnatural', remote and parasitic domination of the three kingdoms by London. The problem with this, and any other federal scheme, was that it stood not the slimmest chance of politically surmounting, or of intellectually pricking, that sturdy edifice of English constitutional tradition: the indivisibility of sovereignty.

London also featured prominently in Fletcher's diagnosis of the economics of union. He believed that economic power would follow political power south. More precisely, since London already acted as a sort of black hole, draining talent, cash and resources from the provinces, he believed that incorporating union would aggravate an existing imbalance. Along with other anti-unionists he flatly rejected the assertion that Wales had prospered under the union; the Welsh, if anything, were poorer.[58] England could not be trusted. Free trade surfaces in this literature not as a boon, but as a snare. The other great snare, of course, was allegedly being set for the Presbyterian settlement.

George Ridpath probably had the secular-minded Fletcher in his sights when he complained that 'most of those who are for liberty have no concern for religion and that many of those who are zealous for religion, are very ill-informed in point of civil liberty'.[59] To Ridpath that was a false and harmful distinction. Union endangered both religion and liberty and both ought to be defended. Presbyterians feared that their establishment, won in 1690, would be compromised, undermined and eventually overturned by a united parliament, committed to an Anglican establishment, and in which bishops sat, as of right, in the upper house. And if any doubted the prevailing temper of the English High Church party they need only look to the sacramental test and the plight of the English, and Ulster, Dissenters who were treated like aliens in their own countries.[60] More than any other issue, the cry of 'Kirk in danger' rallied popular opposition to the union, particularly in the old Covenanter heartlands of the south-west. Copies of the treaty were burned at the crossroads in Dumfries in November 1706, and it was the possibility that Presbyterian mobilisation might escalate into armed resistance that prompted the deployment of troops along the border and in Ulster. 'One thing I must say for the Kirk,' commented Mar, 'if the union fail, it is owing to them.'[61]

Religious contention cut both ways. Some churchmen worried that union posed a threat to episcopacy. Mastering his brief with frank opportunism, Defoe assured his Scottish audience that there was no prospect of toleration for episcopalians and that the Presbyterian settlement would be even more secure after the union, while at the same time in another pamphlet, aimed at an English audience, he argued that a union offered Scottish episcopalians their best hope of obtaining toleration.[62] Across the Irish Sea the double-sided implication of a union for the Presbyterian establishment, so deftly exploited by Defoe, forged a community of opinion every bit as odd as the dalliance of Jacobite and erstwhile Covenanter in Scotland. Opposition to the union in Ireland stemmed from High Churchmen, such as Jonathan Swift and Sir Richard Cox – who feared that it might bolster the Kirk and, by extension, the Presbyterians in Ulster – and from the Presbyterians themselves, who shared in their kinsmen's anxieties about the likely impact of union on the 1690 settlement. Troops were stationed in Ulster for two reasons: to respond to any emergency in south-west Scotland, and in case of trouble in the north of Ireland itself. Always cautious about the Ulster–Scotland connection, in the first years of the eighteenth century the Dublin government was particularly alert after the arrival, during the 1690s, of thousands of new Scots settlers who had fled near famine conditions at home.

Irish public – that is Protestant – opinion generally favoured the union, however, and wished to see it extended to the 'third' kingdom. The old historiographical orthodoxy which saw the 1660 convention as an early marker of an emerging 'colonial nationalism', underpinned by an embryonic sense of 'Anglo-Irish' identity, viewed the Irish parliament's pro-union addresses in 1703 and 1707 as a sort of aberrant footnote. Thus Swift's first pamphlet on Irish affairs, *The Story of the Injured Lady*, which was written in 1707 (though published only posthumously), is allotted its place in the canon of eighteenth-century Protestant nationalism. And while it is true that the pamphleteer's injunction to the lady to buy goods only in her own marketplace (Ireland) prefigures the economic self-help doctrines later championed by Swift himself and by Archbishop King and others, the obvious is usually overlooked: the *Injured Lady* was inspired by a bitter sense of disappointed unionism. The Protestant community's unionist aspirations, and its sense of English identity, both need to be taken more seriously.

Beginning in 1702 the Anglo-Scottish *impasse* presented itself to a number of Anglo-Irish (and one or two sympathetic English) politicians as an opportunity for Ireland. Sir Robert Southwell early on expressed 'great wishes that good may come by attempting an union with Scotland, and the more in hopes it will necessarily draw in a consideration of Ireland'. At the end of 1704, Thomas Coningsby, vice-treasurer in the 1690s, saw 'some advantages' for 'poor old Ireland' opening up in the space created by Anglo-Scottish disagreement, and assured the Lord Lieutenant, the second Duke of Ormond, that 'no opportunities shall be lost to thrust in our claim'.[63] But, while the closely watched crisis in Anglo-Scottish relations undoubtedly revived an interest in union in Ireland, the primary stimuli remained local.

The 1703 Irish parliament met in a state of high dudgeon. Members were agitated by the parlous state of the economy, for which they blamed the English policy of restricting trade. In addition the Resumption Act of three years previously, which granted control of the 'resumed' forfeited estates to Westminster-appointed trustees, still rankled deeply. It was to this exercise of government without consent that the parliamentary resolution referred when, among the 'many grievances', it listed 'the constitution of this . . . kingdom of Ireland [which] hath been of late greatly shaken'.[64] And the remedy to this deplorable situation was either the restoration of ancient privileges and annual parliaments, or else a legislative union with England. The either/or formulation of this resolution has misled historians into inter-preting the union option as the Irish parliament's second choice. However, the desire for union appears to have been strong and genuine,[65] and ranged across the political spectrum, from the anti-clerical Whig, Robert, Viscount Molesworth, to the High Church Tory, Attorney General Sir Richard Cox.[66]

Except for Presbyterian Ulster, opinion 'out-of-doors' is impossible to gauge. Certainly Dubliners, at the very least, could follow the unfolding of 'this great and glorious work'[67] in some detail in the pages of the local newsprints. In Ulster, however, in the admittedly jaundiced words of the Bishop of Down and Connor, 'such as are bigoted to the idol of Presbyterian government in the church are not friends to the union'. The bishop assumed a complete identification between 'our Scots Presbyterians in these parts' and '*their*' country, '*their*' parliament and '*their*' religion. If the Scots in Scotland resisted, then the Scots in Ulster – many of them recent arrivals from the homeland – could be relied upon to join them. Moreover, the Presbyterian community was further unsettled in 1704 by the application of a 'sacramental test' which effectively drove members of their confession out of local government[68] and, as in the Restoration period, there were reports of emissaries from Scotland trying to stir up the opposition of the common people in the north.[69] The Dublin administration responded to the perceived threat, as they had done in the 1670s, by drafting in troops in early 1704 and late 1706,[70] while in the spring of 1705 Ormond toured the north, inspecting the garrison and receiving 'loyal and dutiful' addresses from a number of Presbyterian ministers.[71]

There was then a range of opinions concerning union in early eighteenth-century Ireland. The Protestant elite sought an incorporating union with England, and subsequently inclusion in 'a yet more comprehensive union' in 1707.[72] But some members of this elite, such as Jonathan Swift, opposed an exclusively Anglo-Scottish arrangement which, in their view, empowered Presbyterianism.[73] Presbyterians in Ulster and Scotland were, of course, hostile to the union for precisely the opposite reason. Irish arguments that union would enhance *English* trade and security were simply ignored. This was so because Protestant Ireland, unlike Scotland, could be ignored without an (immediate) price to pay.

Anglo-Scottish relations were tense. The English Junto Whig ministry reacted to Scottish posturing by passing the Alien Act in February 1705, which threatened to treat non-domiciled Scots in England as aliens, and to choke off trade in cattle, linen and coal. That Act in turn elicited a brutal response, the 'show trial' and execution in Edinburgh of three English seamen on charges of 'piracy'. By April Anglo-Scottish relations were moving towards either breakdown or resolution. The Duke of Argyll arrived in the capital at the end of the month and began to construct a 'court' – and unionist – parliamentary majority, supported by the Marquis of Tweeddale's thirty or so 'Squadrone' members. But the critical moment arrived, probably, with the parliament's decision on 1 September 1705 to allow the Queen to appoint *both* sets of the commissioners who were to negotiate the treaty of union. The essence if not the detail of the commissioners' likely recommendations were not in doubt. The twenty-five articles that they subsequently agreed were then presented to the Scottish parliament which opened, for the last time, on 3 October 1706. The opposition achieved only delay, and on 4 November the first articles, enunciating the principle of incorporating union, passed by 116 votes to 83. The same day the ministry placed a bill before the house guaranteeing the Presbyterian settlement of 1690, which passed on 12 November. Parliament finally ratified it on 16 January 1707. After a much shorter, less intense debate, Westminster ratified it on 19 March. The Scottish parliament was formally dissolved by proclamation of the Privy Council on

28 April, and on 1 May 1707 the United Kingdom of Great Britain came into being.

In Scotland the English Whig ministry did treat the 'public sphere' seriously enough to engage by proxy in the pamphlet debate about union, although high political considerations, not mere reasoned argument, determined the outcome. In that sense Riley's Namierite dismissal of the impact of public opinion is accurate. It would be wrong to conclude, however, that public opinion was therefore irrelevant. In Scotland the pro-unionists effectively 'lost' the debate, and this would have profound consequences, not least for the future of Jacobitism. In England the creation of the kingdom of Great Britain on 1 May 1707 appears scarcely to have impinged on English consciousness at all, except perhaps in sharpening Scotophobia. By beginning her story (logically enough) in 1707 Linda Colley's 'success school' account of the forging of Britishness, *Britons*, underestimates the extent to which Anglo-Scottish relations were unresolved by the union. As another historian remarks, the union was not 'accompanied by any ideological consensus . . . there was no real attempt to build a bridge between the Scottish and English political nations to create a common British revolution culture'.[74] The new British state, and the revolution settlement on which it was based, was far from secure.

Notes

1. See the chapter on 'Religious and ecclesiastical union' in Levack, Brian P., 1987, *The Formation of the British State: England, Scotland, and the Union 1603–1707*, Oxford.

2. Cited by William Ferguson in 1977, *Scotland's Relations with England: A Survey to 1707*, Edinburgh, 141.

3. My discussion of the relationship between the Scottish and English crowns draws on Levack, *Formation of the British State*, 51–9.

4. Firth, C.H. and Rait, R.S. (eds) 1911, *Acts and Ordinances of the Interregnum, 1642–1660*, London, iii, 18–20. This Act refers to 'the said crowns of England and Ireland'.

5. *Commons Journal, Ireland*, ii, 341–2.

6. See Shaftesbury's speech on the 'state of the nation', 25 March 1679, in *The Parliamentary History of England*, iv, *1660–1688*, 1116–18. My discussion of

Charles II's Scottish parliaments owes much to Ferguson's chapter   [1 0 3]
'Restoration and reaction' in *Scotland's Relations with England.*

7.   Ormond to Ossory, 21 January 1667, Bodl. Carte Ms. lxx, 415–18; McGuire, James, 1973, 'Why was Ormond dismissed in 1669?', *IHS*, 18: 295–312.

8.   Orrery to Clarendon, 22 June 1661, *Clarendon State Papers in the Bodleian Library*, v, 109; Lord Chancellor Eustace to Secretary Nicholas, *c.* 1 June 1661, Nicholas to Eustace, 4, 11 and 29 June 1661, *Cal S.P. (Ire.) 1660–1662*, 345, 347, 353, 369.

9.   Dow, F.D., 1979, *Cromwellian Scotland 1651–1660*, Edinburgh, 231–2. Kelly, James, 1987, 'The origins of the act of union: an examination of unionist opinion in Britain and Ireland 1650–1800', *IHS*, 99: 238.

10.   Defoe, Daniel, 1709, *The History of the Union of Great Britain*, Edinburgh, 10.

11.   For a discussion of the economic arguments alluded to here see Hont, I., 'Free trade and the economic limits to national politics: neo-Machiavellian political economy reconsidered', in Dunn, J. (ed.) 1990, *The Economic Limits of Modern Politics*, Cambridge, 78–89, 114–19; Andrew Fletcher, *An Account of a Conversation Concerning a Right Regulation of Governments*, reprinted in Daiches, David (ed.) 1979, *Fletcher of Saltoun: Selected Writings*, Edinburgh, 120.

12.   *A Discourse upon the Union of England and Scotland, Addressed to King Charles II March 19th in the Year 1664*, in 1702, *Miscellanea Aulica*, 194.

13.   Ferguson, W., 1974, 'Imperial crowns: a neglected facet of the background of the Treaty of Union of 1707', *SHR*, liii: 22–44.

14.   Oliver St John to Francis St John, 11 March 1689, Cambridgeshire Record Office, Huntingdon dd. M52/1; Connolly, Sean, 1992, *Religion, Law and Power: The Making of Protestant Ireland 1660–1760*, Oxford, 118.

15.   Kilroy, Phil, 1994, *Protestant Dissent and Controversy in Ireland*, Cork, 191; Cox to Nottingham, 13 February 1704, *Cal. S.P. (dom.) 1703–4*, 531.

16.   Barnard, T.C., 1990, 'Crises of identity among Irish Protestants, 1641–1685', *P&P*, cxxvii: 40–2; Smyth, Jim, 1993, ' "Like amphibious animals": Irish Protestants, ancient Britons, 1691–1707', *HJ*, 36, 4: 785–97.

17.   Nicholas Canny's 'Identity formation in Ireland: the emergence of the Anglo-Irish' in Canny, N. and Pagden, A. (eds) 1987, *Colonial Identity in the Atlantic World, 1500–1800*, Princeton, is a classic of that genre.

18.   Rutt, J.T. (ed.) 1828, *Diary of Thomas Bruton*, London, iv, 114, 174, 239; Brewster, Sir Francis, 1698, *A Discourse Concerning Ireland and the Different Interests Thereof; in answer to the Exon and Barnstable petitions; shewing that if a law were enacted to prevent the exportation of woollen manufactures from Ireland to foreign*

parts, what the consequences thereof would be both to England and Ireland, London, 46; [*c.* 1692] *Considerations concerning Ireland in relation to England and particularly in respect of an union*, 2.

19. Orrery, 1662, *An Answer to a Scandalous Letter Lately Printed and Subscribed by Peter Walsh*, Dublin, 10, *Cal. S.P. (Ire.) 1667*, 539.

20. *Miscellanea Aulica*, 203–5.

21. Petty, Sir William, 'An expedient in order to an union of England Ireland and Scotland' in Marquis of Lansdowne (ed.) 1927, *The Petty Papers*, London, i, 14–16.

22. Petty, *c.* 1672, 'Of the future settlement of Ireland, prorogation of rebellions, and its union with England' in O'Donovan, J. (ed.) 1970, *The Political Anatomy of Ireland*, Shannon, 25–35.

23. Ferguson, *Scotland's Relations with England*, 153–4.

24. Riley, P.W.J., 1978, *The Union of England and Scotland: A Study in Anglo-Scottish Politics of the Eighteenth Century*, Manchester, 5.

25. Lauderdale to Moray, 2 November 1669, *Lauderdale Papers*, ii, 154–5. See also pp. 143–5, 149–50, 155–63, and James, Duke of York, to Lauderdale, 28 October 1669, app. lxxvii.

26. Ferguson, *Scotland's Relations with England*, 154.

27. *Ibid.*, 155–7.

28. Wauchope, Piers, 1992, *Patrick Sarsfield and the Williamite War*, Dublin, 34.

29. Miller, J., 1977, 'The Earl of Tyrconnell and James II's Irish policy, 1685–1688', *HJ*, 20: 821–2.

30. Simms, J.G., 'The Patriot Parliament of 1689', in Farrell, B. (ed.) 1973, *The Irish Parliamentary Tradition*, Dublin, 116–27.

31. For example, Hayton, David, 'The Williamite revolution in Ireland, 1688–91' in Israel, J.I. (ed.) 1991, *The Anglo-Dutch Moment: Essays on the Glorious Revolution and its World Impact*, Cambridge, 186.

32. Quoted by Ferguson, 'Imperial crowns', 28.

33. Robertson, John, 'Andrew Fletcher's vision of union' in Mason, Roger (ed.) 1987, *Scotland and England 1286–1815*, Edinburgh, 203–5.

34. Bonnell to Harley, 3 November 1691, *HMC Portland Ms*, iii, 479–81.

35. J.A. Froude dates this pamphlet 1703, Sayle *c.* 1690. From internal evidence it was written before 1702 – the author refers to 'his present Majesty'; before 1697, otherwise his silence on the intended Woollen Act would be inexplicable; and after 1689 because of his allusion to 'the pretended parliament'.

36. Sidney to Nottingham, 6 November 1692, *Cal. S.P. (dom.) 1692 and addenda*, [1 0 5] 217–18.

37. McGuire, J.I., 'The Irish Parliament of 1692' in Bartlett, T. and Hayton, D. (eds) 1979, *Penal Age and Golden Era: Essays in Irish History, 1690–1800*, Belfast, 11, 15, *Cal. S.P. (dom.) 1695 and addenda*, 217.

38. Quoted by Edward Gregg, 1984, *Queen Anne*, London, 130.

39. Hayton, David, 'Constitutional experiments and political expediency, 1689–1725' in Ellis, S. and Barber, S., 1995, *Conquest and Union: Fashioning the British State*, London, 276–305.

40. Froude, J.A., 1895, *The English in Ireland*, London, 338; Fletcher, *An Account of a Conversation*, 120–1.

41. Kelly, P., 1980, 'The Irish Woollen Export Prohibition Act of 1699: Kearney re-visited', *Irish Economic and Social History*, 7: 22–44.

42. Hovell, John, 1698, *A Discourse on the Woollen Manufacture of Ireland and the Consequences of Prohibiting its Exportation*, Dublin, 8; [Annesley] 1698, 1740, *Some Thoughts on the Bill Depending before the Right Honourable the House of Lords for Prohibiting the Exportation of the Woollen Manufactures of Ireland to Foreign Parts*, London and Dublin, 22; both cited by Smyth, 'Like amphibious animals', 794.

43. One contemporary estimated that 80,000 Scottish families had emigrated to Ulster between 1691 and 1698: Brewster, *A Discourse Concerning Ireland and the Different Interests Thereof*, 34; see too Cullen, L.M., 1981, *The Emergence of Modern Ireland*, London, 12, 34, 39.

44. Simms, J.G. (ed. P.H. Kelly) 1982, *William Molyneux of Dublin: A Life of the Seventeenth-century Political Writer and Scientist*, Dublin, ch. vii; Hill, J., 'Ireland without union: Molyneux and his legacy' in Robertson, J. (ed.) 1995, *A Union for Empire*, Cambridge, 271–96.

45. Atwood, William, 1698, *The History and Reasons for the Dependency of Ireland upon the Imperial Crown of England, Rectifying Mr Molyneux's State of the Case of Ireland's Being Bound by Acts of Parliament in England, Stated*.

46. Clement, Simon, 1698, *An Answer to Mr Molyneux's His Case of Ireland . . . Stated: and His Dangerous Notion of Ireland's Being Under No Subordination to the Parliamentary Authority of England Refuted*, London, xxxii; Kelly, P.H., 1979, 'Molyneux and Locke: the anatomy of a friendship', *Hermanthena*, cxxvi, 50–1.

47. Maxwell, Henry, 1703, *An Essay Towards an Union of Ireland with England*, 3.

48. Riley, *The Union of England and Scotland*, 196, 201, 215–16, 219.

[106]   49. Mar to Godolphin, 26 October 1706 in Hume Brown, P. (ed.) 1915, *Letters Relating to Scotland in the Reign of Queen Anne, by James Ogilvy, First Earl of Seafield and Others*, Edinburgh, Scottish Historical Society, 176–7; Mar to Sir David Nairne, 26 November 1706, in *HMC Mar & Kellie Ms*, 333–6.

50. Levack, *Formation of the British State*, 16.

51. Robertson, John (ed.) 1995, *A Union for Empire: Political Thought and the British Union of 1707*, Cambridge, xiii.

52. For example 1706, *Scotland's Great Advantages by a Union with England: Shewn in a Letter from the Country to a Member of Parliament* in *Somers Tracts*, xii, 520–2; Hutchinson, Francis, *A Sermon Preached at Edmund's-Bury, on the first of May, 1707, Being the Day of Thanksgiving for the Union of England and Scotland* in Hutchinson, 1734, *A Defence of the Ancient Historians: With a Particular Application of it to the History of Ireland and Great Britain and Other Northern Nations*, Dublin, 185, 204.

53. The phrase is Andrew Fletcher's in *An Account of a Conversation*, 118.

54. 1707, *A Sermon Preached to the People at the Mercat-Cross of Edinburgh, on the Subject of the Union*, Dublin, 4.

55. Defoe to Robert Harley, 24 October 1706, *HMC Portland Mss 15th rep. App. iv*, 339–41; Defoe, Daniel, 1709, *The History of the Union of Great Britain*, Edinburgh, ch. 3, p. 17.

56. Examples of these arguments may be found in Ridpath, George, 1702, *A Discourse upon the Union of Scotland and England ... Humbly Submitted to the Parliament of Scotland, by a Lover of His Country*, Edinburgh, 74, 83–5; Hodges, James, 1703, *The Rights and Interests of the Two British Monarchies Inquired Into, and Clear'd; with a Special Respect to an United or Separate State*, Edinburgh, 18, 39–40.

57. Fletcher, *An Account of a Conversation*, 127–8, 133, 135–7; see also John Robertson's essay 'Andrew Fletcher's vision of union', 203–5.

58. Fletcher, *An Account* of a Conversation, 120; Hodges, James, 1703, *The Rights and Interests of the two British Monarchies*, Edinburgh, 68.

59. Ridpath to Wodrow, 19 April 1706, NLS Wod. Lett. qu. iv. f. 68.

60. Ridpath, *A Discourse upon the Union of Scotland and England*, 76–7.

61. Hume Brown, *Letters Relating to Scotland in the Reign of Queen Anne*, 101.

62. Riley, *The Union of England and Scotland*, 241.

63. Southwell to Archbisop King, 14 March 1702, in King, C.S. (ed.) 1906, *A Great Archbishop of Dublin*, London, 100–2 (see also Francis Annesley's letter to King in 1706 at pp. 117–18); Coningsby to Ormond, 16 December 1704,

HMC Ormond Mss, viii, 125; Southwell to Godolphin, 25 September 1703, NLI Ormond Entrybook Ms 991/ff 129–131.

64. *Commons Journal, Ireland*, ii, 341–2. The tenor of the controversy raised by the Resumption Act can be sampled in the following pamphlets: 1701, *Short Remarks on the Late Act of Resumption of the Irish Forfeitures, and Upon the Manner of Putting that Act in Execution* in 1814, *Somers Tracts*, London, xi; 1701, *A Letter to a Member of Parliament Relating to the Irish Forfeitures*, London; 1703, *Some Remarks upon a Late Scandalous Pamphlet, Entitled An Address of Some Irish-folks to the House of Commons*, n.p.

65. The chief secretary, Sir Robert Southwell, was struck by the extent of pro-union opinion in parliament: Southwell to Nottingham, 28 September and 9 October 1703, NLI Ormond Entrybook Ms 991/f 139. Same to same, 2 October 1703, *Cal. S.P. (dom.) 1703–4*, 140–1.

66. Molesworth chaired the committee that drafted the resolution. For Cox's views see Cox to Nottingham, 13 February 1704, *Cal. S.P. (dom.) 1703–4*, 531.

67. For example, *Impartial Occurrences*, 26 December 1704, 6, 23 and 27 January, 3 July, 7 and 9 August and 5 October 1705. *Dublin Gazette*, nos 164–91, 12 November 1706, 18 February 1707. The quotation is from the Irish parliament's address published in the *Gazette*, no. 236, 22–6 July 1707.

68. Reid, J.S., 1853 edn, *History of the Presbyterian Church in Ireland*, iii, 25–8, 31–2. Lord MountAlexander to Ormond, 27 April 1707, *HMC Ormond Ms*, vii, 67. Italics added.

69. Edward Smyth, Bishop of Down and Connor to Ormond, 24 May and 14 June 1704, 4 January 1707, *HMC Ormond Ms*, vii, 77–8, 85–6, 274. R. Echlin to Ormond, 26 December 1705, *Ormond Ms*, viii, 203–4.

70. Nottingham to Ormond, 25 December 1703, *Cal. S.P. (dom.) 1703–4*, 243. Ormond to Lt. Gen. Erle, 16 May and 25 July 1704, *HMC Seventh Report pt. 1*, 771, 773. Lord Cutts to Ormond, 16 November 1706, and Edward Smyth, Bishop of Down and Connor to Ormond, 4 January 1707, *HMC Ormond Ms*, viii, 262–4, 274.

71. *Impartial Occurrences*, 10 April, 26 June 1705. Reid, 1828, *History of the Presbyterian Church in Ireland*, iii, Belfast, 33.

72. This phrase is taken from the Irish parliament's resolution presented to Queen Anne welcoming the Anglo-Scottish union: *Commons Journal, Ireland*, ii, 494.

73. See Swift's 'Verses said to be composed upon the Union' in Williams, M. (ed.) 1958, *Swift's Poems*, Oxford, i, 95–6.

74. Kidd, C., 1993, *Subverting Scotland's Past*, Cambridge, 50.

6

JACOBITISM AND THE BRITISH STATE

One effect of the much discussed 'break-up of Britain' in this post-imperial age has been to focus the attention of scholars on the contingent character of that multinational state's construction and on the provisional nature of British identity.[1] It was not always so. In the high Victorian and early Edwardian heyday of empire, historians such as W.E.H. Lecky and (later) G.M. Trevelyan, and the jurist–polemicist A.V. Dicey, celebrated the achievement of the Anglo-Scottish union, assumed its immutability and applauded the statesmanship of the politicians who had made it. That relentlessly Whig rendering of the new British state posited the triumph of the modernity, commerce and political stability that were the foundations of imperial greatness. Hugh Trevor-Roper defended the union along these lines as recently as 1977.[2] Of course, one of the problems with state-building Whig history is that it distorts the past by foregrounding the 'winners' while consigning the losers and the excluded to their fate. Concentration on the eighteenth-century British–Whig–Protestant success story masks the political and cultural diversity of these islands just as surely as it underestimates the scale of the challenge to the new state, particularly in the first four decades after 1707. It has been suggested that the 'multiplicity of minorities in this period may well constitute a majority', and that 'almost half of the population of the British Isles did not conform to jurant Anglicanism'.[3] Formidable numbers of those 'nonconformists' or 'non-jurors' were Jacobite (as were some 'jurant Anglicans'), to whom the British state was anything but preordained, welcome or immutable. Contemporaries, including contemporary Hanoverian governments, understood that, and understood it better, certainly, than some subsequent historians.

The first phase

Jacobitism, a complex, variable and multifaceted phenomenon, rested on a simple principle: the sole legitimacy of the Stuart line. Jacobites therefore rejected the revolution settlement (1688–90), the Act of Settlement (1701), the Act of Union (1707) and the Hanoverian succession (1714) as illegitimate and, strictly, illegal. But denial of the legitimacy of a regime and the withholding of allegiance is only politically significant if other conditions prevail. These may include the existence of a plausible alternative to the rejected *status quo*, numerical support, organisation, some purchase on public opinion or foreign sponsorship. Jacobitism possessed all of these in different combinations at different times. However, domestic support for the cause remained unstable and uncertain in extent, while its foreign backers, mainly France, were self-interested and unreliable. The Jacobites were also unlucky, and a catalogue of failure and ultimate defeat has enabled historians of mainstream Hanoverian Britain to marginalise them. 'The future lay with the Whigs,' writes one historian, 'and nine out of ten Englishmen knew it.'[4] In that scenario the seeing off of the Jacobite challenge illustrates the stability of the Hanoverian succession and the union. Jacobite studies today are thus 'wilfully perverse', an exercise in nostalgia.[5] But that view assumes, if not the inevitability of defeat, then at least the high improbability of any other outcome. Some counter-factual evaluations suggest otherwise. A recent study of the '45 characterises it as 'the most serious crisis to affect the eighteenth-century British state'.[6] Yet, if Charles Edward's fateful decision to turn back at Derby prompts the question 'what might have been?', the issue of Jacobite viability transcends speculation about strategy, logistics and chance. If Jacobitism is moved from the margins closer to the centre of eighteenth-century society and politics, it has the capacity to transform our understanding of the development of that society and polity:

> In place of consensus we have schism. In place of pragmatic or exploitative oligarchy we have contested party rule. In place of political stability we have a society threatened by rebellion and sometimes torn by civil war. In place of an historiography which insisted that 'Britain' was, in a variety of ways, special as a result of the irreversible achievement of 1688–89 we have an historiography which is beginning to examine England's highly problematic relations with its Celtic neighbours.[7]

The crypto-Jacobite, 'Cavalier', MPs elected to the Scottish parliament in 1703 led opposition to the proposed union in unlikely alliance with doctrinaire Presbyterians. But wholly different motives underlay that common cause. The mostly episcopalian Scottish Jacobites were ecclesiastical 'unionists' and political, or more precisely, dynastic, 'nationalists'. Presbyterians were ecclesiastical nationalists and, after the union guaranteed the establishment of the Kirk, political unionists. But acceptance of the union did not come immediately, and as late as 1718 the Pretender, James VIII and III, solicited the support of the Presbyterian extremist Cameronians. In 1719 George Lockhart of Carnwath maintained that Presbyterians were, on the whole, either favourably disposed, or indifferent, to government, but added that 'as the far greatest part of both have an heartie aversion to the union, if once they were thoroughly convinced that the king's prosperity would terminate in the dissolution thereof, there is reason to believe a great many of the first would be converted, at least so far as to be neutral, and most of the others declare for him'.[8] The union's deep unpopularity reinvigorated dynastic nationalism, which, together with the Stuarts' impeccable Scottish lineage, ensured that Jacobitism's greatest strength always lay north of the border. And the probability that a restored Stuart king would have repealed the union is high. After all, in 1660 the Old Pretender's uncle, Charles II, discarded the Cromwellian union and reasserted his prerogatives in each of his three kingdoms. Moreover, French and Jacobite strategists saw the prospect that they offered of reinstating Scotland as an 'independent' kingdom as a stepping-stone towards recapturing the main prize, England.

The centrality of England to French foreign policy and Jacobite strategy also explains the low priority afforded Ireland and Wales in the endless plots and invasion plans. Within less than a year of the Act of Union coming into force, James VIII and III (whom Louis XIV had recognised as king upon his father's death in 1701) and a small French fleet set sail for Scotland on 6 March 1708, reaching the Firth of Forth six days later. But in the event, as the superior forces of the British navy closed in, no landing was attempted and the fleet returned to France. A pattern had been established. The French displayed less than full-blooded commitment; the Jacobites were unlucky; historians are left to speculate on what might have happened. In Jeremy Black's opinion, for example, and as the list of nobles arrested by the government at the time indicates, there was 'more support for the Jacobite cause in Scotland in 1708 than there would be in 1745'.[9]

There were very good reasons, then, for Scots adherence to the Pretender: dissatisfaction with a union that had failed to deliver the promised economic benefits in any obvious way; nationalist resentment at the abolition of the Scottish Privy Council in 1708; the malt tax proposal in 1713; and the compelling ideological appeal of Stuart dynastic legitimism. The strong identification of Jacobitism with Scotland, however, with the Scottish Highlands in particular and with the 'Celtic Fringe' in general, is a primary source of its later marginalisation. The powerful teleology of modernity, civility and enlightenment which relegated the Jacobites to the sidelines of history is profoundly anglocentric. And so, it has been argued, 'Jacobitism naturally lingered longer in the north and west of Britain, for these areas were then in every sense more conservative and backward: their remoteness rendered them less susceptible to changes of ideas and attitudes'.[10] (Revealingly, we are not told from what or from where those benighted backwoods were 'remote'.) In Lord Rosebery's memorable phrase, 'the invasion of England [in 1745] was substantially a Celtic raid'.[11] Rosebery at least had the excuse of writing in the age of Matthew Arnold; it is rather more sobering to discover in a 1960s textbook that 'the highland line . . . marked the limits of civilization', beyond which stretched 'a tribal wilderness'.[12] Jacobitism, in other words, appears as essentially extraneous; implicitly or explicitly, the indigenous English variety is too often treated as relatively less important.

In actuality, Jacobitism had a natural constituency in the Church of England, many of whose members continued to be troubled by 'revolution principles'. In 1689 sufficient numbers of Church–Tories assented to the elegant fiction that James had 'deserted', vacated and thereby abdicated the throne, to avoid civil war – in *England*. But even at that moment, and in spite of James's Catholic design, a significant minority of churchmen, including the Archbishop of Canterbury and others who had earlier defied the ousted king, could not reconcile resistance to the lawful sovereign and head of the Church with doctrine or conscience. These non-jurors refused to swear allegiance to William, and it is no accident that Charles Leslie, the most prolific and intellectually acute critic of the new dispensation, was a nonjuring clergyman. Moreover, the course of events tended to confirm the nonjurors in their conviction and to compound the ambivalences of their jurant fellow-travellers. To some eyes the death of James's daughter Mary in 1696 undermined William's legal standing, and emphasised the foreignness of his court. To others the Act of Settlement, fixing the succession on the German, and Lutheran, electoress of Hanover, raised moral and political qualms. The fragile Whig–Tory consensus which enabled the revolution to take place began to unravel. The Church–Tory interest was also emboldened by the accession of James's younger daughter, Anne, in 1702, a queen whose sympathies were as High Church as her heart was 'entirely English'. For instance, within the first two years of the beginning of Anne's reign, and during the lord lieutenancy of (the future Jacobite courtier) the second Duke of Ormond, the Irish parliament introduced a sacramental test effectively excluding Dissenters from public office. Party divisions and Church–Tory unease are obliquely, but unmistakably, signalled in numerous sermons

[1 1 2]   delivered annually on 30 January, the anniversary of the 'martyrdom' of Charles I. If the rebellion against the father was sinful, then why not the one against the son? Finally, the lightly disguised critique of 'revolution principles' came provocatively close to outright denunciation in a 'Church in Danger!' sermon, preached by the high-flying Dr Henry Sacheverell, at St Paul's, on 5 November 1709.

Sacheverell launched a 'rant against Dissenters and the advocates of toleration', attacked the Lord Treasurer, Godolphin, and castigated the Whig-latitudinarian, and right-of-resistance theorist, Benjamin Hoadly, as 'a monster'. The sermon, subsequently published as *In Perils Among False Brethren*, was voted a 'malicious, scandalous and seditious libel' by the Whig-controlled Commons, which summoned the errant cleric to the bar of the House. If the Whig 'junto' hoped to intimidate its political enemies, then the impeachment of Sacheverell for 'high crimes and misdemeanours' proved a costly blunder. The trial opened on 27 February 1710 before some 2,000 spectators in the great hall of Westminster, specially refitted for the occasion. Sacheverell was accompanied to the bar by Bishop Atterbury, who was himself subjected to withering cross-examination. Transparently an ideo-logically driven political show trial, the arguments turned on the Church-and-Tory doctrines of passive obedience and non-resistance. The Whig prosecutors insisted that Sacheverell had wilfully impugned 'revolution principles'; Sacheverell, in an uncharacteristically restrained, and adroit, defence, fudged the issue of non-resistance and upheld the right of the clergy, not politicians, to decide what to preach. Although found guilty as charged, he received a sentence so light – three years' suspension from preaching and the public burning of his sermons – that it was widely, and correctly, seen as a *de facto* victory.[13]

Sacheverell's 'victory' was a Tory victory, outside the court as well as within. Atterbury's biographer attributed it to 'the unaccountable whim of popular enthusiasm';[14] however, 1710 was not the first, nor would it be the last, time that London witnessed Tory 'mobs'. Far from being aberrant or mystifying, popular support for the doctor sprang from the intersection in contemporary politics where popular and Tory beliefs and prejudices con-verged. Whereas the Godolphin Whigs concentrated their fire on the challenge to 'revolution principles', which included toleration, of course, the high-flyers aimed principally at the danger to the Church posed by Dissenters. Only months before Sacheverell's sermon in May 1709, the Whig Naturalisation Act brought Tory and popular xenophobia and hostil-ity to dissent to a new pitch. The act eased the naturalisation of 'foreign

Protestants', specifically the (Calvinist) Palatine refugees and by late July between 8,000 and 10,000 'poor Palatines' were walking the streets of London, stirring up the usual nativist resentment of parasitic immigrants, and strengthening the connection in popular perceptions between dissent and foreignness. As beneficiaries of the revolution Dissenters, foreign and domestic, were likewise perceived as partisans of the Whig regime. But much more controversially they were associated, in the public mind, with the 'Whig war', and with the financial innovations, the Bank of England and the national debt, used to fund it. The image of Dissenter-as-stockjobber and war-profiteer linked the politics of Church and Tory opposition to popular discontent.[15]

The Sacheverell episode focused discontent; Sacheverell and his friends mobilised it. Estimates of the number of copies of *In Perils Among False Brethren* circulating in 1710 range from 40,000 to 100,000, while up to 600 other 'pamphlets, broadsheets and printed sermons' relating to the case were published that year.[16] Great crowds thronged outside Westminster Hall, jostling peers and MPs in support of their hero. And when, on the night of 1–2 March, the mounting excitement spilled over into the most serious rioting London was to experience before 1780, dissenting meeting houses were the main target of the crowd's fury. Bonfires marked the trial's conclusion on 20 March, in London and elsewhere, and the momentum of popular demonstration and disturbance carried into the autumn and 'the most tumultuous general election of the eighteenth century'.[17] Together with anti-war sentiment, the slogan 'High Church and Sacheverell' helped the Tory party to a sweeping electoral triumph. Was it the revolution settlement that was now in danger?

Neither Tories, even high Tories, nor airborne Anglican high-flyers should be casually conflated with Jacobites. Of the over 330 Tory MPs elected in 1710 probably about fifty were staunch Jacobites.[18] Others were sympathetic, or ambivalent, towards the Jacobite cause; others still were firm Hanoverians. The Pretender, after all, was a Catholic. Thus in Protestant Ireland, which stood to lose most from a Restoration that would surely have reversed the Williamite land settlement, the correlation between Jacobite and Tory weakened to near vanishing point. Episcopalian Scotland lay at the opposite end of the spectrum; there Tory and Jacobite merged. Enough affinities existed between the two, moreover, on the questions of dissent and dynastic legitimacy, to worry Whigs about the security of the Protestant succession and to furnish them with a cache of propaganda *matériel*. The author of *The Jacobitism, Perjury and Popery of High-Church Priests* can scarcely

[1 1 4] be accused of innuendo. He concedes that the High Church clergy had sworn allegiance to William and to the Protestant succession, but alleges that 'these oaths went down with them as glibly as a Bumper of claret to the health of their popish king'. Referring to the abortive expedition of 1708 he observes that:

> Many admir'd the impudence of the Pretender in attempting with so very few forces such a powerful government; but they did not consider how many years the High-Church drummers had been beating up for volunteers on his account. But tho that attempt has happily miscarry'd, yet 'tis very melancholy to consider, how since that time the High Church pulpits have doubled their efforts to make way for another descent.

Other pamphleteers were equally explicit. Just as Whigs were divided 'into conformists and nonconformists', argued one, 'who, however, agree perfectly well in political matters; so the Tories have their particular division; the declared Jacobites refusing to join in commission with the time-servers, who have taken the oath of allegiance, but who, nevertheless, are as great Jacobites as the other'.[19]

Robert Harley's (later Earl of Oxford) Tory ministry of 1710–14 worked to an essentially High Church agenda. Its major legislation included the Occasional Conformity Act (1711), an Act for the toleration of Scottish episcopalians (1712) and the Schism Act (1714) directed against dissenting schools and academies. It also achieved its other great objective, a European peace, by the Treaty of Utrecht in 1713. But throughout these years the succession issue continued to haunt a deeply divided and anxious political nation. Always a wily politician, Harley travelled as far as he did down the High Church road only to placate his hardline and Jacobite backbenchers. Similarly, when he opened secret negotiations with the Pretender in 1712, his motives were probably more pragmatic, and opportunistic, than ideological. If so, the manoeuvre paid dividends when, in 1713, he asked James VIII and III to instruct his followers to support the Tories in the upcoming general election and James complied. James would not comply, however, with his, or subsequently with his ministerial rival Bolingbroke's, request that he open the way to a Stuart restoration by converting to the Church of England.[20] Whatever motivation underlay these negotiations, they had the effect of appearing to leave the succession precariously in the balance.

Rumours of these developments reached a Dublin in the grip of its own 'rage of party'.[21] In fact in no other period did Irish political alignments conform so closely to English patterns than in the closing years of Queen

Anne's reign. Harley's ministry appointed Ormond as Lord Lieutenant in place of the pro-Dissenter Whig grandee Lord Wharton. It was Ormond's new Lord Chancellor, however, the former counsel to Sacheverell, Sir Constantine Phipps, who became the chief antagonist in the ensuing party strife. As one of the lords justices in Ormond's absence, Phipps wielded effective executive power with savage partisanship. Whigs were purged from the Privy Council and the Bench, and most controversially Phipps attempted to impose a Tory candidate as Lord Mayor on the whiggish Dublin corporation.[22] In terms of Church–Dissenter rivalry, Irish Whig–Tory conflict made perfect sense. The combination of fresh Scots immigration from the 1690s and, the sacramental test of 1704 notwithstanding, the more hospitable political and legal context of the post-revolution era, had led to the consolidation and expansion of Ulster Presbyterianism. If anything, from a Church perspective, Irish dissent appeared even more dangerous than its English counterpart, and in 1712 churchmen attacked both the Ulster and Dublin nonconformists on the familiar grounds of their alleged record of disaffection and republicanism. As Phipps's High Church chaplain put it in *Her Majesty's Prerogative in Ireland*, 'the principles of the ancestors are rooted in the progeny'. Meanwhile the Ulster Presbyterians were accused of circulating the works of Milton and Shield's notorious *Hind Let Loose*.[23] Symbolically, in one of its last actions the Phipps administration suspended the payment of *regium donum* stipends to Presbyterian ministers.

In terms of the hidden Jacobite tendency of Tory reaction, Irish Protestant Tories, like Sir Richard Cox, or the ministerial propagandist in England, Jonathan Swift, dared not follow. For obvious reasons the Pretender's Catholicism alienated all possible support from that quarter, and Phipps's career in that respect is instructive. Contemporaries noted his penchant for appointing and promoting Catholic converts in the legal profession. He was successfully thwarted in the stand-off with Dublin corporation, and failed, in the 1713 parliament, and despite an ostensible Tory majority, to secure the nomination of the government candidate for speaker. Phipps's tenure itself then became the defining issue of that short, stormy session. Out of doors, recruitment for the Irish brigades in France increased, spurred on by the promise to the recruits of an early return to their native soil. 'Here is the true source of the zeal and violence of the Protestants of Ireland,' wrote Archbishop King. 'Remove the fear of the Pretender and you may lead them like a dog on a string.'[24] On the question of the succession Irish churchmen and Irish Dissenters were united. 'The Hanover-succession,' observed an Ulster Presbyterian spokesman in 1713, 'is not a meer act of the legislature,

[1 1 6] but an indissoluble covenant: for it is one of the articles of the union of Great-Britain by a positive covenant between the two British nations, upon which they became one.'[25]

Riots, rebellion and conspiracy: the '15 and after

A year passed. Queen Anne died on 1 August 1714. George I was proclaimed, initially without incident. The Irish brigades did not return to their homeland. Indeed, in 1714–16 as the constituent nations of Great Britain were convulsed with rioting and rebellion, Ireland, the main theatre of Jacobite military resistance in 1689–91, did not stir. There were three strands to the crisis of the Hanoverian succession: a ruthless Whig *putsch* at every level of government and administration; successive waves of rioting in English towns and cities; and open rebellion in Scotland and the north of England.

The accession of George I was obviously good news for the Whig minority in parliament. In addition to the taint of suspected Jacobitism, the Tories had earned the new king's enmity by negotiating a separate peace with France, thereby undermining the grand alliance to which the electorate of Hanover belonged. Whig support for George's foreign policy cemented their relationship with the incoming dynasty. An unbreakable Whig–House of Hanover partnership did not appear inevitable at the time, however. On 7 August the Secretary of State for Scotland, John Erskine, Earl of Mar, wrote to his brother that 'Jacobitisme , which they used to brand the Tories with, is now I persum out-of-doors, and the king has better understanding than to make himself but king of one partie, and tho' the Whigs may get the better with him at first, other folks will be in saifty, and may have their turn with him too'.[26] A handful of Tory politicians, notably the Earl of Nottingham, did survive for a while, but by October twenty-five Privy Councillors, including Oxford, Bolingbroke, Ormond and Mar himself, had been dismissed. A wholesale purge of central and local administration followed. County lord lieutenants, Justices of the Peace and revenue commissioners suspected of Tory sympathies were removed and replaced by reliable Whigs.[27] 'In the Scottish administration a complete clearance was made in all the great offices of state' together with a 'purge of officers at shire level'. In the other kingdom the succession 'resulted in a rapid transformation of the Irish political landscape'. On 14 September the two Tory lords justices,

Phipps and Archbishop Thomas Lindsay, were replaced by the soundly Whig Earl of Kildare and Bishop King.[28] Nevertheless the English Tories still enjoyed a hefty majority in the Commons.

When parliament was dissolved in January 1715 Tory MPs outnumbered Whigs by over 200; when the new parliament met in mid-March it had a Whig majority. During the election the Tories campaigned, predictably, on the Church in danger. The party's *de facto* manifesto, Atterbury's anonymous *English Advice to the Freeholders of England*, 'carefully dispersed through the country', warned against the calamities of a Whig regime, forecast standing armies and an end to triennial parliaments; it also managed to link Lutheranism with popery! Government offered a £1,000 reward for information leading to the arrest of the author.[29] The High Church card had delivered a Tory majority in the 1710 election, and increased it in 1713. Moreover, popular receptivity to Atterbury's message is indicated by the 'Sacheverellite' inspiration of the rioting which had swept the English Midlands on George's coronation day, 10 October 1714.[30] What went wrong? Crucially perhaps, the Whigs had the open support of the monarch. It should also be noted that the Tories garnered more votes than the number of seats that they lost might suggest. But the significance of the Whig electoral victory must be acknowledged. Modern re-evaluations of Jacobite or High Church sentiment need not obscure the appeal to English public opinion of the slogan 'the Protestant succession in danger'.

The Whig offensive continued with the impeachment of Lords Oxford, Bolingbroke, Ormond and Strafford. Bolingbroke fled to France and to the court of the Pretender in March, followed by Ormond in August. Both were attainted. From the moment of Queen Anne's death the Whig elite acted swiftly, decisively and with thoroughness. The Tory elite, on the other hand, proved indecisive and reactive. As the trajectories of Bolingbroke's, Ormond's and Mar's slide to rebellion demonstrates, the Jacobite option was thrust upon them. The hounding of High Church Toryism into overt Jacobitism, under the pressure of a relentless Whig take-over, is evident too in the changing political complexion of the anti-Hanoverian riots in 1714–15. In a near rerun of the disturbances of 1710 the coronation day rioters invoked Sacheverell and attacked Dissenter meeting houses. By the summer of 1715, however, the destruction of Dissenter chapels and property in Oxford, Manchester, Bristol, Norwich, Cambridge, Leeds and other towns was accompanied by openly Jacobite sloganeering.[31] No one can have missed the symbolic import, either, of the street disorders that marked the Pretender's birthday on 10 June. The 'Jacobite calendar' had been baptised.

[1 1 8]   This urban unrest did not challenge the existence of the new regime. On the contrary, aside from its cathartic effect for the rioters, the main outcome was the 1715 Riot Act. The real challenge came from the north. Mar returned to Scotland – on the first anniversary of Queen Anne's death – and on 6 September raised the standard of rebellion at Braemar. Discontent with the union, of which, ironically, Mar had been an architect, still ran strong in Scotland, and a Stuart restoration offered a way out. James VIII and III accordingly promised 'to relieve our subjects of Scotland, from the hardships they groan under on account of the late unhappy union, and to restore the kingdom to its ancient free and independent state'. The standard at Braemar bore the inscription 'No Union!'[32] Mar could thus count on substantial support, particularly in the Highlands and in the staunchly Jacobite–episcopalian zone along the north-east coast. Eighteen Scottish lords joined the rebellion, and the Jacobite army enlisted an estimated 16,000 recruits – many of them Lowlanders – vastly outnumbering the 'British' regiments north of the border, and unsurpassed during the '45.[33] But Mar squandered his advantage. By acting unilaterally he failed to coordinate the Scottish rising with a projected landing, led by Ormond, on the south-west coast of England. Typically the Jacobites were also handicapped by bad luck. Despite the Treaty of Utrecht Louis XIV might have provided the Jacobites with covert assistance; they could expect no such help from the Orléans regency, in control after the French king died inconsiderately on 8 August.

Jacobite forces captured Perth on 14 September, and Aberdeen on 25 September. Over the border on 6 October, Thomas Forester, MP, and the Catholic Earl of Derwentwater launched the English rebellion by proclaiming James at Waterfalls Hill in Northumberland. Reinforced by a contingent of Scots under Lord Kenmuir later that month this small English force did not make any attempt on Newcastle, striking out instead towards the north-west, and reaching Lancashire on 7 November. With its strong recusant traditions Lancashire was natural Jacobite territory, and indeed up to 75 per cent of the 1,600 or so Englishmen who shouldered arms for the Pretender in 1715 were Catholic.[34] The major military action on English soil took place at Preston which the Jacobites had occupied on 10 November. Over the coming days they twice repulsed attacks by Hanoverian troops commanded by General Wills. On 14 November, however, fresh troops arrived under General Carpenter and Forester surrendered. That proved to be a fateful day for the Jacobite cause. After failing to deliver a knock-out blow to the Duke of Argyll's greatly outnumbered army at the battle of Sheriffmuir, Mar's troops fell back, undefeated, to the Highlands.

Not even the belated arrival of the Pretender, who landed at Peterhead on 22 December, and was crowned James VIII of Scotland on 23 January 1716, could halt the flow of desertions. From a military standpoint the '15 was over. Within less than two weeks of the coronation Mar and his king set sail for France.

Argyll was no Cumberland or Keppel, but the post-rebellion reprisals were severe enough. Two peers, Lords Derwentwater and Kenmuir, and twenty-six other rebels were executed. Forester escaped from Newgate. Nineteen Scottish peerages were forfeited by act of attainder, and hundreds of prisoners were transported. In 1716 parliament passed the first of the Disarming Acts for Scotland. The crisis of 1714–16 had exposed profound divisions in English society over the first principles of governance and laid bare the shaky foundations of the British state: yet, put to the test, the Hanoverian dynasty emerged not intact merely, but strengthened. One of the ironies of Jacobitism is that it helped to entrench the regime it sought to overthrow. The Act of Settlement providing for the Hanoverian succession, and the Act of Union, designed primarily to extend its provisions north of the border, were conceived in opposition to the Stuart Pretender. The very idea of 'Britain', in other words, together with the ideological core – a Protestant, constitutional, monarchy – of the Whig oligarchy were forged under the shadow of Jacobitism. Jacobitism furnished the pretext for the proscription of the Tories after 1714, and for the maintenance of a one-party state thereafter. Rioting resulted in the Riot Act, while political instability served as an excuse for the Septennial Act in 1716. Elections would now take place every seven rather than every three years. The Whigs consolidated their power as resolutely as they had grasped it.

In the ecclesiastical sphere the Whigs asserted their ascendancy by tightening their control of the episcopal bench. With neatly symbolic timing, that most flagrantly political Low Churchman of the age, Benjamin Hoadly, was appointed Bishop of Bangor in 1715. And the bishop did not disappoint his secular patrons, broadcasting his Erastian and latitudinarian opinions in a pamphlet, *A Preservative against the Principles and Practices of the Nonjurors in both Church and State*, published in 1716, and in a sermon preached before the king on 31 March 1717. The ensuing 'Bangorian controversy' blew up a storm of pamphleteering[35] and drew censure on Hoadly from the high-flying lower house of convocation of the Church of England. But before convocation could proceed further against him it was prorogued; effectively, although no one foresaw this at the time, it had been suppressed. Two years later the Occasional Conformity and Schism Acts were repealed.

[1 2 0] Irish dissent finally got its Toleration Act. The rout of High Church Toryism seemed complete.

After 1715 the political prospects of the Jacobites receded rapidly. James Stanhope's Whig ministry reached a rapprochement with France, shutting down in the process French financial or military support for the Pretender for decades to come, and nudging his court-in-exile out of the papal state of Avignon, over the Alps, to the Italian city of Urbino. During these lean years Jacobite diplomacy operated as a footnote to European power politics which were none of its making. Intrigues with Britain's and Hanover's rivals of the day, Sweden in 1716–17 and Spain in 1718–19, came to grief; fizzling out with the small Spanish landing in Scotland and, at Glenshiel, the last military action on British soil before the '45. 'By the summer of 1719,' wrote G.V. Bennett, 'English Jacobitism was utterly dejected.'[36]

By this time the essential weakness of Jacobitism was that it could only react to political opportunities, not create them. One such opportunity appeared to open up in the spring of 1720 when the bursting of the 'South Sea Bubble' precipitated a grave financial and political crisis. At one level that spectacular stock market implosion could be read as a vindication of standard Tory and Jacobite critiques of the 'monied interest' at the rotten heart of the Whig new order; at another, panic and the financial ruin of investors, if translated into political discontent, had the potential to undermine the Whig regime. However, Jacobite inactivity in 1720 revealed just how poorly prepared and positioned they were to capitalise even on a ministry in disarray. James III, it is true, issued a declaration calling his subjects to their proper allegiance, and in a pointed allusion to his sister, Anne, reminding them of his 'entirely English heart'.[37] But the political unreality of that gesture is underlined by its place of origin: Rome, to where the Pretender's peripatetic court had moved the previous year.

Early in 1721 the train of events that culminated in the so-called Atterbury plot were set in motion, remarkably enough, by Secretary of State Sunderland. Sunderland stood to lose, and his rival, Robert Walpole, to gain, in the ministerial reshuffle likely to result from the South Sea company's collapse. He therefore approached the Jacobite leadership, Orrery, Atterbury and others in England, and George Lockart in Scotland, with an eye, presumably, to outflanking Walpole by building an alternative, majority coalition, in parliament. As bait for these unlikely allies he dangled before them the prospect of a Stuart restoration, probably upon George I's death. The improbability, secrecy, double-bluff and double-dealing of these negotiations would have led to nowhere, but for that by now inevitable adjunct to

Jacobite conspiracy – a projected military intervention from the Continent. Sunderland did not foresee that once he had initiated contact, he would also trigger plans for another 'invasion', to be led, once again by Ormond, and to coincide, once again, with a national uprising. Once more, too, the English Jacobites were found wanting in terms of organisation, preparation and recruitment.

Walpole became the chief beneficiary of the 'plot'. Beginning with the interception of easily decodable seditious letters in April 1722, he skilfully stage-managed a bogus national emergency. The leading conspirators, Atterbury, Lord Orrery, and Lord North and Grey were arrested in August and September, followed on 17 October by the suspension of *habeas corpus*. The most useful catch, however, turned out to be Christopher Layer, a Norfolk lawyer, and Lord North and Grey's legal agent, busily orchestrating a parallel 'plot', much, but by no means all, of it within the confines of his own luxuriant imagination, and much of it obligingly committed to paper.[38] The Layer papers provided enough 'evidence' to hang him, but not enough to bring Atterbury before a court of law. Instead, after the reading of a special committee report which 'confused and conflated quite separate Jacobite correspondences and thereby created the impression of a single widespread conspiracy',[39] parliament passed a bill of pains and penalties on the bishop who, on 18 June 1723, went into exile.

Walpole's brilliant manipulation of a half-imaginary Jacobite plot took him to the heights of political power, and he never forgot the lesson. If Jacobitism had not existed, Walpole would have invented it. The era of 'political stability' with which Britain's 'first prime minister' is so intimately associated rested, in part, upon the post-Atterbury eclipse of Jacobitism as a serious political force. For the Jacobites themselves had learned a hard lesson: the bishop's fate demonstrated the virtues of silence and caution. More surprisingly, its impact seems to have filtered down into popular culture: after 1723 'the Jacobite ballad press disappeared'.[40] But that decline cannot be attributed solely to the Atterbury affair. The countervailing force of inertia should not be underestimated. With each passing year the simple fact of survival, of ordinariness and familiarity, deepened the rootedness of the Hanoverian dynasty. In that respect what did not happen upon the succession of George II in 1727 is eloquent testimony to the basic security of the regime, and to the ineffectiveness of its opponents.

The undoubted political ascendancy of the Walpoleian Whigs in this period has led some historians virtually to ignore Jacobitism. The articulation of political opposition devolved along a court–country, rather than a

[1 2 2] Whig–Tory, axis. Moreover, the 'prime minister' exercised so tight a grip on patronage within parliament that the focus of opposition shifted out-of-doors. Both the cross-party nature of the country platform and its extra-parliamentary dimension are epitomised by the career of Bolingbroke, who had secured a pardon in 1723, but remained debarred from the House of Lords. In December 1726, Bolingbroke launched a paper, *The Craftsman*, in the pages of which he denounced Walpoleian corruption (or 'craft') and called for the abandonment of the old party labels as obsolete and divisive. He did, in fact, win the cooperation of a number of anti-Walpole Whigs, notably William Pulteney, and steered clear of the Tory MP William Shippen's 'irrelevant Jacobitism'.[41] Walpole, of course, only stood to lose if party distinctions and the Jacobite bogey were allowed to lapse. The prime minister routinely and indiscriminately smeared his opponents with accusations of Jacobitism. Bolingbroke, of course, presented a particularly easy target for this form of political abuse, and its effective deployment contributed to his second 'exile', this time voluntary, to France in 1735.[42] Historians have characterised this tactic as obsessive, unscrupulous, cynical and successful. They have also been struck by the amounts of time, money, energy and resources devoted to uncovering supposed Jacobite plots. Integral to the Walpoleian system was a far-flung espionage network, constantly recycling rumours, half-truths and conjectures from the capitals of Europe. Walpole, they are agreed, had a genuine fear of the Jacobite threat. 'The need to circumvent Jacobitism,' concludes his biographer, 'was one of the fundamental principles that guided . . . decisions in domestic and foreign affairs.'[43]

As the spectre of Jacobitism receded in the political and military spheres it deposited numerous traces in British and Irish culture and society. For example, James VIII and III continued to exercise ecclesiastical patronage in the Scottish episcopal and Irish Catholic Churches.[44] In Ireland the anti-recruitment statute of 1722 and the execution of 'scores – if not hundreds' did not prevent the annual enlistment of thousands in the service of the Pretender in the armies of France and Spain. Some 400 of these 'wild geese' later formed the professional core of Charles Edward's army and 'fought with distinction' at Falkirk and Culloden.[45] Jacobite sentiments were also transmitted in Gaelic verse, above all in the irredentist heartlands of the south-west. The *aisling*, or vision poem, was aristocratic, prophetic, Catholic-millenarian and nationalist. At the same time the more plebeian drinking song likewise looked forward to a Stuart restoration.[46] Welsh Jacobitism, in contrast, appears to have lacked a nationalist component.[47] In England Jacobite symbolism has been tracked across plasterwork, glassware, poetry

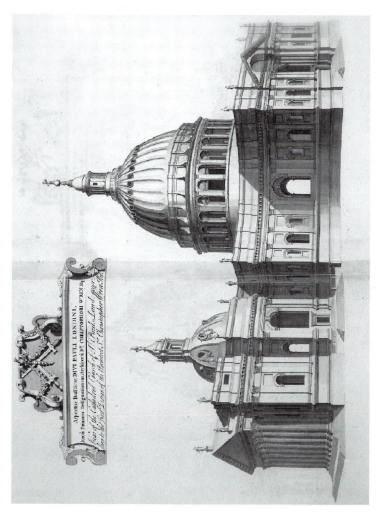

Plate 1
St Paul's, symbol of the 'near-confessional' state.
Source: Royal Academy of Art Library London/The Bridgeman Art Library

THE PARLIAMENT HOUSE, DUBLIN

Plate 2
Parliament House, Dublin
Source: Courtesy of the National Library of Ireland

Plate 3
Sawney Scot and John Bull
Source: The British Library

Plate 4
March to Finchley – Hogarth
Source: Mary Evans Picture Library

Plate 5
Fort George – securing the British State
Source: National Monuments Record of Scotland

Plate 6
Map of Great Britain and Ireland
Source: Mary Evans Picture Library

Plate 7
'Baptism from the jail at Stonehaven': post-Culloden repression of the Scottish
Episcopal Church.
Courtesy of the Rt. Rev. Neville Chamberlain, Bishop of Brechin

and folkways.[48] Approaching Jacobitism as a 'culture' or subculture, rather than as a continuous coherent political 'movement', represents a valuable conceptual advance, but leaves the difficulty of how to evaluate such evidence unresolved. How is commitment to be measured? How subversive, ultimately, were the white roses and oak boughs of the House of Stuart? Did poetry, toasts or 'seditious words' matter? Linda Colley's dismissal of these diverse and often coded manifestations of support for the Pretender as merely 'passive Jacobitism'[49] deserves consideration. Yet if the extent and depth of Jacobite sympathies in England, Wales and Ireland remains open to dispute, in Scotland those sympathies were put to the severest of tests.

Challenge and consolidation: the union, the House of Hanover and the '45

The revival of Jacobitism as a political and military force in the 1740s owed everything to the changing international situation and especially to the renewal of Anglo-French rivalry. Under domestic political pressures Walpole reluctantly committed Britain to war with Spain in 1739. The next year Frederick of Prussia occupied Silesia, sparking off the war of the Austrian succession (1740–48), and the 'logic' of the balance of power ensured that sooner or later both Britain and France would be drawn into the European conflict. The Pretender instructed his supporters in parliament to ally with opposition Whigs, and thereby helped to speed Walpole's downfall in 1742. In 1743 the premier Welsh Jacobite Sir Watkin William Wynn travelled to France to solicit foreign aid, and Ormond's illegitimate son, James Butler, travelled to England, to gauge Jacobite strength. By the beginning of 1744 the French were proceeding with invasion plans, but were thwarted, as they had been thwarted in 1692 and would be again in 1796, by a 'Protestant wind'. Nevertheless the prospect of French intervention provides the essential context for Charles Edward's daring expedition, which set sail from Nantes on 5 July 1745.[50]

While the young prince embarked on this enterprise without seeking the sanction of either his father or, more importantly, the French, he could soon claim the sanction of success. Landing at Eriskay in the Western Isles on 3 August, the Jacobite army, daily supplemented by Highland clansmen, raised the standard of rebellion at Glenfinnan on 19 August. Within less than a month, on 17 September, it entered Edinburgh, and Charles declared 'the

[1 2 4]   pretended union' at an end. Edinburgh was a great symbolic prize; crucially, however, the Jacobite forces failed to capture the castle. Four days later, though, they won their first significant military victory by routing General Cope's troops at the battle of Prestonpans. Prestonpans changed perceptions of 'this romantic expedition' south of the border. George II, in Hanover at the time of the original landing, signalled the initial lack of urgency by his leisurely rate of return. An English MP confessed that 'this affair in Scotland taken by itself gives me no great terrors'. After Prestonpans few doubted the gravity of the crisis, and the British troops stationed at Ostend were recalled.[51] By as early as October ripples of panic were unsettling the city. 'It is almost incredible what a severe blow this rebellion has given to trade and public credit,' declared an alarmed Londoner, 'Merchants dare do nothing. The bank won't discount any bills.'[52] Reports surfaced in the provincial press of Catholic agents and 'mendicants in various disguise' stalking the land by night.[53] In Ireland the Scotophobic Lord Lieutenant Chesterfield found that 'all my good subjects here are unanimously zealous, but unanimously frightn'd too'. Although he himself continued not to entertain 'the least apprehension', he did take the precaution of stepping up the country's defences, and of sending a spy – 'a trusty smuggler' – to infiltrate the Jacobite MacDonald clan. But undoubtedly Chesterfield's greatest contribution to the Hanoverian state during this crisis was to keep Ireland calm by refusing to crack down on the Catholics.[54]

    The Lord Lieutenant also displayed an elementary grasp of geopolitics. Noting dryly that Irish Protestants 'think themselves of so much importance as to be the principal objects of the designs of our enemies', he took the view that 'our enemies are well enough informed to know that this country must necessarily follow the fate of England'.[55] Charles Edward concurred. Victory or defeat, restoration or exile, hinged finally on control not of Edinburgh but of London. On 8 November the Jacobite army crossed the border into England. The Jacobites opted for the western route south to London, bypassing the Hanoverian army under General Wade drawn up on the north-east coast at Newcastle. As in Scotland earlier they enjoyed the tactical advantage of speed and mobility, assisted in the Scottish case by the military roads in the Highlands, constructed ironically by Wade between 1724 and 1740 to safeguard against a future Jacobite rising. But unlike Monck in 1660 the Jacobites failed to secure their rear properly before marching south. As well as Edinburgh Castle, the Hanoverians retained control the Highland forts, William and Augustus. More dangerously, perhaps, Scotland was far from united in the Pretender's cause. Nor was this simply a

Highland–Lowland divide. In addition to the staunchly Whig allegiance of the mighty Clan Campbell–House of Argyll, the political alignments of the clans generally tended to split along religious lines: the episcopalians and the numerically small Catholics rallying to the prince's standard; the Presbyterians remaining loyal to Hanover.[56] Jacobitism did mobilise considerable numbers of Lowlanders, if not in the Presbyterian strongholds of Glasgow, the borders or the south-west, and Lowlanders were represented disproportionately among the officer cadres and in Charles Edward's council of war and Privy Council.[57] It is therefore possible to argue that in 1745–46 Scotland witnessed both a 'national uprising' and a civil war.

The complexity of Scottish allegiances need not obscure the facts that Jacobitism commanded the support of the majority of the clans, and that the Highlanders bore the brunt of the fighting, comprising an estimated 67 per cent of the 6,000 soldiers who marched into England, for instance.[58] Moreover, the ubiquity of tartanry – not only Lowlanders but Mancunians were decked out in plaid – broadcast the Highlandism of the Jacobite army. But like the swords that the clansmen used to such devastating effect at Prestonpans, the symbolism was double-edged. Whereas tartan signified steadfast patriotism to its wearers, to loyal Hanoverians it connoted treason and backwardness. Perceptions of a cultural–ideological dichotomy, of a struggle between (English) Protestant civility on the one hand, and 'Celtic', Catholic barbarism on the other, are conveyed succinctly by the MP who detected the working of providence in early rebel successes. Thus emboldened, he maintained, they would be 'draw[en] . . . from their native mountains and fastnesses that in the plain country they may become an easy sacrifice to his majesty's just vengeance'. Subsequently, a Whig *apologia* for the slaughter at Culloden explained that 'the rebels had enraged the troops; their habit was strange, their language still stranger, and their way of fighting was shocking to the utmost degree'.[59] Meanwhile the 'otherness' of the Jacobite acted as a brake on English recruitment.

For, again unlike Monck's army in 1660, which advanced through the open door of the English political nation, Charles Edward's troops ventured into the political unknown. English Jacobites had risen in the north in the '15, and the Stuart papers are stuffed with optimistic assessments of English Jacobite support thereafter: but would words now be translated into actions? There is no question that, except for Lancashire, with its substantial Catholic minority, the English responded very tardily to the call. It is equally true, however, that the Jacobite army met little active resistance, occupying Carlisle on 9 November, Preston on 26 November and Manchester on

[1 2 6] 29 November, before reaching Derby by 4 December. To some historians inaction is evidence of neutrality and of the absence of enthusiasm for the ruling dynasty. To others it indicates a 'sullen' quiescence by a resentful civilian population helpless before a fierce invader.[60] And while the Jacobite army has been described as 'remarkably restrained and relatively disciplined [on the] march south', that did not prevent the spread of rumours and stories about plundering and pillage. *Faulkner's Dublin Journal* reported the 'shocking villainies of the Highlanders' at Carlisle, and fear of large-scale violence, it is suggested, undermined popular attachment to the Jacobite cause.[61] Fear of popery and France also loomed large, and to judge from the pages of the English provincial press Charles Edward confronted 'a nation of defiant loyalists'. On the other hand, it has been pointed out, 'newspapers printed only Whig propaganda' and, as a contemporary observed of the loyal addresses, 'the gazettes about the time of the Revolution were filled with very handsome ones to King James'.[62]

The issue of English and Welsh allegiance is critical to any answer that might be given to one of the great counter-factual questions of the '45 – and indeed of British history: what if the prince, and not his military commander, Lord George Murray, had prevailed in the debate at Derby and the Jacobite army had continued its advance south?[63] Murray did prevail, however. He and a majority on the council of war could argue from the lack of large-scale English mobilisation or of French intervention. They did not know that the French had reactivated invasion preparations. They were unaware too of the ramshackle character of London's defences, satirised memorably in Hogarth's print *The March to Finchley*. On 5 December the Jacobites turned back. As they retreated northwards anti-Jacobite rioting broke out in Manchester, a city that only a week earlier had welcomed the Young Pretender with ringing bells. Attacks on the straggler, the wounded and the left-behind have been claimed as 'unambiguous' evidence of the real sentiments of the 'English poor',[64] but they can just as credibly be read as proof of opportunism – as a sort of popular verdict on which side was likely to win.

London may have been vulnerable when the Jacobite army turned back, but England by no means lay at its feet. To the east Wade's forces had shadowed the prince's march south; while directly to the south an army under the command of George II's younger son, the Duke of Cumberland, had reached Staffordshire. By 8 December Cumberland had selected a force of 1,500 mounted troops ready to begin a rapid pursuit of his 'quarry' – as he thought of it . Cumberland's men did move quickly in appalling winter conditions, although they were slowed down by a Whitehall nervous that the south-east now stood exposed to French invasion. The Jacobites crossed back into Scotland on 20 December, and exactly one week later the Hanoverians began to bombard the 350-strong garrison left to defend Carlise.[65] During the siege four Jacobite prisoners had been hung outside the castle; when, after three days' shelling, the garrison surrendered, those who had been captured at Prestonpans and joined the Jacobites were executed immediately. 'Cruelty was to be used as a policy.'[66] Edinburgh meanwhile had been retaken and Charles Edward headed for the chill Whig–Presbyterian environs of Glasgow.

Cumberland returned to London. Events did not permit any lengthy respite in the capital, however, as on 17 January 1746 Murray inflicted the last big defeat of the campaign on the Hanoverians, under General Hawley at the battle of Falkirk. The Jacobites now fell back, to the north and the Highlands. Then, on 16 April, at Culloden moor, four miles east of Inverness, came the final confrontation, the last great battle fought on British soil. Cumberland commanded some 9,000 soldiers, including the Campbells of the Argyll militia; the mainly Highlander Jacobites numbered approximately 5,000. Within half an hour or so it was over, the fabled Highland charge cut to shreds in hails of cannon and musket fire. The slaughter commenced. Exact figures are impossible to obtain, but probably more than 2,000 Jacobite soldiers and camp-followers were killed that day. Another 1,000 were taken prisoner. Estimates of Hanoverian fatalities range from as low as 44 up to 350, with 250 wounded.[67] Most, perhaps twice as many, Jacobites were killed after the battle, and by several eye-witness accounts corpses were strewn from Culloden moor to the streets of Inverness.[68] Despite a brief rally of the remnant at Ruthven, the Jacobite cause was broken. 'Bonnie Prince Charlie' gave the order to disperse, and departed into hiding, exile, drunkenness and legend. His loyal clansmen, left behind, were less fortunate.

In the closing weeks of April, news of Culloden was greeted with jubilation across England. Bonfires, illuminations and the ringing of church bells marked Cumberland's triumph. Parliament granted the duke £25,000 per annum; Handel set to work on his oratorio *Judas Maccabaeus* in honour of the 'conquering hero'; St Paul's held a service of national thanksgiving. What did these celebrations mean? According to the author of a 'winners'' history of the '45, 'like the previous manifestations of loyalty, the demonstrations after the battle cannot be dismissed as contrived set pieces stage-managed by the court'. And yet the note of scepticism sounded by Horace Walpole suggests that precisely like 'previous manifestations of loyalty' – whether for

[128] George II or James II – the post-Culloden displays can indeed be dismissed as, at the very least, inconclusive evidence of firm popular loyalty to the ruling regime. One 'Mr Dodington', wrote Walpole, 'on the first report came out with a very pretty illumination: so pretty, that I believe he had it by him, ready for any occasion'.[69]

In Scotland the raids and reprisals mounted after Culloden have been described as 'systematic state terrorism, characterized by a genocidal intent that verged on ethnic cleansing'.[70] Others, sympathetic to the 'Butcher' Cumberland, as he was already being called by the summer of 1746, deny the charge. Exaggerated, allegedly, by subsequent Jacobite 'lies', the 'admittedly harsh' pacification of the Highlands and western islands is attributed, in their view, to the 'reluctant' royal duke's military subordinates or political superiors, to 'excesses . . . committed by the soldiery', to the previous merciless behaviour of the Jacobites, to the norms of European warfare and so on.[71] Cumberland himself oversaw these operations between late April and mid-July. Homes, episcopal chapels and Catholic meeting houses were burned, cattle driven off and ploughs smashed. Armed rebels were shot. Captured rebel 'thieves' and 'vermin' were shipped south to await their fate. In total the number of prisoners rose above 3,000. As in 1716 it was the peers tried for treason who attracted most public attention. Two, Lords Kilmarnock and Balmerino, were beheaded on 18 August. A third nobleman who suffered the ultimate penalty bore the title Derwentwater; his older brother had been executed in 1716. In all around 120 prisoners were hanged, including thirty-eight British army deserters and twenty-four men of the Manchester regiment, singled out, as English Jacobites, for exemplary punishment. The remainder were transported to the West Indies and American colonies or, more often, died of prison fevers and disease.[72]

The effort at military extirpation, continued with equal brutality after Cumberland's departure, by William Anne Keppel, second Earl of Albemarle, was soon carried on by other means – a legislative package which represented a concerted attempt to eradicate the 'Highland problem' once and for all, and a renewed programme of fortification. The legislation consisted of an Act of Attainder and the forfeitures of rebel properties, another Disarming Act, an Act outlawing Highland dress, swords and bagpipes, the effective suppression of 'that seminary of Jacobitism' the non-juring episcopal church, and finally, in 1747, the abolition of heritable jurisdictions. The last Act – which violated article 20 of the union treaty – by dismantling the 160 surviving Baron courts, courts of reality and sheriffdoms, further eroded Scottish particularism. Aimed at undercutting the local power bases of the clan chiefs, thus subordinating an unruly Gaeldom to the sovereign authority of central government, this 'modernising' legislation provides a classic example of what Michael Hechter terms 'internal colonialism'.[73] The process of legal and administrative integration rested on physical domination. In order to prevent another '45 General Wade's military roads network was expanded, the Highlands were carefully mapped and, in 1748, nine miles to the east of Inverness, work began on Fort George.

By the time of its completion in 1767 the spent force of Jacobitism no longer justified Fort George's massive cost and scale. But in the immediate aftermath of Culloden, neither the finality of Jacobite defeat nor the implications of the rebellion and its suppression were clear. To the extent that legislative union had not been accompanied by a union of sentiment or of peoples, it is hardly surprising that a Scottish-based and Scottish-led rebellion provoked outbursts of English Scotophobia. The fact that a majority of Scots, particularly Lowland Scots, were either neutral or loyal Hanoverians failed to blunt hostility or assuage suspicions. If the Argyll militia saw action at Culloden, the newly formed Highland Blackwatch company, stationed near London in 1745, was held pointedly in reserve. And just as Irish Protestants had earlier complained of the English habit of seeing all Irishmen, Protestant and Catholic, settler and native, 'in the gross',[74] so in 1746 some Englishmen deemed all Scots 'natural hereditary Jacobite[s]'. Chesterfield, who had operated an embargo on supplies from Ireland to Scotland, did not even pretend to that conflation in advocating a complete blockade, declaring 'I would starve the loyal with the disloyal.'[75]

In the longer term Fort George can be seen as a symbol of Hanoverian ascendancy, the security of the union and the power of the British state. The benign version of the effects of the post-Culloden onslaught presents it as 'that general pacification which smoothed the path of national commerce and development, and secured to Scotland the first fruits of the Act of Union'.[76] Herein lies the central paradox of the entire Jacobite challenge: it strengthened the Whig–British state it sought to overthrow. Jacobitism forced the ideological underpinning of Whiggery – the revolution settlement – to the fore, and acted as a catalyst for the Act of Union. Along with Catholics and the French, Jacobites, heavily stigmatised with Catholicism and French sponsorship anyway, served as the 'other' against which Britishness defined itself. Finally, it has been noted, 'the physical authority of the state also expanded. The standing army more than doubled in size, the fiscal "sinews of power" were enormously strengthened and the overseas and domestic intelligence network of His Majesty's government became truly formidable'.[77] With hindsight, the crushing of the Jacobite threat and the consolidation of the union and the state seem the obvious outcomes of the '45. What is more, from a 'British' four nations perspective, the defeat of Scottish (dynastic) nationalism at Culloden appears more comprehensive than the 'shipwreck' of its Irish counterpart at the Boyne and Aughrim over fifty years before. Fort George would, eventually, be pressed into service against rebellion: as a prison for leading United Irishmen after 1798.

Notes

1. Nairn, Tom, 1981, *The Break-up of Britain*, London. See also the comments of Raphael Samuel, 'Grand narratives in 1990', *History Workshop*, 29: 129.

2. The Anglo-Scottish union, reprinted in Trevor-Roper, 1992, *From Counter-reformation to Revolution*, London, 287–302.

3. Pittock, Murray G.H., 1997, *Inventing and Resisting Britain: Cultural Identities in Britain and Ireland, 1685–1789*, Houndsmills, 1, 5.

4. Ayling, S.E., 1966, *The Georgian Century 1714–1837*, London, 81.

5. For example Cannadine, David, 1987, 'British history: Past, Present – and Future?' *P&P*, 116: 189–90.

6. Black, J., 1990, *Culloden and the '45*, New York, xiii.

7. Clark, J.C.D., 'On moving the middle ground: the significance of Jacobitism in historical studies' in Black, J. (ed.) 1988, *The Jacobite Challenge*, Edinburgh, 181–2.

8. Pittock, M.G.H., 1998, *Jacobitism*, Houndsmills, 31. Lockhart to George Keith, April 1719, in Szechi, D. (ed.) 1989, *Letters of George Lockhart of Carnwath, 1698–1732*, SHS Edinburgh, 141.

9. Black, *Culloden and the '45*, 18.

10. Thomas, P.D.G., 1962, 'Jacobitism in Wales' *Welsh History Review* 1:3, 279.

11. Pittock, M.G.H., 1995, *The Myth of the Jacobite Clans*, Edinburgh, 54.

12. Ayling, *Georgian Century*, 193.

13. Bennett, G.V., 1975, *The Tory Crisis in Church and State 1688–1730: The Career of Francis Atterbury, Bishop of Rochester*, Oxford, 110–17; Holmes, Geoffrey, 1973, *The Trial of Doctor Sacheverell*, London, 228–32.

14. Bennett, *Tory Crisis in Church and State*, 117.

15. Holmes, Geoffrey, 1976, 'The Sacheverell riots: the crowd and the Church in early eighteenth-century London', *P&P*, 72: 61–4; Dickinson, H.T., 1967, 'The poor Palatines and the parties', *EHR*, lxxxii: 464–85.

16. Bennett, *Tory Crisis in Church and State*, 113; Holmes, *The Trial of Doctor Sacheverell*, 75; Holmes, 'The Sacheverell riots', 68.

17. Holmes, 'The Sacheverell riots', 55.

18. See appendix, Szechi, D., 1984, *Jacobitism and Tory Politics, 1710–14*, Edinburgh.

19. [John Toland] 1710, *The Jacobitism, Perjury and Popery of High-Church Priests*, London, 6, 11; Anon., 1710, *Mr Toland's Reflections on Dr Sacheverell's Sermon*, London, 3.

20. Szechi, *Jacobitism and Tory Politics*, 182–91, 200–3.

21. It was reported there that the Pretender was daily showing 'coldness and indifferancy' to the Catholic Church and intended 'to build a chapel . . . for those of his family that are of the Church of England': Margaret Dean to Henry Boyle, 23 June 1713, PRONI Cal. Shannon Papers, D 2707/A1/2/1B.

22. The best account of the mayoral dispute is in Hill, Jacqeline, 1998, *From Patriots to Unionists: Dublin Civic Politics and Protestant Patriotism, 1660–1841*, Oxford, 71–8; For general treatments of this period see James, F.G., 1973, *Ireland in the Empire, 1688–1760*, Cambridge, Mass., 71–82 and Hayton, D.W., 1981, 'The crisis in Ireland and the disintegration of Queen Anne's last ministry', *IHS*, xxii: 193–215.

23. Trapp, Joseph, 1712, *Her Majesty's Prerogative in Ireland*, London, 4–5; Tisdell, William, 1712, *The Conduct of the Dissenters of Ireland, with Respect to Both Church and State*, Dublin, 67–9; a Presbyterian minister, James Kirkpatrick, replied to Tisdell in 1713, *An Historical Essay upon the Loyalty of Presbyterians in Great Britain and Ireland from the Reformation to this Present Year 1713*, Belfast.

24. Cited by J.G. Simms, 'The Irish Parliament of 1713' in Hayton, D. and O'Brien, G. (eds) 1986, *War and Politics in Ireland, 1649–1730*, London, 285.

25. Kirkpatrick, *An Historical Essay upon the Loyalty of Presbyterians*, ix.

26. *HMC Mar and Kellie Ms*, 505–6.

27. For accounts of the Whig take-over see Speck, W.A., 1977, *Stability and Strife, England, 1714–1760*, Cambridge, Mass., 169–84; and Colley, Linda, 1982, *In Defiance of Oligarchy: The Tory Party 1714–60*, Cambridge, 177–83.

[1 3 2]   28. Riely, P.W.J., 1964, *The English Ministers and Scotland, 1707–1727*, London, 257–9; McNally, Patrick, 1997, *Parties, Patriots and Undertakers: Parliamentary Politics in Early Hanoverian Ireland*, Dublin, 58, 67–9.

29. *Cobbett's Parliamentary History of England*, vii, 25; Bennett, *Tory Crisis in Church and State*, 192–3.

30. Monod, Paul, 1989, *Jacobitism and the English People, 1688–1788*, Cambridge, 173.

31. *Ibid.*, 173–94.

32. Pittock, *Jacobitism*, 38, 41.

33. MacInnes, A., 1996, *Clanship, Commerce and the House of Stuart, 1603–1788*, East Lothian, 162–3.

34. Monod, *Jacobitism and the English People*, 321–2.

35. One estimate puts the number of publications related to Hoadly at 1,000: Bennett, *Tory Crisis in Church and State*, 215.

36. Bennett, 'Jacobitism and the rise of Walpole' in McKendrick, N. (ed.) 1974, *Historical Perspectives: Studies in English Thought and Society in Honour of J.H. Plumb*, London, 70–92, at 73. My account of the Atterbury plot is based mainly on this essay and on the relevant chapters in Bennett, *Tory Crisis in Church and State*, 223–75.

37. James III to the People of England, 10 October 1720: *HMC Various Collections*, v, 242–3.

38. Plumb's (see n. 41) and Bennett's treatment of Layer as an unlucky crank is challenged by Eveline Cruickshanks in 'Lord North, Christopher Layer and the Atterbury Plot: 1720–23' in Cruickshanks, E. (ed.) *The Jacobite Challenge*, 92–106.

39. Bennett, 'Jacobitism and the rise of Walpole', 89.

40. Monod, *Jacobitism and the English People*, 67.

41. The phrase is J.H. Plumb's: 1960, *Sir Robert Walpole, the King's Minister*, London, 195.

42. Quentin Skinner's 'The principles and politics of opposition: the case of Bolingbroke versus Walpole' in McKendrick, N. (ed.) *Historical Perspectives: Studies in English Thought and Society in Honour of J.H. Plumb*, London, 93–128, remains the best analysis of this phase of Bolingbroke's career.

43. Plumb, *Sir Robert Walpole*, 326–7; Dickinson, H.T., 1973, *Walpole and the Whig Supremacy*, London, 158.

44. Lockhart to James III and VIII, 25 April 1720, 7 December 1722, Szechi, *Letters of George Lockhart*, 145–7, 180–5. Fagen, Patrick (ed.) 1995, *Ireland in the Stuart Papers*, 2 vols, Dublin, *passim.*

45. O'Buachalla, Brendan, 1993, 'Irish Jacobitism in official documents', *Eighteenth Century Ireland*, 8: 128–38; Murtah, Harmon, 'Irish soldiers abroad, 1600–1800' in Bartlett, Thomas and Jeffrey, Keith (eds) 1996, *A Military History of Ireland*, Cambridge, 296–9, 308, 310–12.

46. O'Buachalla, Brendan, 'Irish Jacobitism and Irish nationalism: the literary evidence' in Whelan, Kevin and O'Dea, Michael (eds) 1995, *Studies on Voltaire and the Eighteenth Century*, Oxford, 103–16; O'Buachalla, Brendan, 1992, 'Irish Jacobite poetry', *The Irish Review*, 12: 40–9.

47. Pittock, *Inventing and Resisting Britain*, 53.

48. The classic, most detailed and far-ranging example of this style of analysis is Monod's *Jacobitism and the English People.*

49. Colley, Linda, 1992, *Britons: Forging the Nation, 1707–1837*, New Haven.

50. The European background is sketched in by Jeremy Black in *Culloden and the '45*, 46–65.

51. Black, *Culloden and the '45*, 74, 80–5.

52. Henry Hastings to Earl of Huntingdon, October 1745, *HMC Hastings Ms*, iii, 52–3.

53. Harris, B., 1995, 'England's provincial newspapers and the Jacobite rebellion of 1745–1746', *History*, 80: 256, 10.

54. Chesterfield to Andrew Stone, 31 August, Chesterfield to Newcastle, 2 September, 5 October, 25 November 1745, 1930, *Private Correspondence of Chesterfield and Newcastle, 1744–46*, London, RHS, 61–3, 72–3, 87. McLynn, F.J., 1979, 'Ireland and the Jacobite Rising of 1745', *Irish Sword*, xiii: 53, 339–52. McLynn, F.J., 1981, '"Good behaviour": Irish Catholics and the Jacobite rising', *Eire–Ireland*, xvi: 2, 43–58.

55. Chesterfield to Newcastle, 5 October 1745, *Private Correspondence of Chesterfield and Newcastle*, 72–3.

56. The political and religious geography of the clans is expertly delineated in MacInnes, *Clanship, Commerce and the House of Stuart*, 163, 173–6, n. 182.

57. Pittock, *Myth of the Jacobite Clans*, 61.

58. MacInnes, *Clanship, Commerce and the House of Stuart*, 163.

59. *Parliamentary History of England*, xiii, 1315; Henderson, Andrew, 1748, *History of the Rebellion*, 117.

[134] 60. Contrast Colley, *Britons*, 76–7 and Speck, W.A., 1995, *The Butcher: The Duke of Cumberland and the Suppression of the '45*, Caernarvon, with Cruickshanks, Eveline, 1979, *Political Untouchables: The Tories and the '45*, London.

61. MacInnes, *Clanship, Commerce and the House of Stuart*, 165; *Dublin Evening Post*, 30 Nov.–3 Dec. 1745; Colley, *Britons*, 76.

62. Harris, 'England's provincial newspapers and the Jacobite rebellion', 14–16; Cruickshanks, *Political Untouchables*, 81, 88.

63. For an entertaining and frankly partisan counter-factual history of the 'second restoration' see Petrie, Charles, 1926, 'If: a Jacobite fantasy', *The Weekly Westminster*, 30 Jan.

64. Colley, *Britons*, 77.

65. Whitworth, Rex, 1992, *William Augustus, Duke of Cumberland: A Life*, London, 64–8.

66. Black, *Culloden and the '45*, 132.

67. For example Black, *Culloden and the '45*, 174; Whitworth, *William Augustus*, 87; Speck, *The Butcher*, 145.

68. Black, *Culloden and the '45*, 165; Speck, *The Butcher*, 145.

69. Speck, *The Butcher*, 158; Charteris, Evan, 1913, *William Augustus, Duke of Cumberland: His Early Life and Times (1721–1748)*, London, 20.

70. MacInnes, *Clanship, Commerce and the House of Stuart*, 211.

71. For example Whitworth, *William Augustus*, 89, 90, 99; Charteris, *William Augustus*, 276–7, 282–3, 285.

72. My account draws on Lenman, Bruce, 1980, *The Jacobite Risings in Britain, 1689–1746*, London, 261–78.

73. Hechter, Michael, 1975, *Internal Colonialism*, London.

74. Anon, *c.* 1692, *Considerations Concerning Ireland in Relation to England and Particularly in Respect of an Union*.

75. Lenman, *The Jacobite Risings in Britain*, 264, Chesterfield to Newcastle, March, 1746, *Private Correspondence of Chesterfield and Newcastle*, 123.

76. Charteris, *William Augustus*, 287. Charteris, it is worth noting, was himself a Scot.

77. Szechi, D., 1994, *The Jacobites, Britain and Europe, 1688–1788*, Manchester, 137.

CONVERGENCE AND DIVERGENCE: IDENTITY FORMATION AND POLITICS IN THE EIGHTEENTH CENTURY

At the beginning of the eighteenth century the majority of Scots opposed an incorporating union with England. In addition to the religious, Jacobite-legitimist, and constitutional reasons for such opposition, Scottish antipathy to the union project drew on national sentiment. In 1706, as we have seen, the Edinburgh 'mob' proclaimed its Scottishness and 'condemned the name of Britains'. Lord Belhaven trembled at the imagined fate of 'our ancient mother, Caledonia'. In striking contrast to that patriotic rhetoric, Irish Protestants, insisting on their English blood and heritage, pleaded to be admitted to 'a yet more comprehensive union'.[1] By the last decade of the century these positions were utterly reversed. In 1792 Dr William Drennan drafted an address on behalf of the radical Dublin Society of United Irishmen to their fellow parliamentary reformers, gathered at a convention in Edinburgh. Drennan, a Belfastman, had studied medicine at Edinburgh University in the late 1770s, and knew his Scottish history. The address combined fraternal greetings with a call to action. Its militancy perturbed the more moderate 'Friends of the People', but Drennan's real offence lay in his appeal to an imagined Scottish nationalism. 'We rejoice,' he wrote, 'that you do not consider yourselves as merged and melted down into another country, but that in this great national question you are still Scotland – the land where Buchanan wrote, and Fletcher spoke, and Wallace fought.' The assembled delegates reacted angrily, rejecting the address as, in the words of one of its critics, 'high treason against the union betwixt England and Scotland'.

Amazingly, within months the Belfast Society of United Irishmen dispatched a second address to the Scottish reformers, again presuming to stroke their national pride:

That Scotland, for ages, the asylum of independence, and equally renowned in arms and arts; that Scotland, the modern nurse of literature and science, whose seminaries have supplied the world with statesmen, orators, historians, and philosophers . . . that this same Scotland should have so long forgotten her degraded state as a nation, slept over her political insignificance, or silently acquiesced in the mockery of a popular representation, among senators of another people, hath long filled us with an inexpressible astonishment . . . [the union] set upon your independency and blotted your name from among the nations of the earth.[2]

Aside from the doubtful efficacy of condescension as a means of persuasion, Drennan and the Belfast radicals badly misjudged their audience. They assumed that, like themselves, Scots reformers were motivated in part by national feeling, and that the union would therefore be a legitimate and a popular target. They were wrong. By the 1790s the union was no longer a political issue, and except for a few individuals, such as Thomas Muir and James Thompson Callender, who were moving in a nationalist direction, Scottish 'democrats' wished to reform the *British* parliament.[3]

During the eighteenth century, then, Scottish senses of identity evolved towards a new dual allegiance, as Scots and North Britons. In Ireland during the same period a contrary trajectory can be traced. There the Protestant community which at the beginning of the century identified itself by formulae such as 'the English Interest' or (simultaneously) 'the people of Ireland', came to describe itself, simply, as 'the Irish nation'. This chapter explores those processes of identity formation, their political contexts and how they shaped constitutional relationships within these islands.

Divergence: Ireland

Any account of the forging of new collective identities in eighteenth-century Ireland must necessarily concentrate on the 'Protestant nation'. Irish Catholic allegiance did not stand still: it changed, rather, from traditional adherence to Jacobitism in the first half of the century, to endorsement of the Hanoverian regime in the second half. As the founder of the Catholic Committee, Charles O'Conor, put it in 1786, 'we are all become good Protestants in politics'.[4] What he meant was that educated Catholics now accepted the 1688 revolution as a victory of parliamentary liberty over tyranny, not as a defeat of Catholics by Protestants. And although there is no reason to question O'Conor's sincerity about this, he understood also the strategic necessity of shaking off the Jacobite millstone. Catholic relief would never make any headway in a Protestant state while it remained. Then, in the revolutionary 1790s, some among the essentially conservative Catholic community advanced to republican separatism. But there is no evidence to suggest that any of these changes in political orientation were either prompted by, or effected, corresponding shifts in Catholic senses of national identity. They were Irish; most of the rural poor were Gaelic-speaking; they had nowhere else to go. Nevertheless the changing position of the Catholics under the penal laws shaped – even determined – the development of Protestant nationalism.

There is nothing surprising, to paraphrase Francis Hutcheson, about colonies becoming independent. Time, distance from the 'mother country', resentment at second-class status and attachment to place conspire, with the passing of generations, in the fabrication of distinctive colonial, provincial or 'national' identities. These, in turn, are part cause, part rationale, and part justification for concrete re-orderings of the political and constitutional arrangements between 'centres' and 'peripheries'.[5] This is not to posit an iron law of colonial nationalism. Each case is different: distance is obviously less important in the history of Anglo-Irish relations than it is in the genesis of American colonial rebellion; equally obviously, equidistant British Canada harboured less resentment of the metropolitan power than its neighbours to the south; Ireland was not, strictly, a colony anyway, and so on. Nevertheless, the tendency of dissimilar settler communities towards cultural and political differentiation is marked by enough similarities to suggest a pattern, so much so that rather than asking why a particular colony asserted its independence, we might ask: what, hitherto, *prevented* it from arriving at that destination; what, as it were, slowed the process down? In the case of Protestant Ireland an answer readily presents itself: the rhetorical equation, still strong at the beginning of the eighteenth century, of the categories 'native Irish' and 'papist'.

The casual conflation of Irish with Catholic is nicely conveyed by the title of Sir Richard Cox's 1698 pamphlet, *An Essay for the Conversion of the Irish, Showing that 'tis their Duty and Interest to Become Protestants.* Cox also illustrates the dichotomy in the Irish Protestant position, addressing Catholics as 'my countrymen' before proceeding to advocate their 'total conversion and conformity to the laws, language, habit, manners and religion of England'. After all, he inquires of these benighted recusants, 'what greater honour can you desire, than to be accounted English?'[6] The corollary of that attitude is clearly stated in 1712 by the Whig grandee, Alan Broderick: 'I shall be thought', he wrote, 'and perhaps told, that I am (what of all things I least chuse to be) an Irishman'.[7] In addition to a horror of popery, Protestants in this period were as yet psychologically unprepared to embrace the appellation 'Irish' because they shared their English co-religionists' racial prejudices.

[1 3 8]   English images of the native Irish as an inferior, lazy, feckless and warlike people can be traced back to Giraldus Cambrensis in the twelfth century. The stereotype also had a lighter – though not always less offensive – side in the 'stage Irishry' which achieved sharper definition during the eighteenth century. But the transition, in English characterisations, from 'Barbarism to Burlesque' was never completed, and an ingrained sense, among Protestants, of cultural superiority over the 'original inhabitants' acted as a barrier on the road to an Irish self-identification.[8]

So long as the Catholic threat retained a military edge England and its 'bulwark' in Ireland, the English Interest, were mutually dependent. And the imperatives of physical survival combined with shared Protestantism and a compelling – if sometimes precarious – sense of a privileged joint propri-etorship in unique Saxon liberties, to lock Irish Protestants into the English connection and English identity. However, the eclipse of the Catholic mili-tary threat after 1691, and the elimination of the Old English as a rival polit-ical elite, slackened Irish Protestant dependence on their English guarantors, enabling the articulation of a more assertive politics, and clearing a space for the fashioning of a more distinctive corporate identity. Protestant nationalist aspirations and Protestant appropriation of Irishness thus rested, ultimately, on the broken back of Catholic Ireland and on its continued subjugation under the penal laws. That is, the necessary self-confidence that underpinned these developments derived from a long unchallenged monopoly in the state and a near monopoly in the acknowledged source of political power: landed property. Henry Maxwell put the matter simply: 'there is no danger', he wrote in 1703, 'to be apprehended from the popish Irish'. Almost thirty years later Swift remarked that 'the papists are wholly disarmed. They had neither courage, leaders, money, or inclination to rebel.'[9]

The burgeoning self-confidence of what is often (though anachronistically) termed the 'Protestant Ascendancy', manifested itself through architecture, notably the great country houses, like Carton, Castletown and Powerscourt, through the equally imposing public buildings, particularly in Dublin, and above all in the parliament house itself, constructed between 1729 and 1739. The long peace of the eighteenth century also imparted a sense of security to the ruling elite, expressed, for example, by the fashions for landscape gardening and agricultural 'improvement'. Landed gentlemen, in other words, were prepared to invest in their own and in their country's future.[10] But it is important not to overstate the firmness of Protestant confidence. Swift's seemingly complacent assessment of Catholic impotence is polemical. Penal laws affecting dissent need not be relaxed, nor need churchmen concern themselves with Protestant solidarity, he implied, since the 'common enemy' posed no real danger. Others were less sanguine. An unmistakable thread of anxiety can be detected in Protestant attitudes throughout the eighteenth century: apprehension about popish infiltration of the Phipps administration in 1711–14, for instance, or the panicked closure of Catholic mass houses during the invasion scare of 1744, and the instant attribution by some of agrarian unrest after 1760 to papist conspiracies and French intrigue, all indicate a somewhat nervous disposition.

The erosion of a dependence mentality must not be overstated either. English arms remained the guarantee of last resort for Protestant control in Ireland, and the Protestants knew it. That is one reason why, before 1707, the Dublin parliament dared not emulate its Edinburgh counterpart by threatening to opt out of the Hanoverian succession. That is the reason, too, that not until the 1790s did (a minority of) Protestants push constitutional nationalism to the logical terminus of separation. And before that could happen prejudices towards Catholics had to moderate and accommodations had to be reached. Moreover, no matter how much Irish Protestants railed at English injustice, it was always tempered by a keen grasp of *Realpolitik*. Maxwell began his *Essay* in 1703 with the frank admission that 'it is not the design of this discourse to examine whether laws made in England ought to bind Ireland; it being sufficient for those of that nation [Ireland] to know that this is a power which England claims, and is *able to vindicate*'. In 1720 a pamphleteer, protesting against the impending Declaratory Act (6 Geo. I), acknowledged that if the parliament of Britain enacts that the British House of Lords 'shall be the supreme court of judicature over the kingdom of Ireland; no doubt but we must submit to it, because we cannot help so doing'; while in 1749 Sir Richard Cox, grandson of the Tory (and unionist) lord chancellor earlier in the century, replied to Charles Lucas's alleged desire for 'independency' by insisting that there was no point 'in disputing a sovereignty which they [England] are in possession of, are able to hold, and doubtless resolved to do so'.[11]

Confidence and security, based on dominance in the domestic political sphere, was one face of the Protestant elite; a sense of grievance at English maltreatment was the other. Protestant resentment turned on three basic issues: the disbursement of patronage; commercial restrictions on the Irish economy; and limitations on Irish sovereignty. The first was a function of the wider British political spoils system perfected by Walpole. J.G.A. Pocock describes eighteenth-century Irish (and Scottish) politics as 'those of ... locally administered province[s] of the Whig empire of parliamentary

[1 4 0] patronage', while towards the end of this period the Irish radical, Theobald Wolfe Tone, observed, 'our benches were filled with English lawyers; our Bishoprics with English divines; our custom-house with English commissioners; all offices of state filled, three deep, with Englishmen in possession, Englishmen in reversion and Englishmen in expectancy'.[12] Walpole and his successors were naturally more attuned to English political advantage than to Anglo-Irish sensitivities, but the appointment of Englishmen to key positions in the Irish Church and administration also represented a means of political control. As Archbishop Hugh Boulter wrote to the Duke of Newcastle in the aftermath of the 'Woods halfpence' crisis: 'have none but Englishmen put into the great places for the future'.[13] And many of the chief offices of Church and state, including the lord chancellorship and the primatial see, were in fact occupied by Englishmen for most of the century. Two primates particularly stand out: Boulter (1724–42) and George Stone (1747–64). Not only did the archbishops of Armagh usually act, with the Lord Chancellor and the Speaker, as lords justices in the Lord Lieutenant's absence; they were active parliamentary managers as well. According to a contemporary critic, Stone, 'that refined politician', was 'intoxicated with the unnatural interest he has by every kind of corruption obtained in the house of commons . . . all favours are dispensed through his benign influence, and without Wolsey's interposition it is in vain to look after honours or any kind of preferment'.[14]

By Boulter's time the term 'English Interest' had ceased to denominate the Protestant community in opposition to the Catholic majority, and indicated instead the upholders of English policy in Ireland against the 'Irish Interest'. But to the extent to which this was a matter of metropolitan rhetoric, suspicion and perception, as much as of real political differences, the Protestants had their nationalism thrust upon them. 'Unfortunately for this kingdom,' lamented one commentator, 'it still bears the name of Ireland, and the Protestant inhabitants, the denomination of Irish, with old ideas annexed to them of opposition to the interest of England.'[15] The Woods halfpence episode began in 1722 when George I granted a patent to coin copper halfpennies and farthings for Ireland (which lacked that symbolic attribute of sovereignty, a mint) to his mistress the Duchess of Kendal, who in turn sold it to William Woods, an ironmonger from Wolverhampton. It is symptomatic of evolving Irish perceptions, however, that resistance to this flagrant, if routine, piece of graft soon escalated into a national crusade. As the 'Drapier', Swift famously rallied 'the whole people of Ireland' – a revealing description of conforming Protestants. Moreover, the successful campaign against the coins, which were withdrawn in 1725, illustrates how political, economic and constitutional grievances could combine. Irish 'public opinion' objected to the 'corrupt' origins of the patent, to the supposedly disastrous impact the halfpence would have on the currency and, above all, to the arbitrary manner of its imposition by the English ministry without the consent of the Irish people or parliament.

From Swift's injunction in 1719 to 'burn every Thing that came from England, except their *People* and their *Coals*', through the agitation for 'free trade' in 1779, to the non-importation movements of 1784 and 1792, denunciations of mercantilist restrictions on Irish commerce, principally the Woollen Act (1699), persisted throughout the eighteenth century.[16] However, neither the blame for, nor the solution to, economic backwardness was laid solely at England's door. Beginning with Swift's *Proposal for the Universal Use of Irish Manufactures*, 'Patriot' writers produced a considerable body of 'self-help' literature, enjoining Irish consumption of Irish goods, non-consumption of imported 'luxury' items, taxes on absentee landlords, and agricultural improvement. These writers included Robert Viscount Molesworth, *Some Considerations for the Promoting of Agriculture and Employing the Poor* (1723), Thomas Prior, *A List of the Absentees of Ireland* (1729), Arthur Dobbs, *An Essay on the Trade and Improvement of Ireland* (1729–31), Bishop George Berkeley, *The Querist* (1735–37), and Samuel Madden, *Reflections and Resolutions Proper for the Gentlemen of Ireland* (1738). A number of them were likewise founders of the Dublin Society in 1731, which offered premiums and prizes for new agricultural technologies and practices. The 'patriotism' of men like Prior and Madden denotes a practical public spirit, indistinguishable from, say, the promoters of Edinburgh's Honourable Society of Improvers in the Knowledge of Agriculture set up in 1723. Nevertheless, the self-help project had profounder implications: the conceptual framework that Molesworth and the rest adopted – the unit to which their remedies were to be applied – was the 'nation'. To be sure, concern for the wretched conditions of the Catholic 'natives' often smacked of colonial paternalism, but it also inched the would-be paternalists towards identification with what Berkeley called 'the whole inhabitants' of the island, as part of a wider national community distinct from England.[17]

To Anglo-Irish eyes, of course, the root of all jobbery and economic retardation could be traced back to constitutional subordination. The Drapier invoked 'the famous Mr Molyneux' and repudiated the assertion that Ireland was 'a depending kingdom'. Over twenty years later, the Dublin radical, Dr Charles Lucas, recycled the arguments of 'that strenuous asserter of truth and liberty', 'that most illustrious, venerable patriot' the author of the 'invaluable' *Case of Ireland being Bound by Acts of Parliament in England Stated.*[18] Presumably Lucas was behind the reprinting of the *Case* in 1749, as it was republished at each moment of tension in British–Irish relations during the eighteenth century. Certainly, Lucas's debt to Molyneux is plain.

In the tenth of his twenty addresses to the freemen and freeholders of Dublin in 1749 Lucas proclaimed that

> it has been long, as artfully, as falsely and wickedly, dinned in the ears of every subject of this kingdom, that we are a conquered people, absolutely dependent upon, and subject to, the government of England, or Great Britain; that our parliament is inferior, subordinate, or subservient, made in the British parliament without our consent, or knowledge.

Whereas 'Ireland [is] . . . effectually, totally, separated and alienated from the *crown* of England; and was indisputably established as new complete kingdom, absolutely remote and distinct, from the crown of England, and free and independent of its power and authority, to all intents and purposes.' He then goes on to condemn Poynings' Law and the Declaratory Act as infringements of Irish sovereignty.[19] This was all familiar territory by the 1740s, of course. But Lucas went further. In his controversial eleventh address he sketched a version of Irish history which came perilously close to a Catholic–Gaelic inter-pretation of the divisive national past. 'With what shame and grief I tell it!' he wrote, 'the Mexicans were never used worse, by the barbarous Spaniards, than the poor Irish were, for some centuries, by the English.'[20] No friend to popery, Lucas nonetheless came close to justifying the 1641 rebellion as the outcome of English oppressions. As they came to think of themselves as 'the Irish nation', Irish Protestants began to appropriate the Gaelic past.

Again, it would be a mistake to overburden the radical Doctor's rhetoric with too much interpretative weight. The autonomy of the Irish kingdom and parliament remained one of a range of concerns; one aspect of the corporate privileges, immunities and liberties which, like all good Whigs, he sought to defend. Nor, unlike later Protestant radicals, did he ever seek an accommodation with the Catholics. Moreover, in addition to Molyneux, Lucas drew freely on English intellectual sources, such as Sir Edward Coke and John Locke. Some of his many publications were signed 'Britannicus' – his associate, James Digges LaTouche, adopted the pseudonym 'Hibernicus' – and he even, in exile in London in 1756, proposed union for Ireland on the Scottish model.[21] The oft-professed loyalty of Protestant 'Patriots' or 'nationalists' to the crown and to the British connection was both sincere, and not, in their view, in any way inconsistent with their attachment to Ireland or demands for greater constitutional rights.

Declared 'an enemy of the country' by parliament, Lucas fled to England in 1749 (he would return at the beginning of George III's reign in 1760 and win election as a Dublin city MP the following year). The great majority of the conservative and landed members were as offended by the presumption of a mere apothecary inciting the 'mob' to political action, as by his stirring up of jealousies between the two kingdoms. But as the events of the 1750s soon showed, it was Lucas, not the parliament, who more accurately reflected the direction in which public opinion was by then moving. Those events were the money bill dispute of 1753–55 and the Dublin anti-union riot in 1759.[22] The first episode was, in practice, a straight power-political contest between parliamentary factions led by the Speaker, Henry Boyle, on the one hand, and by Primate Stone on the other. However, and significantly, Boyle contrived to present the occasion of the dispute – the 'sole right' of parliament to initiate money bills – as a defence of 'national rights'. The second episode demonstrated the depth of popular hostility to the idea of a legislative union in Dublin when, early in December 1759, crowds reacted to rumours of an intended union by barracking MPs and peers, before breaking into the parliament chambers. The contrast with Irish Protestant attitudes on this question in 1707 could not be sharper.

By 1760, then, a broadly 'national' standpoint had become entrenched in Irish politics. Nationalist iconography and insignia bedecked the uniforms and banners of the volunteer army which sprang up, in the context of the American war, in 1778, and a 'nationalist' agenda underlay the great constitutional conflicts of 1779–82, which culminated in the repeal of Poynings' Law and the Declaratory Act. In retrospect the 'legislative independence' secured by the 'revolution' or 'constitution' of 1782 represents the high tide of eighteenth-century Protestant nationalism – the point beyond which many Protestant politicians, patriots and volunteers were not prepared to venture. Yet it was an incomplete 'revolution', which failed to challenge, or remove, a London-appointed executive. Radicals, such as Wolfe Tone, later scorned it. As the very first public declaration of the Society of United Irishmen announced in 1791:

> We have no national government; we are ruled by Englishmen and the servants of Englishmen, whose object is the interest of another country, whose instrument is corruption, and whose strength is the weakness of Ireland; and these men have the whole of the power and patronage of the country as a means to seduce and to subdue the honesty and the spirit of the representatives in the legislature.[23]

[1 4 4] If the United Irish analysis was correct and little indeed had changed after 1782, why then did the Protestant elite not push on? Why did they not emulate their admired American counterparts and assert their complete independence? The main answer, as so often in Irish history, is denominational. Protestant nationalism was limited, conditional, confessional and, ultimately, transitory. Protestant Ascendancy, underwritten by the British connection, mattered more to most Protestants than the restrictions on sovereignty which that connection inevitably entailed. Separatism, or even parliamentary reform, if it advanced the prospects of Catholic political power, proved simply too risky to contemplate. Stalling in the mid-1780s, and retreating to unionism in the late 1790s, Protestant nationalism receded in inverse proportion to the revival of the Catholic nation.

Still, not all Protestants, perhaps not even a majority, endorsed the union at first; nor did they hop lightly from an Irish to a British sense of identity. On the contrary, in Ireland the term 'British', while used occasionally by Protestants – Lucas for example – as a self-description, tended to be applied to the 'Ulster-Scot' Presbyterians. 'Britain' and 'Great Britain' also enjoyed occasional use, but politicians and pamphleteers referred much more often to 'England' and the 'English government'. The northern Presbyterians themselves were at ease with the British designation in the early decades of the century, before developing, like their Church of Ireland rivals, a more Irish sense of identity. After all, it was a Presbyterian, William Drennan, who coined the phrase 'Emerald Isle'. But it is no accident that 'Britishness' only took hold in the areas of Scottish settlement in Ulster, for nowhere in these islands, with the exception of Wales, was that concept stronger than in Scotland itself.

Convergence: Scotland

The Old Pretender, and later Charles Edward, repudiated the 'pretended union', first, because they wished to restore the traditional prerogatives of the House of Stuart in its ancient kingdom of Scotland, and second, because they believed such a policy would attract popular support in Scotland. The second calculation was certainly true for the episcopalian core of Jacobites along the north-east coast; it may even have been true in 1715 for some Presbyterians, particularly the Cameronian remnant which continued to reject as sinful the Anglican–Erastian polity created, as they believed, by the hated union. By 1745, however, as the dismal record of Jacobite recruitment in Glasgow and the south-west showed, the Stuart cause had lost its residual appeal for old-style Presbyterian nationalism. The incentive of a restored kingdom no longer outweighed the deterrent of a popish king. Charles Edward's experience in 1745 serves as a reminder of a basic fact which should never be underestimated in any assessment of the 'success' of the union or the progress of North Britishness: the simple passage of time consolidated the United Kingdom. Like the Hanoverian succession, the longer the union lasted the more 'natural' and non-reversible it must have seemed. Inertia, though, is scarcely a sufficient explanation for the survival of the union. In other circumstances the passing of time weakened the bonds between the American colonists and the mother country, and attenuated Irish Protestant senses of their Englishness.

A principal argument in favour of the union had been the projected economic benefits of ready access to English and English colonial markets. In the short and medium terms the advantages accruing to Scotland from expanded commercial opportunities were far from clear to contemporaries, and continue to perplex historians. It is generally agreed, however, and it seemed to contemporary observers, that the union facilitated modest economic advances – in the export of live cattle south, in the tobacco trade and in the linen industry. One revealing indicator of comparative economic health is the country's ability to feed itself during the harsh winter and crop failures of 1740–41.[24] The contrast with Ireland, which was decimated by famine at this time,[25] and with Scotland's own 'hungry years' in the 1690s, is as marked as it is poignant. But even these straightforward propositions about post-union economic trends turn out, upon closer scrutiny, to be problematic.

The surviving data are patchy and therefore any generalisations based upon them are necessarily inconclusive. For example, the growth of cattle exports during this period has been questioned. That is an empirical issue. The broader interpretative difficulties are more intractable still; where economic growth can be clearly measured, in the tobacco and linen trades for instance, is it attributable to the union, to indigenous conditions – in the case of tobacco to efficient smuggling – or to a combination of both? As Richard Brinsley Sheridan pointed out during the 1799 Westminster debates on a British–Irish union, the undoubted fact that Edinburgh had flourished under the union did not prove that it had flourished *because* of the union.[26] In other words, there was no necessary correlation between union and economic development. Yet, although Sheridan's logic is impeccable, it was perception, not logic (or the 'actual' situation subsequently pieced together by economic historians), that determined the extent to which Scots associated the union with 'improvement'.

[1 4 6]   In his 'Observations on the present circumstances of Scotland', composed in 1730, Sir John Clerk of Penicuik (one of the commissioners who had negotiated the union in 1706) detected increases in the export of 'black catle' to England since 1707, and in 'the value of the lands which produced them'. He likewise noted 'considerable' growth in the linen trade – which was certainly the case in the years following the founding of the Board of Trustees for manufactures in 1728. But overall his estimate of the state and prospects of the economy is only cautiously optimistic. It is just as well the linen and cattle trades are thriving, he observes, because otherwise 'we wou'd be in no condition to live in this part of Britain, by reason of the vast sums which are drawn yearly out of the country for the support of our people who live in England, or for purchasing the commodities we want from that country'. [27]

The allusion to absenteeism has obvious parallels with contemporary Irish analysis, and, indeed, there are other striking similarities. The Board of Trustees appears to have been modelled on the equally successful Irish Linen Board; Patrick Linesay discussed Irish examples in his improving *Interest of Scotland Considered* (1733), and some Scottish 'Patriots' echoed Irish calls for local consumption of home-produced textiles. [28] But the comparison is not exact. Whereas both sets of improvers extolled the merits of national self-help, the Scots, who enjoyed free trade with England and the colonies, were unable, in addition, to blame English-imposed commercial restrictions for a less than buoyant economic performance. 'If since the union of the kingdoms we have not improven our opportunities of encreasing in trade and riches as we might have done,' Clerk concluded bleakly, 'it is intirely oueing to want of industry or perhaps honesty amongst ourselves, and to the obstinat neglect of the welfare of our country.' [29]

In one specific instance, however, Scots could legitimately pin an economic grievance on England and the union: the detested Malt Tax. First extended north of the border in the teeth of fierce Scottish parliamentary resistance in 1713, and exploited by Jacobite propagandists thereafter, London only attempted to enforce it in 1725. This time resistance spread to the streets – rioting in Glasgow and a brewers' strike in Edinburgh. Secretary of State Roxburgh and Lord Advocate Robert Dundas were dismissed for refusing to cooperate in the implementation of the tax, and the office of the secretaryship, hitherto the preserve of local 'Squadrone' politicians, simply ceased. Into its place stepped Archibald Campbell, Earl of Islay (from 1743 the third Duke of Argyll) and his brother John, the second duke, to whom the 'management' of Scottish society devolved. As his first service to Walpole as *de facto* minister for North Britain, Islay suppressed opposition to the Malt Tax. By birth, education (Eton, but also the universities of Glasgow and Utrecht), residence (Whitton estate, Middlesex) and inclination, Islay was an Englishman; nevertheless it is significant that he tackled the crisis of 1725 in his capacity as leader of a powerful domestic political faction. Viewed from an Irish angle, where English lord lieutenants had failed, at precisely that moment, to impose another unpopular economic measure, Woods halfpence, the resolution of the Malt Tax episode seems to illustrate the greater integration – or subservience – of Scottish political elites into the Westminster power nexus.

That is only partly true. Eighteenth-century Scotland has been described as a 'client society', to be sure, and Islay did Walpole's – and later Henry Pelham's – bidding. Like his Irish 'undertaker' counterparts, notably Speaker Boyle, he delivered parliamentary votes and controlled the levers of patronage in return, but with this crucial difference: both the legal autonomy of Scottish law and of the Kirk, and the distinctive practices and traditions of those institutions in terms, respectively, of jurisprudence and theology, ensured that, in marked contrast to Ireland, posts at the Bar, on the Bench or in the Church could not be colonised by Englishmen. The law and the Kirk amounted, in effect, to a 'private reserve of power and patronage for well-connected North Britons',[30] and as institutional repositories of Scottish identity, which negotiated and mitigated the full force of anglicisation.

Not that anyone would accuse Islay of fretting unduly about Scottish identity. Rather he ran the country in a hard-headed pragmatic manner, as a sort of fiefdom within the Hanoverian patronage empire. The earl prudently distributed employments, preferments and favours across a range of crown offices and public bodies, including the Royal Bank of Scotland, of which he was a governor, the Board of Trustees, the Custom House, the Post Office, Edinburgh town council and the convention of Royal Burghs.[31] Through his agent, Patrick Cummings, and the mechanism of the Patronage Act, Islay also exercised enormous influence over the appointment of Presbyterian ministers; directly in the case of the one-third or so in the gift of royal patronage, and less directly in numerous other instances through individual lay patrons tied in a hundred ways to the Argyll interest. The installation of politically safe, or docile, clerical candidates contributed, in turn, to the rise and eventual dominance of the moderate party within the Kirk. The days when the Kirk might compete with, or challenge, the state were emphatically over.

So long as Scotland behaved itself a semi-detached English ministry was generally content to delegate control to a semi-independent manager. But realignments in English politics, or the intrusion of Scottish affairs – the Malt Tax agitation, the Porteous riots in Edinburgh in 1736, or the '45 for example – upon ministerial attention quickly exposed the ultimate source of political power. When Walpole fell, Islay fell, to be replaced between 1742 and 1746 by the Marquis of Tweeddale, installed in the temporarily revived office of secretary of state. When 'Scotland' misbehaved spectacularly in 1745 it prompted the most sweeping legislative intervention from Westminster since 1707. Islay (now Argyll), who returned as unofficial minister for Scotland in 1746, a role he fulfilled until his death in 1761, proved unable to delay or mitigate the abolition of heritable jurisdictions in 1747, the effects of which reached far beyond the Highlands. Much of the time the London government had no 'policy' for, and less interest in, Scotland. When impressed by the need to act, however, it displayed both the capacity and the will to do so.

The eradication of the heritable jurisdictions and the suppression of clanship is often represented as the dismantling of backward 'feudal' and Gaelic obstacles on the march to modernity, politeness and commerce. After 1747 the union began to deliver tangible results, or so the story goes.[32] In fact, the dynamics of cultural, political and economic change are certainly more complex than the conventional Whig-unionist, and anglocentric, narrative allows, even if there is little doubt that at mid-century Scottish society shifted gear. Sir Gilbert Elliott's proposal for Edinburgh New Town, published in 1752, exudes optimism. 'At no period, surely,' he argued, 'did there ever appear a more general, or a better directed zeal for the improvement and prosperity of this country, persons of every rank and denomination seem at length to be activated by a truly public and national spirit.' Moreover, Elliott predicted, accurately as it turned out, that the growth of Edinburgh would have a 'multiplier effect' on the economy as a whole, commenting that 'the national advantages which a populous capital must necessarily produce, are obvious . . . the certain consequence is, general wealth and prosperity: the number of useful people will increase; the rents of land rise; the public revenue improve; and in room of sloth and poverty, will succeed industry and opulence'.[33]

Like the parallel development of Dublin, the construction of the New Town in the 1760s and 1770s testified to a new-found – and in the Scottish case more firmly based – sense of political stability. But whereas Dublin's residential squares and public buildings are usually read as an architectural analogue of 'Ascendancy' self-confidence, Edinburgh's Georgian grids, with their Hanover, George and Frederick streets, stand as a monument, a sort of civic version of Fort George, to Scotland's incorporation into the British state. The New Town was also, of course, a triumph of taste, planning and modernity. Meanwhile intellectuals were constructing models of 'civil society' as quintessentially 'eighteenth century' as any classical building by Sir

James Craig or James or Robert Adam, and as securely located in a British context.

In an oft-quoted passage from the first issue of the *Edinburgh Review* in 1755 (the publication of which is in itself a sign of cultural vigour), Alexander Wedderburn remarked that 'if countries have had their ages with respect to improvement, North Britain may be considered in a state of early youth, guided and supported by the more mature strength of her kindred country'. Why, at this stage, did intellectuals turn more decidedly towards a British identity? One answer may lie in the suppression of the '45, which appeared finally to settle the union question – notwithstanding the fact that the 'question' was rarely posed publicly before then. Another clue is contained elsewhere in the *Review* essay itself. 'The communication of trade,' it asserts, 'has awakened industry.' Scots actually were experiencing the birth pangs of modern industrial and urban society. From a lower base line Glasgow grew more rapidly even than the capital, and by the 1770s overtook London as the leading tobacco entrepôt in Britain. By the 1780s the historic shift from linen to cotton production had begun. Again, the origins and motor forces of industrialisation are endlessly debated, and raise questions about labour skills, technologies, entrepreneurship and capital investment. Still, 'there is general agreement that it was during the period *c.* 1740–1780 that the union played its most unambiguously favourable role in Scottish economic development, although generally in a permissive rather than an active manner'.[34] Crucially for the process of identity formation there were perceived connections between union, empire – 'the communication of trade' – and economic growth – 'awakened industry'.

Nor was this simply a matter of a healthy economic balance sheet. 'Commerce', in addition, stood for 'politeness', 'modernity' and 'civilisation', in a word, for 'progress'. Adam Ferguson for one, the author of *An Essay on the History of Civil Society* (1767), took a more complicated view than that, and others worried that the 'luxury' created by commercial development corroded public 'virtue', but on the whole the equation may be allowed to stand. 'Commerce' and 'modernity' were Whig shibboleths, and like increased economic productivity, the spectacular productivity in ideas about man, moral character, history and society, known as 'Scottish sociology' or as 'the Scottish Enlightenment',[35] resulted from the complex interplay of distinctive local and British contexts.

Some of the most important local contexts were institutional: the moderate wing of the Kirk, the universities and the Edinburgh clubs. The so-called 'father' of the Scottish Enlightenment, the Ulsterman Francis Hutcheson,

[1 5 0] was both a Presbyterian minister and a university professor, occupying the chair of moral philosophy at Glasgow between 1730 and 1743. Ferguson began his career as an army chaplain, later giving up the cloth and holding the chair in moral philosophy at Edinburgh University. Other clergymen, or sometime clergymen, who belonged to the 'moderate literati' include Alexander Carlyle, the historian William Robertson and John Home. David Hume stands out, not just as the towering figure of the Enlightenment, but as a religious sceptic. Nevertheless, he was able to exchange ideas with his contemporaries in the Select Society, a sort of polite debating club set up in Edinburgh in 1754, or later in the Poker Club, founded in 1762 to agitate for a Scottish militia.

Intellectually and politically the militia episode confirms the Scottishness of the Enlightenment project. Indeed it has been suggested that Ferguson's *Civil Society* 'may be read as an extended commentary on the themes he and Carlyle had articulated in their [earlier] militia pamphlets'.[36] County militias were embodied in England and – without comment – in Wales in 1757. The new arrangements did not, however, extend to Scotland, thus, allegedly, leaving North Britain defenceless at the time of the Seven Years War (1756–63). Ferguson had published a pamphlet on the desirability of such an institution in 1756, to no discernible effect. It took the invasion scare of 1759 to trigger public debate. Beginning in Argyll in October that year a number of counties and burghs petitioned parliament for the introduction of a militia to Scotland. Carlyle penned an anonymous pamphlet, *The Questions Relating to a Scots Militia Considered*, which was quarried for excerpts and arguments by the Scottish press, and would be reprinted when the agitation revived in late 1762. At Westminster Sir Gilbert Elliott introduced a bill for a Scottish militia on 24 March 1760, but this was decisively defeated at the second reading on 15 April. Significantly though, only two of the twenty-five Scots MPs, Robert Dundas and Hope Weir, voted against. Further pamphlets followed rejection, including the allegory *The History of the Proceedings in the Case of Margaret, Commonly Called Peg, Only Lawful Sister to John Bull*, which is usually attributed to Ferguson and has been recently claimed for Hume.[37] Ferguson, Hume, Carlyle and others formed the Poker Club in 1762 to continue the campaign, but without success, either then, or later, during the American war between 1776 and 1783.

There were two basic issues at stake for the literati: the reconstruction of Scottish society on 'civil' principles, and equality for Scotland within the union. The first aspiration looked back to, without directly replicating, the ideas of the great Scottish commonwealthman and advocate of militias,

Andrew Fletcher. Whereas Fletcher proposed militias as a replacement to standing armies which threatened liberty, Carlyle and the others accepted the need for an *imperial* army, most usefully deployed abroad, which the militia would complement at home. At a more sophisticated level, they sought to resuscitate Scotland's traditional martial spirit, and through the public participation of the armed citizen secure the nation from 'a return to the oppressions of the Gothic past and . . . a descent into the corruption of the commercial future'.[38] The emphasis on a martial past reveals the specifically Scottish coloration of their analysis, and this emerges even more strongly on the other front of the debate, the issue of militia and loyalty.

There had been opposition to the original English militia bill, a 'patriot' measure hitched to the rising star of William Pitt, in 1756–57. Opponents objected, for instance, that the militarisation of the able-bodied would cause unnecessary economic dislocation. It is not surprising, then, that the same voices were raised against an extension of the system north of the border in 1760. But opposition to, and rejection of, the Scottish militia bill also had implications for the union and tainted the Scots with suspected disloyalty. As the Scotophobic Horace Walpole afterwards remarked, 'the disaffected there [could not] obtain this mode of having their arms restored'.[39] It is not surprising either that Scots bridled at the imputation of ineradicable Jacobitism. *Sister Peg* consists largely of a repudiation of the charge. Another pamphlet, written by the Whig historian of the '45 and eulogist of the 'illustrious' Duke of Cumberland, Andrew Henderson, rebuts 'false prejudices against the north part of the United Kingdom' and asks if the militia had not been extended to Scotland 'from any fear an insurrection in favour of the Pretender, why was not the same exception made to Lancashire'? Trade, intermarriage and geography, he contends, have blended the inhabitants of the north of England and Lowland Scotland into virtually one people. Why, then, 'should the people of Northumberland, which jutts in among the southern counties of Scotland, be entrusted with arms, while the other, tho' containing a track of territory, no less extended, nor less populous than Yorkshire and Westmorland, put together, are denied the privilege'?[40]

The militia debate thus brought to the surface both a sense of nation-hood rooted in martial traditions, and an acute sensitivity about Scotland's constitutional status within a union between supposedly equal partners. Furthermore, the demand for equality of treatment within the union – not renegotiation, restructuring or, least of all, withdrawal – rested upon an assumption of permanence. A tenacious sense of Scottish identity may have underpinned arguments for a militia, yet that in no way conflicted with the

[1 5 2] literati's avowed North Britishness. This was never a simple duality, however. One man's North Britishness is another man's anglicisation:[41] how else, for example, is the hunting down of 'Scotticisms' to be characterised?

As David Hume confessed to Gilbert Elliott in 1757, they and their countrymen were 'unhappy in our accent and pronunciation [and] speak a very corrupt dialect of the tongue which we make use of'. Adherence to English standards was explicit. After the passing of the union, reasoned William Robertson, 'the English naturally became the sole judges and lawgivers in language, and rejected, as solecisms, every form of speech to which their ear was not accustomed'.[42] One provocative suggestion is that this sort of cultural hegemony (or internal colonisation) may have resulted not so much from English economic and military might, as from an overlooked 'autonomous Welsh or Scots cultural collapse'.[43] Certainly, a number of Scottish historians have discerned a 'lack of pride' – or is it self-confidence – among eighteenth-century patriots and improvers. And there is evidence, too, of provincial cringe, of the 'high road to London' variety. Both Adam Smith and the architect Robert Adam described their native land as 'too narrow' for their talents.[44]

On the theoretical or intellectual plane, as distinct from these broader cultural processes, the articulation of North or Anglo-Britishness, represents an intellectually nimble adaptation of Whig ideology to Scottish conditions. According to the stadial model of history and society, nations progressed, to use Ferguson's terms, from a 'rude' to a 'polished' state, from the barbarous and feudal to the civil and commercial. Mid-eighteenth-century Scotland, the literati believed, had achieved the benefits and liberties of a modern commercial society, but not on its own. It had been achieved, rather, by the 'accidental acceleration' of historical development consequent upon assimilation to the more advanced (or 'mature') economy and polity of England.[45] That analysis enabled post-1707 Scotland to appropriate the history of English liberty and the English – now British – parliament, while discarding a past that, from a Whig perspective, had little use. In this view union and, even more perhaps, the reformist legislation of 1747 which swept away the 'feudal' encumbrances of heritable jurisdictions, had propelled Scotland into the modern world one hundred or more years ahead of its time.

Precisely because he is a less sophisticated thinker than Hume, Ferguson or Carlyle, Andrew Henderson illustrates the way in which that modernising narrative came to shape the Scottish Whig outlook – and, incidentally, to anticipate twentieth-century whiggish readings of 1747 as a great watershed in Scottish social and political history. 'Everything has been done,' he wrote in his militia pamphlet, for establishing that constitution which the rebellion was intended to subvert; the most wholesome laws have been provided against any future insurrection, and the people are no longer under that slavish vassalage to their chieftans, which drowned them in ignorance, fettered them with strong chains of bondage and oppressions, and irrevocably sunk them in an abyss of misery and want; they know that they are free, and sensible of that liberty which their ancestors never dream'd of.[46]

Political and theoretical endorsement of 'reform', the eclipse of Jacobitism and, seemingly, the resolution of the 'Highland problem', commercial and career opportunities provided by partnership in empire, the stirrings of industrialisation, close political management and a politically tame Kirk, all conspired by the second half of the eighteenth century to cement the union and secure a North British identity. But this had a negative side. Bruce Lenman describes Scotland in this era as 'the most undemanding and subservient of British provinces', while an Irish historian of the period is struck by its 'quite stifling complacency'.[47] Loyalty to the (Hanoverian) crown often translated into political conservatism. The contrast between Irish radicalism and nationalism and Scottish unionism in the 1790s has already been noted. The same is true of the late 1770s. Whereas Irish Protestants and volunteers and English reformers and Dissenters expressed support for the colonists, particularly in the early stages of the American war, with the exception of some of the 'Popular party' within the Kirk, Scots generally supported the government. Adam Ferguson and Alexander Carlyle, for example, both wrote pamphlets in favour of prosecuting the war.[48] From the ministerial standpoint, of course, complacency, conservatism and subservience looked like stability, order and obedience to lawful authority. And if the Belfast United Irishmen were baffled in 1792 by the fact, as they saw it, that Scotland had 'long forgotten her degraded state as a nation [and] slept over her political insignificance', the Scots themselves could discern no puzzle: the union had been tested, it had survived, it had worked and it had delivered on its promise.

English nationalism, British empire

Eighteenth-century Irish, Anglo-Irish, Scottish and North British identities were richly various, complex and contingent, but they had one thing in common: all of them were, in either a positive or a negative way, defined by their relationship to England and the English. The English, on the other hand, were often as indifferent as they were hostile to their 'Celtic' neighbours. It is no accident that the term 'South Britain', ridiculed by the self-proclaimed Englishman Jonathan Swift, never took hold. As Tobias Smollett's *Humphrey Clinker* remarks, 'between want of curiosity, and traditional sarcasms, the effect of ancient animosity, the people at the other end of the island know as little of Scotland as of Japan'. Dr Johnson claimed to have met 'a man of eminence [who] had no idea of the existence of the Act of Union'. And later William Cobbett inscribed that anglocentric view in the formal historical record, when he reported in the *Parliamentary History of England* that during the 1760 session, the session during which members rejected Elliott's Scottish militia bill, 'there were no debates on any public measure'.[49]

Indifference, or 'want of curiosity', indicates supreme national self-assurance. Not only, as Milton knew, is God an Englishman; but as the admittedly deranged poet Chistopher Smart confirmed, 'English cats are the best in Europe'.[50] It also reflected the distribution of power within 'these islands'. Whereas the union altered the structures of Scottish society and politics, after 1707 the Westminster parliament remained the locus of sovereignty with twenty-five additional MPs and sixteen peers tacked on. The concentration of wealth and authority in London increased. No one worried about the scotticisation of English culture. At the level of politics, jurisdiction and administration, if not of language and culture, Wales was totally integrated into the English system. Johnson volunteered the scarcely credible, but revealing, opinion that 'Wales is so little different from England that it offers nothing to the speculation of the traveller'.[51] Hostility to the 'Celt', then, stemmed from contempt, and sometimes resentment, rather than fear.

The 'free born Englishman's' 'want of curiosity' about other nations reflects insularity and a lack of anxiety about his axiomatic superiority to foreigners. 'England' was taken as given. Completely confident in their national identity, the English felt little need to reflect upon or define it, and that in turn helps to explain the 'extraordinary blind spot in English historiography' on the subject of nationalism. Although this is beginning, slowly, to change, to judge from the endlessly expanding historical and political science literature on the topic, England, it would seem, somehow managed to escape the nationalist condition that has afflicted the rest of humankind.[52] The purist might reasonably object that since the concept and term 'nationalism' is anachronistic when applied to the eighteenth century, 'patriotism' is a more appropriate word. But patriotism, with its contemporary resonance of public-spiritedness and improvement, fails to convey the xenophobia, bellicosity and chauvinism that undoubtedly characterised English popular attitudes during this period.

Xenophobic prejudices towards Irish, Scottish and Welsh immigrants, or 'domestic foreigners', were stamped on the national stereotypes portrayed on stage, and in cartoons and prints.[53] 'Taffy' the Welshman, sometimes astride a goat, and almost always replete with leeks and toasted cheese, hailed from the 'fag end of creation',[54] and was noted for his poverty, dirt and dishonesty. The invariably kilted Scot was known for his poverty, clannishness, unsanitary habits (the cause of the 'itch') and fondness for arbitrary power. Irish 'bogtrotters' were notoriously poor, popish, disaffected and prone to violence. All of these immigrants were inferior, competed for English jobs, and were distinguished by accents so thick as to render them next to incomprehensible.

Irish labourers were targeted by London rioters in 1736. A 1762 print depicted 'The Caledonians arrival in Money-Land'.[55] Brogues rivalled Scotticisms for the derision with which they were received. Swift, reflecting on 'Barbarous Denominations', observed that:

> the Scotch cadence, as well as expression, are offensive enough. But none of these defects derive contempt for the speaker; whereas, what we call the Irish Brogue is no sooner discovered, than it makes the deliverer, in the last degree, ridiculous and despised; and, from such a mouth, an Englishman expects nothing but bulls, blunders and follies.[56]

Edmund Burke's oratory stank of 'whiskey and potatoes'. When the last Speaker of the Irish parliament, John Foster, took up his seat at Westminster, English MPs were 'astonished' at the strength of his brogue. One of them, William Wilberforce, called him 'Mr. *Spaker*'.[57] Clearly national caricatures, by definition crude, made little allowance for social, or confessional, let alone regional, variation among the caricatured.

Equally clearly the diffusion of 'patriotic xenophobia' made it a very 'marketable commodity' in a commercialising society.[58] But it would be wrong to mulch down such attitudes into a generalised, unchanging, genetically transmitted animus towards the lesser breeds. In fact chronologies of the rise and (relative) decline of anti-Welsh, anti-Scottish and anti-Irish sentiment can be traced, and related to changing political contexts. When a Wilkesite paper observed in 1769 that 'the Welsh and the Scotch, who inhabit the remote ends of this kingdom, are the very opposite in their principles. The former are hot, generous, and great lovers of liberty. The latter are violent and tyrannical,'[59] it registered a real shift in public perceptions. By mid-century Scots generally attracted greater hostility than either the Welsh or the Irish, and there are identifiable reasons for that.

As the miniature scale of English Jewry (5,000–8,000-strong in 1753) suggests, there is no direct correlation between fear and prejudice on the one hand, and the actual size of the community towards which it is directed on the other. Nevertheless, the blunting of English depictions of 'Taffy' after about 1740 may owe something to the comparatively small numbers of the Welsh. More people lived in London than in Wales. 'Alien' minorities can be perceived as dangerous to the 'national interest', however, when they are seen to infiltrate positions of influence – classically banking, – strike a visible political profile or filch 'native' jobs, usually, in the process, driving down wage rates. Luckily for the Welsh they scored handsomely for innocuousness on all counts. They had never figured as villains in high finance. That role was reserved for Huguenots and other foreign Protestants earlier in the century, passing, at the time of the Jewish Naturalisation Act in 1753, to a more familiar scapegoat. In politics the Welsh were tainted by Jacobitism. Yet Welsh constituencies were as likely to return Whigs as Tories and, crucially, the twenty-four Welsh MPs never cohered into a parliamentary interest, unlike the usually pliant Scots, who were capable of voting along national lines, as on the militia bill in 1760. Finally, it is true that the labouring poor made their way from the valleys to London in search of work, though not, it seems, in sufficient numbers to provoke the sort of backlash to which the Irish were subjected in 1736. But perhaps the principal reason for the receding of anti-Welsh sentiment is its submergence under the rising tide of Scotophobia.

English antipathy towards the Scots peaked between the mid-1740s, when many – quite inaccurately – equated Jacobite rebellion with Scottish treason, and the 1760s, when the Wilkesite opposition stigmatised the king's first minister, the Earl of Bute – a Scottish peer who gloried in the surname of Stuart! – as a conspirator against English liberty. The Duke of Cumberland may have gone down in history and legend as the 'Butcher' of Culloden; but at the time this national deliverer and hammer of the Scots was honoured by more commemorative pottery, 'plates, bowls, mugs and punchbowls', than any other English popular hero of the period, probably, except Admiral Vernon. Bute, in contrast, found himself at the sharp end of 'the most scurrilous press campaign of the century', and the be-thistled butt of an unprecedented outpouring of satirical prints.[60]

John Wilkes rose to prominence as a scourge of Bute, founder of the opposition paper *North Briton* and critic of the 1763 Peace of Paris which brought the Seven Years War to a conclusion. Fleeing into exile after a 'general warrant' was issued for his arrest for allegedly libelling ministers in no. 45 of the *North Briton*, he returned at the end of the decade to contest, successfully, the 'open' parliamentary constituency of Middlesex. Upon his election to Westminster, however, and in a rerun of the Lucas episode in Dublin almost twenty years earlier, he was not permitted to take his seat. Echoing to the slogan 'Wilkes and Liberty!' this 'unconstitutional' action sparked off street disturbances and one of the greatest out-of-doors political agitations that London – and beyond – had yet witnessed. Re-elected twice, he finally took his seat in 1771.[61] From a purely English perspective the Wilkes episode is important as a pivotal moment in the history of press freedom and the development of extra-parliamentary popular politics. From a British perspective it manifested itself, in David Hume's words, as a 'rage against the Scots'.

The *North Briton* claimed that parliament had fallen into the hands of a 'knot of Tories, Scottish members, and Scottified English'. Nor when Wilkes promised 'to write plain English, and to avoid ... Scotticisms'[62] was this simple racial prejudice – although it was that as well. Rather, by associating Bute and his countrymen with the Stuarts, Jacobitism and arbitrary power, anti-Scottish propaganda formed part of the radical agenda. Moreover, grossly exaggerated though they were, accusations of Scottish cronyism were not entirely groundless. Bute, for instance, hired the London-based Scot Tobias Smollett to edit the pro-government newspaper *The Briton*. By the 1760s the Caledonians *were* arriving in 'Money-Land' in increasing numbers, and, like most immigrant communities, establishing their own jobs networks. It is worth noting too that, virulent as the 'rage' could be, it did not, unlike the anti-Irish riots in 1736 or the anti-Catholic Gordon riots in 1780, result in overt violence.

The same is true in relation to the other main resident 'foreigners', the Jews. An anti-Jewish campaign arose in reaction to the Naturalisation Act in 1753. Designed, like the naturalisation of foreign Protestants earlier in the century, to attract inward investment and bolster the economy, as with opposition to the Huguenots and Palatines, agitation against the 'Jew Bill' drew on a Little England, Tory, High Church ethos – or, in the formula of a contemporary toast, 'Church and King, without mass, meeting, or synagogue!'[63] In so far as opposition politicians exploited the issue to embarrass the government, and force it to repeal the Act, this was politics as usual. But in view of the print caricatures of hook-nosed, long-bearded Israelites used in the repeal campaign, it seems extraordinary to conclude that 'most of the *ostensible* anti-semitism of the clamour was aimed *wholly* at the court politicians, and was surely understood in that spirit'.[64] The point, surely, is that whether or not the agitators were themselves anti-semitic, they were able to use anti-semitism to mobilise public opinion. Similarly, both the country party in the 1690s and the Jacobites struck a popular xenophobic chord by harping,

[158] respectively, on King William's 'Dutch favourites' and on the first two Georges' German origins.

Scots, Irish, Welsh and Jews were 'the Other' within, whose otherness helped to define English identity. The most important Other, however, was French. Linda Colley sees rivalry with Catholic France as the vital element in the forging of British Protestant solidarity. But it also continued to shape older understandings of 'national character'. As Seamus Deane observes, 'what the English thought of the French was a reflection of what the English thought of the English'.[65] British, or Anglo-French, rivalries were kept alight by imperial competition and war. Britain and France were at war at some point in every decade between 1689 and 1814 except the 1720s and 1730s. Hanoverian supporters attempted to stir up public opinion against the Pretender in 1745 by insisting that if he were victorious England would be reduced to a French province – an horrific fate, since France was everything – popish, poverty-stricken and despotic – that England was not.

John Andrews' booklet, *A Comparative View of the French and English Nations* (1785), provides an accessible compendium of eighteenth-century stereotypes. The 'exterior glare' of Paris's dazzling façade, he states, deflected attention from the underlying realities of rural hardship and political oppression. 'The French', moreover, 'are silent on the affairs of state', cowed by the 'multitudes of spies . . . that swarm the coffee houses and other places of public resort; much in the same manner as the emissaries of the Grand Vizar of Constantinople.' And while the 'poorer sort' wallow in their own dirt, the other ranks are in 'intellectual bondage' to every passing fashion. Yet it is not all bad. The French esteem education, and notwithstanding the inordinate number of 'priests and monastics' encountered by travellers, the author detects a decline in Romish extremism. Implicitly, explicitly and continuously, Andrews compares France unfavourably with England. For Gallophobia, like all the other phobias, had a positive as well as a negative side. Even when it is not spelt out, depictions of the failings, misfortunes and vices of the foreigner are a commentary on English freedom, religion and laws. Liberty and property are opposed to absolute monarchy, 'plain and unaffected' manners to Gallic frivolity and flattery, and so on.[66]

The contrast functioned on at least two levels: confirming popular patriotic myths, and as a political, quasi-philosophical discourse. Popular images of English superiority and French inferiority were a staple of prints and cartoons such as William Hogarth's 'The Gates of Calais, or the Roast Beef of Old England' (1748), and were personified by that enduring eighteenth-century invention, 'John Bull'.[67] John Bull first strutted out upon the national stage in a pamphlet written, ironically, by a Scot, John Arbuthnot, in 1712. He reappeared in 1760, again courtesy of a Scottish author, in *Sister Peg*, but, not surprisingly in that Wilkesite decade when he 'choaked by inadvertently swallowing a thistle',[68] he soon turned against his nearest neighbour. His cartoon career, as a named character, began perhaps in 1762, rising to new heights during the war against revolutionary France in the 1790s and the Napoleonic empire in the 1800s. John Bull served many purposes. It was not unknown for him to be over-burdened with taxes by his own government, for example. Nevertheless, certain abiding characteristics stand out. Arbuthnot's creation is described as 'an honest plain-dealing fellow', and so he remained. A sturdy yeoman farmer, or shopkeeper, well fed no doubt on Hogarth's roast beef, John Bull embodies the native virtues of fairness, firmness and patriotism. Finally, he is the antithesis not merely of the emaciated, craven and superstitious Frenchman, but also of dandified home-grown cosmopolites.[69]

At the political level the 'superior excellence', as Andrews put it, of Britain's mixed constitution as it had evolved after 1688 appeared obvious, unmatched, unique and the envy of the world. The element of self-satisfaction in the great surge of loyalist propaganda in the 1790s – the heyday also of John Bull – is unmistakable. Britain boasted trial by jury, the rule of law, a free press, religious toleration, limited monarchy and government by consent of the governed. Before 1789 Protestant liberty had been contrasted with French Catholic absolutism; after 1789 the focus shifted. Now the practical, concrete freedoms, grounded in experience and tradition, protected by law and secured by the constitution, were emphasised, together with the maintenance of property, order and social hierarchy. The 'false liberty' of the French Revolution, on the other hand, had unleashed violence, anarchy and levelling, exposing thereby the folly and arrogance of attempting to reconstruct society upon the flimsy foundations of abstract principles and philosophical 'speculation'.

Even parliamentary reformers were persuaded of the blessings of a mixed constitution which they sought, not to overturn, but to restore to its pristine state. English liberties had existed in their pure form, they believed, in Saxon times, only to be shackled to a 'Norman Yoke' by William the Conquerer. English history since then had been the story of the unfolding struggle to reassert lost rights and reclaim the original constitution. Magna Carta, the conflict between parliament and the Stuart kings in the seventeenth century and the Bill of Rights in 1689 were all milestones in that great Whig struggle.[70] But as the experience of so many European kingdoms clearly demonstrated, constitutional liberties were precarious. In England too they were under constant threat, usually from corrupt and power-hungry ministers

[160] and courtiers. That sense of insecurity explains, for instance, the suspicions about Bute's secret designs. Similarly, American colonists in the 1760s and 1770s feared that their liberties were endangered by a ministerial plot.[71]

The Saxon foundation myth permeates the rhetoric of radical politics and parliamentary reform. It is central to Obadiah Hulme's popular *Historical Essay on the English Constitution* (1771), and to John Baxter's *New and Impartial History of England* (1796), wherein, E.P Thompson wryly notes, the 'Saxons were Jacobins and *sans-culottes* to a man'.[72] And, although Scottish Whig intellectuals were able to enrol 'our Saxon forefathers' in a useable past, the 'birth-rights' bequeathed by those forefathers were specifically English. It is true that during the 1790s 'English national feeling was overwhelmingly a conservative force'. Indeed, against a background of war with revolutionary France from 1793 onwards, reformers were castigated as traitorous 'Jacobins'. But conservatives did not hold a monopoly on patriotic sentiments. The 'theory of the Norman Yoke' after all, 'is the theory of the English nation'.[73]

Britishness and empire

John Bull had an iconographic companion, Britannia, who likewise symbolised the popular patriotic fever generated by the long contest with France. The anthem 'Rule Britannia!' was written in 1745, and its naval motif – Britannia rules the waves – celebrates the triumphs of a proud island people and a maritime empire. The capture of Porto Bello from Britain's other European Catholic rival, Spain, by the hero Admiral Edward Vernon in November 1739 was greeted with jubilation, in Lowland Scotland as well as England. More commemorative medals were struck in his honour than for any other public figure in the entire eighteenth century.[74] The lionising of Vernon had an oppositional, anti-Walpoleian, dimension – the first minister had been reluctant to declare war in the first place – and stirred the imperial imagination.

It was still possible in the 1740s, though technically inaccurate, to think of an 'English' empire. By the time of the Seven Years War, however, the Britishness of the imperial project had become increasingly manifest. Revealingly, the patriotic leader in that war, Pitt the Elder, has been claimed as the emblem both of rising English nationalism and of the new, post-Culloden, British partnership.[75] Certainly, contemporary perceptions of the character of Pitt's patriotism notwithstanding, the war was fought by a

British army. Army recruitment, in fact, played an immensely important role in assimilating the once recalcitrant Highlands to the British state. The 78th Fraser's Highlanders regiment, raised by Simon Fraser in 1757, set the precedent. The Fraser clan had fought for the Pretender in the '45. Simon's father, Lord Lovat, was executed and the family's estate forfeited to the crown. Now, little over a decade later, 1,400 men, uniformed in traditional tartan, served under the Culloden veteran General James Wolfe and the union flag, in Novia Scotia and Quebec. Fraser recovered the family estate. Between the beginning of the Seven Years War in 1756 and the end of the Napoleonic War in 1815 it is estimated that over 48,300 Highlanders (excluding the Black Watch formed in 1739) saw service in twenty-three regular and twenty-six fencible regiments of the British army.[76]

The thoroughly multinational composition of the British army made it the most comprehensively, successfully British institution of the eighteenth century. A Protestant Anglo-Irishman, General Wade, acted as Commander-in-Chief in Scotland in the 1730s and early 1740s; a Scot, General Sir Ralph Abercromby, served for a brief time as Commander-in-Chief in Ireland in the 1790s; the Black Watch were stationed in Ireland between 1749 and 1756, as were Scottish and Welsh fencible regiments at the end of the century; Tobias Smollett began his career as a surgeon in the British navy, Adam Ferguson as a chaplain in the army; the United Irishmen Lord Edward Fitzgerald, Thomas Russell and Matthew Tone were previously British officers in America and India; the examples could be multiplied. Irishmen were well represented among the ranks of generals as early as Queen Anne's reign, and by mid-century up to one-quarter of regimental officers were Scottish.[77] So insatiable did the imperial appetite for manpower become that in the 1770s Whitehall began to cast a covetous eye upon Irish Catholics, at that point debarred from the armed forces by the penal laws. Two decades later the '"Hibernicization" of the British regular infantry continued apace'.[78] It may be overstating the matter to claim that shared experience of soldiering 'superimposed a form of British identity over those national and regional loyalties which had hitherto served only to highlight division and conflict within British society',[79] but the ever-extending reach of the recruiting sergeant, and thus of the state, is remarkable. To many in this period, if Britishness had any practical meaning at all, it wore a red coat.

In addition the Welsh, Scottish and Irish (convicts[80] and indentured servants as well as emigrants) helped to people the colonies of settlement. The Pennsylvania Welsh and the Ulster Presbyterians, known to American history as the Scotch-Irish, are well-known examples of the multinational

[1 6 2]   character of British immigration. Scots and Irishmen also made their mark, at home and abroad, as colonial merchants and administrators. Arthur Dobbs, formerly an Irish MP, and advocate of Ireland's incorporation in the union, completed his career as governor of North Carolina (1754–65). In 1768 Scottish merchants formed a North British Society in Halifax, Nova Scotia.[81] But it is in India that Irish and Scottish participation and preferment within the empire is most conspicuous. Laurence Sulivan, born in County Cork, made his way from Bombay in the 1730s up to the London-based chairmanship of the East India Company in 1756. Another Irishman, George Macartney, governor of Madras between 1780 and 1785 was succeeded by a Scot, General Sir Archibald Campbell. In 1772 thirty civil servants and 250 of the 800 British army officers in Bengal were Scots.[82] Ultimately, however, imperial policy was still made in London.

The transition from an essentially English to a British empire, the development of imperial perspectives, priorities and consciousness by the British ruling elite, and the reciprocity of empire and Britishness – the ways in which the spoils of empire, trade, prestige and employments, bedded down the union – are personified by the greatest manager of Scottish politics since Islay, Henry Dundas. Dundas, elected MP for Midlothian in 1772 (and Edinburgh in 1790), appointed Lord Advocate in 1775, went on to achieve a prominence in British politics and imperial administration of which the wily Islay could only have daydreamed.[83] By 1782 he had gained control of Scottish patronage, and although Scotland remained an important power-base for him, it proved too narrow to contain his ambitions. It is significant that Dundas chose to make his maiden speech in parliament on the most pressing imperial issue of the day, strongly opposing conciliation of the American colonists.[84] Under the terms of the India Act in 1784 he became a member of the East India Company's Board of Control, whose affairs he in practice dominated long before his formal assumption of the presidency of the board in 1793. Predictably, and not without foundation, Dundas's political clout with the company soon provoked accusations of Scottish cronyism in the filling of new posts. In 1791 he became Home Secretary and in 1794 Secretary of War. Elevated to the peerage as Viscount Melville in 1802, First Lord of the Admiralty in 1806, Dundas was finally driven out of public life by an, albeit unsuccessful, impeachment for financial misapprobation in 1806. Remembered in Scottish history for his 'despotic' rule in the 1790s,[85] Dundas surfaces in Irish history as a liberal Home Secretary who pressured an unwilling Protestant Ascendancy into granting Catholic relief Acts in 1792 and 1793.

Like any able politician, Dundas's capacity for aggrandising power, collecting offices and accumulating titles can be attributed to force of character,
luck, intelligence, oratorical skill and other political assets. Specifically, in his
case, it owed a good deal to his close relationship with the leading politician
of the age, William Pitt the Younger. Yet this Scottish lawyer's tenure at the
top of the British establishment has wider meaning than an individual ascent
of the greasy pole. Rather, it is emblematic of the changing configuration
and possibilities of British (and imperial) politics and society in the late
eighteenth century. Older senses of national identity persisted tenaciously,
as the continued popularity in Scotland of the 'nationalist' medieval ballads,
Wallace and *Brus*, suggests. In Ireland senses of nationhood crossed confessional lines in new ways, strengthened, and continued to exert centripetal
force on a composite British identity. But, not least because of a shared imperial project, those identities were now articulated within a sturdy British
superstructure.

Notes

1. See Chapter 5.

2. Both addresses are reprinted in McFarland, E.W., 1994, *Ireland and Scotland in the Age of Revolution: Planting the Green Bough*, Edinburgh, 248–55.

3. Brims, J.D., 'The Scottish "Jacobins", Scottish nationalism and the British union' in Mason, R. (ed.) 1987, *Scotland and England, 1286–1815*, Edinburgh.

4. O'Conor to Joseph C. Walker, 31 January 1786 in Ward, C.C. and Ward, R.E. (eds) 1980, *The Letters of Charles O'Conor of Belanagare ii: 1772–1790*, Ann Arbor, 236–7.

5. For wide-ranging discussions of these issues see Canny, N. and Pagden, A. (eds) 1987, *Colonial Identity in the Atlantic World, 1500–1800*, Princeton; Greene, J.P., 1986, *Peripheries and Center: Constitutional Development in the Extended Polities of the British Empire and the United States, 1607–1788*, Georgia.

6. Cox, Richard, 1698, *An Essay for the Conversion of the Irish, Showing that 'tis Their Duty and Interest to Become Protestants*, Dublin, 1, 10, 12–13.

7. Quoted by Isolde Victory, unpublished PhD dissertation, Trinity College, Dublin, 1985, 'Colonial nationalism, 1692–1725: from common law to natural rights', xiv.

[164]   8. Transitions in Protestant identities in this period are explored in Hayton, David, 1987, 'Anglo-Irish attitudes: changing perceptions of national identity among the Protestant Ascendancy in Ireland, 1690–1750', *Studies in Eighteenth-Century Culture*, 17: 145–57; Hayton, David, 1988, 'From Barbarian to burlesque: English images of the Irish *c.* 1660–1750', *Irish Economic and Social History*, xv: 5–31; Smyth, Jim, 1993, '"Like amphibious animals": ancient Britons, Irish Protestants, 1690–1707', *HJ*, 4: 785–97; Leersson, Joep, 1997, *Mere Irish and Fíor-Ghael: Studies in the Idea of Irish Nationality, its Development and Literary Expression Prior to the Nineteenth Century*, Cork, esp. 294–376.

9. Maxwell, Henry, *An Essay Towards an Union*, 12; Swift, Jonathan, 1732, *Queries Relating to the Sacramental Test* in Davis, H. (ed.) 1939–68, *Prose Writings of Jonathan Swift*, Oxford, xii: 259.

10. The achievements of the eighteenth-century Protestant elite are celebrated in Beckett, J.C., 1976, *The Anglo-Irish Tradition*, London. On the transformations in the landscape in this period see Cullen, L.M., 1981, *The Emergence of Modern Ireland 1600–1900*, London.

11. Maxwell, *Essay Towards an Union*, 3; Anon., 1720, *A Letter from a Member of the House of Commons in Ireland to a Gentleman of the Long Robe in Great-Britain: Containing an Answer to Some Objections Made Against the Judictory Power of the Parliament of Ireland*, Dublin, 4; Cox, Richard, 1749, *The Cork-Surgeon's Antidote No. 2*, 7–8.

12. Pocock, J.G.A., 1982, 'The limits and divisions of British history', *AHR*, 87, 328–9; Moody, T.W., McDowell, R.B., Woods, C.J. (eds) 1998, *The Writings of Theobald Wolfe Tone, 1763–1798*, vol. i: *Tone's Career in Ireland to June 1795*, Oxford, 95.

13. Quoted by James, F.G., 1973, *Ireland in the Empire*, Cambridge, Mass., 129.

14. *HMC Charlemont Ms*, I: 5, 189.

15. Anon., 1731, *An Inquiry into Some of the Causes of the Ill Situation of the Affairs of Ireland*, Dublin, 11.

16. Swift, Jonathan, 1720, *Proposal for the Universal Use of Irish Manufactures* in McMinn, J., 1991, *Swift's Irish Pamphlets*, Dublin; for the continued prominence of the Woollen Act as a source of complaint see Hely-Hutchinson, John, 1779, *The Commercial Restraints of Ireland*, Dublin.

17. Leersson, *Mere Irish and Fíor-Ghael*, 305.

18. Lucas, Charles, 1751, *The Political Constitutions of Great Britain and Ireland Asserted and Vindicated; the Connection and Common Interest of Both Kingdoms, Demonstrated*, London, 113–14.

19. *Ibid.,* 113, 118, 126, 143.

20. *Ibid.,* 132–7.

21. Lucas, 1756, *An Appeal to the Commons and Citizens of London by Charles Lucas, the Last Free Citizen of Dublin,* London, 8.

22. Donovan, Declan, 'The money bill dispute' in Bartlett, T. and Hayton, D. (eds) 1979, *Penal Age and Golden Era,* Belfast; Murphy, Sean, 'The Dublin anti-union riot of 3 December 1759' in O'Brien, G. (ed.) 1989, *Parliament, Politics and People: Essays in Eighteenth-century Irish History,* Dublin, 49–68.

23. Declaration and Resolutions of the Society of United Irishmen of Belfast, 18 October 1791, reprinted in Moody, McDowell and Woods, *The Writings of Theobald Wolfe Tone,* i: 139–40.

24. Smout, T.C., 'Where had the Scottish economy got to by the third quarter of the eighteenth century?' in Hont, I. and Ignatieff, M. (eds) 1983, *Wealth and Virtue: The Shaping of Political Economy in the Scottish Enlightenment,* Cambridge, 45–72; Whatley, C.A., 1989, 'Economic causes and consequences of the union of 1707: a survey', *SHR,* lxviii, 2: 186, 150–81.

25. Dickson, David, 1997, *Arctic Ireland: The Extraordinary Story of the Great Frost and Forgotten Famine of 1740–41,* Belfast.

26. *The Parliamentary History of England,* xxxiv, 299.

27. Smout, T.C. (ed.) 'Sir John Clerk's observations on the present circumstances of Scotland, 1730', 1965, *SHS, 4th ser., vol. 2, Miscellany x,* 195–6.

28. Mitchison, R. 1978, 'Patriotism and national identity in eighteenth-century Scotland', *Historical Studies,* xi, Belfast, 73–95.

29. Smout, 'Sir John Clerk's observations', 212.

30. The phrase is Bruce Lenman's, 'A client society: Scotland between the '15 and the '45' in Black, J. (ed.) 1992, *Britain in the Age of Walpole,* Houndsmills, 72.

31. For the range of jobs potentially at the disposal of a Scottish manager at this time see Murdoch, Alexander, 1980, *'The People Above': Politics and Administration in Mid Eighteenth-century Scotland,* Edinburgh, appendix II, 140–50. For the operation of patronage generally, see Murdoch, *'The People Above', passim*; Shaw, John Stuart, 1983, *The Management of Scottish Society, 1707–1764: Power, Nobles, Lawyers, Edinburgh Agents and English Influences,* Edinburgh; and Simpson, John M., 'Who steered the gravy train, 1707–1766?' in Mitchison, R. and Phillipson, N.T. (eds) 1970, *Scotland in the Age of Improvement,* Edinburgh, 47–72.

[166]   32.   For example, see Basil Williams' comments on the completion of 'the good work of the union': 1939, 1974, *The Whig Supremacy, 1714–1760*, Oxford, 285; and Cowie, L.W., 1966, *Hanoverian England*, London, 213. A more balanced and sceptical assessment is offered by Langford, P., 1992, *Polite and Commercial People*, Oxford, 218.

33.   Cited by Murdoch, '*The People Above*', 124; and Smout, 'Where had the Scottish economy got to by the third quarter of the eighteenth century?', 58.

34.   Whatley, 'Economic causes and consequences of the union', 176.

35.   The term 'Scottish sociology' is used by Colin Kidd, 1993, *Subverting Scotland's Past*, Cambridge. The term 'Scottish Enlightenment' was coined, apparently, by William Robert Scott in 1900: Lenman, Bruce, 'Union, Jacobitism and Enlightenment' in Mitchison, R. (ed.) 1991, *Why Scottish History Matters*, Edinburgh, 55.

36.   Robertson, John, 1985, *The Scottish Enlightenment and the Militia Issue*, Edinburgh, 121. My account of the militia episode is based mainly on Robertson. See also Western, J.R., 1965, *The English Militia in the Eighteenth Century: The Story of a Political Issue, 1660–1802*, London.

37.   The problem of authorship is explored by David R. Raynor, who decides unequivocally for Hume: Raynor, 1982, *Sister Peg: A Pamphlet Hitherto Unknown by David Hume*, Cambridge.

38.   Robertson, *The Scottish Enlightenment and the Militia Issue*, 145.

39.   Brooke, John (ed.) 1985, *Horace Walpole's Memoirs of King George II*, New Haven and London, iii, 108.

40.   Henderson, Andrew, 1760, *Considerations on the Question Whether the Act of Parliament Establishing a Militia thro England Ought to Extend to Scotland in Time of War*, London, 4–5, 10–11.

41.   See the opening comments of Nicholas Phillipson, 'Politics, politeness and the anglicisation of early eighteenth-century Scottish culture' in Mason, R. (ed.) 1981, *Scotland and England, 1286–1815*, Edinburgh, 226.

42.   Adam Smith, Janet, 'Some eighteenth-century ideas of Scotland' in Mitchison, R. and Phillipson, N.T. (eds) 1970, *Scotland in the Age of Improvement*, Edinburgh, 110–12.

43.   Clark, J.C.D., 1989, 'English history's forgotten contexts', *HJ*, 32: 232.

44.   Mitchison, R., 'Patriotism and national identity in eighteenth-century Scotland' in Moody, T.W. (ed.) 1978, *Historical Studies XI*, Belfast, 79; Smith, 'Some eighteenth-century ideas of Scotland', 108.

45. The phrase 'accidental acceleration' is Colin Kidd's, *Subverting Scotland's Past*, 207. This book elaborates Scottish Whig analysis most astutely. See also Phillipson, 'Politics, politeness and the anglicisation', 227.

46. Henderson, *Considerations on the Question*, 27.

47. Lenman, Bruce, 1981, *Integration, Enlightenment and Industrialization: Scotland, 1746–1832*, London, 58; Cullen, L.M., 'Scotland and Ireland, 1600–1800: their role in the evolution of British society' in Houstan, R.A. and White, I.D. (eds) 1989, *Scottish Society, 1500–1800*, Cambridge, 244.

48. Robertson, *The Scottish Enlightenment and the Militia Issue*, 129; for English opposition to the war see Bradley, James E., 1990, *Religion, Revolution and English Radicalism: Nonconformity in Eighteenth-century Politics and Society*, Cambridge.

49. Swift, Jonathan, *The Tatler*, 258 (30 Nov.–2 Dec. 1710) in Davis, H. (ed.) 1939–68, *Prose Writings of Jonathan Swift*, Oxford, iii, 247; Martz, Louis L., 1942, *The Later Career of Tobias Smollett*, New Haven, 108; Lenman, Bruce, 'Union, Jacobitism and Enlightenment', 50; *Cobbett's Parliamentary History of England vol xv, 1753–1765*, 966.

50. Smart cited in Cannon, John, 1994, *Samuel Johnson and the Politics of Hanoverian England*, Cambridge, 242.

51. Cannon, *Samuel Johnson*, 243.

52. Newman, Gerald, 1987, *The Rise of English Nationalism: A Cultural History 1740–1830*, London, xvii–xix, 190; Hobsbawm, E.J., 1997, *Nations and Nationalism since 1780*, Cambridge, 11.

53. Duffy, Michael, 1986, *The English Satirical Print, 1600–1832: The Englishman and the Foreigner*, Cambridge. Duffy uses the term 'domestic foreigners', 18.

54. Ward, Ned, 1701, *A Trip to North Wales*, cited in Jenkins, Geraint H., 1987, *The Foundation of Modern Wales, 1642–1780*, Oxford, 87.

55. Print reproduced in Colley, Linda, 1992, *Britons: Forging the Nation, 1707–1837*, New Haven, 121.

56. Davis, *Prose Writings of Jonathan Swift*, iv, 280–1.

57. MacPherson, C.E., 1980, *Burke*, London; Malcomson, A.P.W., 1987, *John Foster: The Politics of the Anglo-Irish Ascendancy*, Oxford, 432.

58. Duffy, *The English Satirical Print*, 13.

59. Quoted in Lord, Peter, 1995, *Words and Pictures: Welsh Images and Images of Wales in the Popular Press, 1640–1860*, Aberystwyth, 61.

60. Wilson, Kathleen, 1995, *The Sense of the People: Politics, Culture and Imperialism in England, 1715–1785*, Cambridge, 175, 211.

[1 6 8]
61. Brewer, John, 1976, *Party Ideology and Popular Politics at the Accession of George III*, Cambridge; Rudé, George, 1962, *Wilkes and Liberty*, Oxford.

62. Nobbe, George, 1939, *The North Briton: A Study of Political Propaganda*, New York, 173; Colley, *Britons*, 116.

63. Perry, Thomas W., 1962, *Public Opinion, Propaganda and Politics in Eighteenth-century England*, Cambridge, Mass., 74.

64. *Ibid.*, 75. Italics added.

65. Deane, Seamus, 1988, *The French Revolution and Enlightenment in England, 1789–1832*, Cambridge, Mass., 1.

66. Andrews, John, 1785, *A Comparative View of England and France*, London, 26–8, 31, 34, 49, 90.

67. My discussion of John Bull is indebted to Taylor, Myles, 1992, 'John Bull and the iconography of public opinion in England *c.* 1712–1929', *P&P*, 134; and Surel, Jeannie, 'John Bull' in Samuel, Raphael (ed.) 1989, *Patriotism: The Making and Unmaking of British National Identity*, vol. iii: *National Fictions* London, 3–25.

68. *North Briton*, 17 July 1762, quoted by Taylor, 'John Bull', 103.

69. Newman sees the reaction against cultural cosmopolitanism as a key factor in the emergence of English nationalism, e.g. *The Rise of English Nationalism*, 63–8.

70. Hill, Christopher, 'The Norman Yoke' in Hill, 1968, *Puritanism and Revolution*, London, 58–125.

71. Woods, Gordon, 1982, 'Conspiracy and the paranoid style', *William and Mary Quarterly*, 39.

72. Thompson, E.P., 1964, *The Making of the English Working Class*, London, 86–7.

73. Dinwiddy, Ohn, 'England' in Dann, Otto and Dinwiddy, Ohn (eds) 1988, *Nationalism in the Age of the French Revolution*, London, 69; Newman, *The Rise of English Nationalism*, 190.

74. Wilson, *Sense of the People*, 140–6.

75. Newman, *The Rise of English Nationalism*, 169–70; but see Colley on the Britishness of the Seven Years War, *Britons*, 101–2.

76. Clyde, Robert, 1995, *From Rebel to Hero: The Image of the Highlander, 1745–1830*, Edinburgh, 150–2.

77. Holmes, Geoffrey, 1982, *Augustan England: Professions, State and Society, 1680–1730*, London, 270; Hayes, James, 1958, 'Scottish officers in the British Army, 1714–63', *SHR*, 37: 23–33.

78. Bartlett, T., 'Defence, counter-insurgency and rebellion: Ireland, 1793–1803' in Bartlett, T. and Jeffrey, K. (eds) 1997, *A Military History of Ireland*, Cambridge, 257.

79. Bowen, H.V., 1996, *Elites, Enterprise and the Making of the British Overseas Empire, 1688–1775*, London, 157.

80. Up to 30,000 were transported to the American colonies between 1718 and *c.* 1776: Lloyd, T.O., 1996, *The British Empire, 1558–1996*, Oxford, 63.

81. Bowen, *Elites, Enterprise and the Making of the British Overseas Empire*, 166.

82. For Macartney's extraordinary career see Roebuck, Peter (ed.) 1983, *Macartney of Lisanoure, 1737–1806*, Belfast; Bryant, G.J., 1985, 'Scots in India in the eighteenth century', *SHR*, lxiv: 177, 22–41.

83. Murdoch, *'The People Above'*, 133.

84. *The Parliamentary History of England*, xviii, 332.

85. Fry, Michael, 1992, *The Dundas Despotism*, Edinburgh.

8

CATHOLICS, PROTESTANTS AND DISSENTERS: RELIGION AND POLITICS IN THE EIGHTEENTH CENTURY

National and supranational identities coexisted and overlapped with regional and confessional allegiances. Eighteenth-century Ulster, for instance, provides numerous examples of a tight correlation between confessional and national, or 'ethnic', self-identification. Catholics were Gaelic-Irish 'natives', while 'planters' of Scottish and English stock were Presbyterian and Episcopalian respectively. For Linda Colley, Protestantism is the bedrock of Britishness. Politics and religion were likewise intertwined. English Dissenters and Scottish Presbyterians were Whigs almost to a man or woman; non-jurors were usually Tories, if not outright Jacobites. Indeed, in a society and 'near-confessional state' in which the rights of full citizenship were reserved to members of the established Church only, political change – and the mere act of political participation – inevitably raised issues of Church polity. The prominence of Dissenters in radical politics, particularly from the 1760s onwards, was as obvious to contemporaries as it is to historians. A variety of explanations have been advanced to account for that high visibility, but no one has invested the well-known Dissenter–radical intersection with more interpretative significance than J.C.D. Clark. In his vigorous 'revisionist tract', *English Society* (1985),[1] Clark proposes that the indivisibility of Church and state, at the level of official theory if not so comprehensively in practice, is crucial to an understanding both of the nature of the state and of the challenges to it. Put simply, he insists that radical politics during this period originate in religious heterodoxy. Clark's thesis provoked controversy, yet even his critics agree that he has succeeded in returning religion to the centre of an historiography long dominated by the related themes of 'Enlightenment', 'modernity' and nascent secularisation.

Orthodoxy: the Church of England

The Dissenter minorities of eighteenth-century Britain and Ireland have received almost as much attention as the radical minorities with whom they so often intersected. Yet it could be argued – in both cases – that neither their numbers, nor their influence on society at large, justify so much printer's ink. It might also be argued that to understand the critics, we need to understand better the criticised; and, in fact, all the signs are that the Hanoverian state-Church is finally being afforded the scrutiny it deserves. Until fairly recently perspectives on the Church of England (and on the Moderate regime in the Church of Scotland) in this period were distorted by hostile critiques nurtured by an entirely contrary religious culture. From their divergent standpoints nonconformists, Evangelicals and Tractarians in the 1820s and 1830s concurred in dismissing the eighteenth-century Church (in Scotland as well as England) as Erastian, worldly and spiritually impoverished, and to a remarkable degree the negative image has stuck.[2]

An Anglican apologist might respond effectively to both the eighteenth- and nineteenth-century faultfinders in a number of ways. First, there is the enormity of the pastoral task that confronted the Church. It has been suggested that before 1745 'jurant Anglicans' may have amounted to less than 50 per cent of all churchgoers in these islands. However, to arrive at that arresting statistic we must factor in Irish Catholics and the non-jurors at their peak. If Ireland is subtracted from the equation, and we move forward a few years to 1750 when the non-juring generation in England was almost extinct and Scottish episcopalianism in steep decline, startlingly different figures emerge: over 90 per cent of all churchgoers in Britain at mid-century, it is estimated, belonged to the 'established churches'.[3] Moreover, in the face of rapid demographic growth, and shifting demographic patterns, with which an inherited parochial infrastructure failed to keep pace; despite problems of manpower, clerical pluralism and limited resources; and despite – after 1739 – swingeing condemnation by itinerant Methodist lay preachers of widespread pastoral delinquency, in terms of numbers the established Church held the line.

Second, it is perhaps too easy when navigating the intellectual rapids of eighteenth-century heterodoxy, revivalism and dissent to overlook the fact that, in terms of doctrine, the Church of England again held the line. From the onslaught of the deists and anti-Trinitarian Socinians and Arians in the 1690s, through the intermittent sniper fire from Old Dissent, down to the theological challenge mounted by Rational Dissent and Unitarianism in

[1 7 2] the late eighteenth century, the Church survived intact, emerging in the 1790s ideologically retrenched. After the major non-juring schism of the 1690s it experienced serious debate, to be sure, such as the Bangorian controversy in the late 1710s, but only a trickle of defections. Even the secession of non-subscribers following parliament's rejection of the Feathers Tavern petition in 1772–74 involved a mere handful of disaffected churchmen.

The notion of 'orthodoxy', over which the Church stood guard, smacks of dogmatism, brittleness and rigidity. Anglicanism, however, managed to hold competing emphases, High Church and Low, Caroline and 'Puritan', in creative tension. In part this dextrous balancing act turned on a shrewd 'unwillingness to define tradition too closely'.[4] And in a sense it was always thus. Strictly a 'Catholic' Church claiming unbroken apostolic succession, it repudiated the authority of Rome and the 'Roman' doctrine of transubstantiation. It belonged to the reformed tradition, adopting elements of Calvinist theology, although for many of its members, as well as its rivals and critics without, the Church of England was never Protestant enough. The ejection of the 'Puritan' ministers in 1662 on the one hand, and the departure of the high-flying non-jurors after 1688 on the other, reduced the inevitable tensions generated by those competing conceptions. Those differences did not go away, of course, as the distance separating a Hoadly from an Atterbury demonstrates. But, as with the preoccupation with dissent, by focusing on differences within the Church we risk underestimating the stability that the Church achieved during the eighteenth century, the extent of the 'underlying consensus'[5] upon which it rested, and the success of the *via media* – between Rome and Geneva. The Anglican calendar, for instance, commemorated Charles the Martyr on 30 January, thus distancing its communicants from regicide-tainted sectaries, and 5 November, anniversary of the gunpowder plot and King William's deliverance, distancing them equally from popish sedition.[6] It was a broad Church, then, whose equipoise, appropriate, it is suggested, to the 'classical and enlightenment ideals of balance, proportion and harmony', accommodated both latitudinarianism and reverence for the Caroline divines.

Such accommodations were rendered possible by a certain amount of judicious fudging; by a strategic 'unwillingness', as we have seen, 'to define tradition too closely', or to superintend too closely the opinions of the clergy. The parameters of orthodoxy were set by the canons, liturgy, prayerbook and thirty-nine articles, to which articles all clerics as well as members of the universities were required to subscribe. Nevertheless a surprising number of churchmen were able in good conscience to square their reservations with their subscription, not least Samuel Clarke who, when reprimanded by Convocation in 1714 for his heretical tract, *The Scripture Doctrine of the Trinity* (1712), agreed to preach no further on that doctrine, yet remained within the Church. A similar readiness to compromise is evidenced by the decision of all but nine of the 250 Feathers Tavern petitioners not to secede upon the rejection of their petition. From one standpoint those episodes testify to the flexibility of the Church and to the overriding loyalties of the dissidents; from another it looked like organised hypocrisy. The nonconformist Micaiah Towgood went so far as to attribute 'the growth of infidelity' to

> a general apprehension that the clergy themselves are not thoroughly persuaded of the truth and importance of the Christian religion, inasmuch as they solemnly subscribe articles, which they do not really believe; and declare publickly, in God's presence, their unfeigned assent and consent to forms, in divine worship, which they highly disapprove; perhaps heartily condemn.

'It is men of principle and conscience only,' he concludes with some justice, 'that these subscriptions are ever capable of keeping out of the Church.'[7]

Edmund Burke took a different view. Although at the time still in favour of limited toleration for Dissenters, in 1772 he broke with his Whig colleagues and aligned himself with Lord North to defend clerical subscription. His grounds for doing so are very revealing. 'It is not conformity of private but of public opinion that She [the Church] requires in teachers,' he asserted. 'In their closets they may embrace what tenets they please, but for the sake of peace and order, they must inculcate from the pulpit only the religion of the state.'[8] 'More than a system of faith', religion in this period served – or was widely believed to serve – as the foundation of the state and society, and as the 'primary means of creating political and ideological cohesion, and the language through which such cohesion was discussed and challenged'.[9] The Church establishment, including subscription, had therefore to be defended as *the* bulwark of peace, order and rightful authority. Lord North's claim that 'when the church tottered, the state had tottered likewise; and that the ruin of the former had regularly preceded the ruin of the constitution'[10] is a working politician's statement of that 'orthodox Anglican political theology', identified by J.C.D. Clark, which also enjoined 'Christian submission, [the] divine origin of government, [and the] sinfulness of rebellion'.[11]

Gathering pace during the North administration, particularly in reaction to the rebellious American colonies, the conservative, monarchical and loyalist message broadcast by the 'Anglican pulpit' perhaps achieved its widest

dissemination during the counter-revolutionary 1790s. That political trajectory is faithfully reflected, moreover, by the stance – anti-American, anti-
radical and anti-Jacobin – of the Scottish Moderates.[12] Orthodox Anglican
political theology, in fact, bears a striking resemblance to the refurbished
Toryism enabled by the eclipse of Jacobitism and the ending of proscription
by George III: the 'sinfulness of rebellion' owes more to a High Church,
even non-juring, ethos, than to the Whig Erastianism to which clergy in this
period supposedly adhered. And there is a good deal of evidence to suggest
that at some demotic level the Anglican pulpit chimed with popular prejudices. From the Sacheverell riots in 1710 to the Priestley riots in 1791,
the eighteenth century is punctuated by High Church, quasi-Jacobite and
'Church and King' crowd actions against dissenting meeting houses (in
1714–15, 1745, 1791) or Catholic chapels. Certain dramatic episodes
stand out, such as the anti-Catholic Gordon riots in London in 1780, or
the assault on the Birmingham home of the Unitarian spokesman Joseph
Priestley in 1791; but there were other, less spectacular disturbances. Some
of the countless attacks on itinerant Methodist preachers in the 1740s and
1750s appear to have been instigated by the parochial clergy. Two Catholic
chapels were burned during an election campaign in Preston in 1768, while
the Cross Street meeting house in Manchester was ransacked on three
occasions: 1715, 1745 and 1792.[13] Nonconformity could be a risky affair.

Heterodoxy, subscription and dissent

'Dissenters as such,' remarked Priestley, have 'nothing in common but
dissent from the established church.'[14] One line, between conformity and
nonconformity, divided Anglicans from the various sects; another line,
between orthodoxy and heterodoxy, cut across all denominations. Unlike
the Unitarian Priestley, most Dissenters were orthodox – defined here as
affirming the doctrine of the Trinity – as were most Anglicans. But minorities within both the established Church and the dissenting communities
were not. Both the Toleration Act (1689) and the Blasphemy Act (1697)
contained Trinitarian clauses, and almost one hundred years after their
enactment a supporter of Anglican ascendancy could claim in parliament that
orthodox Dissenters actually opposed the extension of toleration, 'because,
under the pretext of relieving them from subscription [to thirty-five of the
thirty-nine articles] it would let in the anti-Trinitarians, the Anabaptists, and
all manner of sects'.[15]

If, as Bishop Chillingworth insisted in 1637, the Bible is 'the religion of [1 7 5] the Protestants', then scripture supersedes tradition, and individual judgement, not authority, is the ultimate arbiter of its meanings. And since the Bible is, in Burke's phrase, 'one of the most miscellaneous books in the world',[16] the potential range of interpretations is infinitely elastic. It is not surprising therefore that since the time of the Reformation Protestants had argued about the sacraments, ceremonial, Church polity and doctrine. In the 1690s in England, however, these debates-without-end took a distinctive lurch into the realms of radical heterodoxy. The reasons for the outbreak of the Trinitarian and deist controversies in the late seventeenth and early eighteenth centuries are less than transparent, but they had something to do, surely, with the new learning and the spirit of scientific inquiry in which intellectual historians discern the origins of 'the Enlightenment'. It is no coincidence, in that respect, that graduates of Cambridge, the university of Isaac Newton, figured so prominently in these doctrinal disputes.[17]

At its most extreme, heretical opinion substituted 'natural religion' for 'revealed religion', and a corpus of polemical literature, from John Toland's *Christianity Not Mysterious* (1696) to Matthew Tindal's *Christianity as Old as the Creation* (1730), renounced superstition and priestcraft, and sought the mind of God in the works of nature. More threatening to orthodoxy perhaps than such theological exotica, because grounded in scriptural exegesis, were the doubts expressed about the core doctrine of Christianity – the Holy Trinity. Non-Trinitarians – who faced up to three years' imprisonment for their beliefs – were either Arians, who believed that the Son was consubstantial with and subordinate to the Father, or Socinians, who denied the pre-existence and divinity of Christ. The challenge to orthodoxy was in no sense a popular movement, and the Church-state authorities dealt with it robustly. In 1714 Convocation silenced the latitudinarian divine, Samuel Clarke. Earlier, in 1705, the Dublin-based Presbyterian minister Thomas Emlyn landed himself in gaol for his *Humble Inquiry into the Scripture Account of Jesus Christ*. Meanwhile, skilled controversialists such as Daniel Waterland and Jonathan Swift led the ideological counter-attack. By the 1730s the challenge had either 'withered' away, according to one view, or suffered 'intellectual defeat', according to another.[18] And yet the longer-term implications and consequences of these seemingly arcane debates were far-reaching and profound.

First, in an age when the theoretical foundations of the state were explicitly Christian, rejection of the central tenets of Christianity – the Trinity and revelation – constituted, *ipso facto*, an attack on the state itself. We shall

[1 7 6]   return to this point later. Second, 'intellectual defeat' did not prevent re-covery later in a century that witnessed the re-emergence of deism, the founding of the non-Trinitarian Unitarian sect (and, conversely, the reasser-tion of Trinitarian orthodoxy). This other 'revival' had a political impact too. Finally, it is arguable that the true significance of heterodox opinion lay not in questions of Christology or the status of revelation, but in the related issue of subscription.

Subscription – to the thirty-nine articles in the case of Church of England clergy, and Oxford and Cambridge; to thirty-five of those articles in the case of 'licensed' teachers in the dissenting academies; and to the 1643 Westminster Confession of Faith in the case of the Church of Scotland and Presbyterian Synod of Ulster – remained a source of contention throughout the eighteenth century. The arguments may be briefly summarised. All Pro-testants accepted scripture as the basis of belief and practice. But since the Bible is 'miscellaneous' and, in the words of the Belfast Presbyterian minister John Abernathy, 'diversity of judgement is a natural consequence from humane imperfection', it followed that 'agreement in our opinions' was out of reach. 'Must the peace of the church on that account,' he asked, 'be broken?'[19] Subscriptionists and non-subscribers gave different answers.

To its defenders subscription represented an essential safeguard against the growth of heresy, heterodoxy, deism, scepticism and even atheism. Diversity, while inescapable, had to be restrained. 'If we would preserve in the Church any order, any decorum, any peace,' observed Burke in opposi-tion to the Feathers Tavern petition, 'we must have some criterion of faith more brief, more precise and definite than the scripture.'[20] For objectors to subscription that argument controverted the first principles of the Reformation: the sufficiency of scripture and the right to private judgement. Man-made formularies and creeds were rejected as authoritarian, reduction-ist, redundant, impertinent and an invitation to hypocrisy. In other words, subscription *per se* was the issue, rather than, or more than, the orthodoxies that such creeds affirmed.

In one of the key texts on subscription, *The Confessional: or a Full and Free Inquiry into the Right, Utility, Edification and Success of Establishing Systematical Confessions of Faith and Doctrine in Protestant Churches* (1766), Francis Black-burne cites his intellectual forerunner, Chillingworth. 'This vain conceit . . .' warns the bishop, 'this deifying our own interpretations and tyrannous inforcing them upon others . . . is and hath been the only fountain of all the schism of the church.'[21] And it is true that questions of subscription were, in some form, rarely far away from the religious controversies of the eighteenth century. English dissent confronted the problem publicly and directly during the Salters' Hall debates in London in 1719. In 1716 the Devon and Cornwall Association of Ministers sought 'advises' from their London brethren on how to proceed against an Exeter Presbyterian minister, James Pierce, and three others who, influenced, it seems, by the writings of Samuel Clarke, were suspected of Arianism. The Dissenters – Baptist, Congregationalist and Presbyterian – who gathered subsequently at Salters' Hall to settle the matter split not on the substantive issue of the Trinity but on the probity of subscription: a slim majority of the one hundred or so delegates asserting the absolute primacy of scripture over any forms or confessions devised by human hand.[22]

Later that same year John Abernathy preached a sermon in Belfast entitled 'Religious obedience founded on personal persuasion' (published in 1720), which in its championing of the individual conscience over inessential 'ceremonial injunctions' and 'mere ecclesiastical authority' echoed Bishop Hoadly's controversial views, and can be seen as the opening shot in a subscription dispute which led eventually to schism.[23] Like almost all of Ulster's Presbyterian ministers, Abernathy had attended the University of Glasgow (and more unusually of Edinburgh too). After his 'call' to the congregation of Antrim in 1705, with like-minded clergy and laymen he formed a discussion and reading group soon to be known as the Belfast Society. The society explored matters of theological concern, such as the basis of Church unity, but its real significance lay in its spirit of rational inquiry. It is no coincidence, perhaps, that the Belfast Society was established at the same time as the Emlyn heresy trial. In reaction to that trial the Synod of Ulster passed a second Act requiring subscription to the Westminster Confession, which it had earlier adopted from the Scottish Church in 1698. The inherent tension between synodical orthodoxy and the more liberal attitudes of Abernathy and his cohort finally surfaced in the shape of Abernathy's sermon and in the refusal the following year by the Revd Samuel Haliday to subscribe.

Haliday had travelled in Protestant Europe and attended the Salters' Hall debates. Another minister, from the south of Ireland, also in London in 1719, accused Haliday of Arianism. Cleared of that charge, the Synod attempted to smooth his installation as minister of the Belfast 'First' congregation by passing the so-called 'Pacific Act', allowing an incoming minister to rephrase troubling clauses of the confession and leaving it to individual congregations to determine his suitability thereafter. Haliday, however, refused to sign *any* confession. Controversy erupted, generating the publication of

[1 7 8] up to fifty pamphlets over the next five or six years. In 1721 eleven other ministers, led by Abernathy and another Belfast Society veteran, James Kirkpatrick, joined Haliday in refusing to subscribe. Finally, after repeated failed attempts to resolve the crisis, the non-subscribers, or 'New Lights' as they had come to be known, seceded to found the Presbytery of Antrim.

Still, as Ian McBride remarks, it was 'an odd sort of schism'. The seceders could no longer sit in the Synod, but communication and generally good relations were maintained between the two groups, and, crucially, there was no attempt to deprive the seceders of their share of the *regium donum*. The subscription requirement was finally dropped in 1783. McBride notes a further important dimension of this episode: the prominence, on the orthodox side, of the laity, whether as Church elders voting at Synod, or as members of congregations defecting from New Light ministers. The subscription crisis had a geographical and a social structure. Non-subscribers were strongest in east Ulster and in the urban setting of Belfast; the 'conservatives' in the rural hinterland.[24] To reconstruct this split as one between elite learning and popular piety would be to oversimplify; nevertheless the imperatives of 'politeness' for the New Lights should not be underestimated. And here a connection with Scotland might be suggested. As Abernathy has been called the 'father of non-subscription', his fellow Ulsterman, and Glasgow alumnus, Francis Hutcheson, is sometimes claimed as the 'father of Scottish moderatism': and the logic of both their positions privileged learning and, consequently, social 'respectability', over piety or 'enthusiasm'.

The third great subscription controversy of the eighteenth century disrupted the Church of England in the early 1770s and had its roots deep within the venerable tradition of latitudinarianism.[25] The 'latitude-men' never constituted a movement or even a faction within the Church; they represented rather a style, a loose body of opinion, which stressed the essentials that united, over the inessentials that divided, Protestants. Castigated by their detractors for being too close to the Dissenters or for straying into heresy, it might be more accurate to see them as promoters under eighteenth-century conditions of the old aspiration to 'comprehension'. The latitudinarians did indeed concur with Old Dissent in their emphasis upon scripture and wariness of Church authority; but were nearer to Rational Dissent (and to the 'New Lights') in their insistence upon the essential simplicity and rationality of the Christian message. Their intellectual cradle was Cambridge, which produced the luminaries – and many of the rank-and-file – of this tendency, including Samuel Clarke, William Whiston and Edmund Law.

The spirit of latitudinarianism ran counter to the imposition of subscription. In 1766 Francis Blackburne subjected the practice to an extended critique in his book *The Confessional*, and his son-in-law, Theophilus Lindsey, played a key role in the Feathers Tavern petition against subscription in 1772. Parliament, as we have seen, rejected that petition, prompting Lindsey, John Jebb and others to secede (like most of the petitioners, however, Blackburne remained within the Church of England). Lindsey went on to set up a Unitarian church in Essex Street in London. Unitarianism's theological lineage lay in the Socinian and Arian heresies and drew its original adherents from among the English Presbyterians (a Church in long-term decline, but the other party, suggestively enough, to the comprehension project in 1660–62). Coming out of a completely different institutional context and ecclesiastical tradition, Lindsey thus carried the latitudinarian affinity with Rational Dissent to its logical terminus. Again the small numbers involved in these developments should be registered, if only to underline the extraordinary political impact of this dissident intelligentsia.

The twin problems of heterodoxy and subscription, then, were common to both the established and the dissenting Churches. But the old divisions between the established Churches and Dissenters remained. These turned on the establishment principle itself, the proper role of the state (or, to use the contemporary short-hand, the magistrate) in ecclesiastical affairs, and the limits of toleration. The structure of the 'near-confessional' state, it is often assumed, predisposed nonconformists, who were denied the rights of full citizenship, to radical politics. It should be remembered, though, that Dissenters were 'natural' supporters of the Hanoverian dispensation. The Protestant succession, the triumph of the Whigs and the great purge of the High Church Tory party from central and local government in 1714–15 gave the Dissenters a vested interest in maintaining the *status quo*. The Toleration Acts of 1689, and in Ireland 1719, permitted freedom of worship. Non-Anglican education flourished, ostensibly under licence, in the famous dissenting academies. Dissenter merchant elites infiltrated local government in important urban centres like Bristol, Norwich and Newcastle. Indeed the combination of Tory proscription and Dissenter loyalty to the regime encouraged accommodation rather than confrontation. Walpole, moreover, cultivated the nonconformist constituency, in 1723 granting a *regium donum* of £500 (later rising to £1,000) to the widows of English and Welsh dissenting ministers.

The Dissenter problem receded during the reigns of the first two Georges without being entirely defused. Infinitely preferable as the Low Church

[1 8 0] Hanoverian regime undoubtedly was to the revanchist Tory alternative witnessed in the last years of Queen Anne's reign, or worse still, to the waking nightmare of a popish Jacobite restoration, for the Dissenters the burden of civil exclusions and disabilities remained: the Test and Corporation Acts in England and Wales, and the Sacramental Test in Ireland. This amounted, in their view, to a gross injustice. As Abernathy argued strenuously in his pamphlet urging the repeal of the Sacramental Test, the Presbyterians' unblemished record of fidelity to the Protestant cause and succession entitled them to legal equality.[26] And the same reasoning applied, of course, to all Protestant Dissenters in these islands.

From the legislature's standpoint, penal laws debarring Dissenters from public office were justified by the principle of a state Church. In 1731 Abernathy refrained, presumably for tactical reasons, from attacking that underlying principle, standing instead on the case for civil liberties. In 1746, however, Towgood, an alumnus of Taunton Academy, restated the perennial objections to Erastianism in *The Dissenting Gentleman's Answer to the Rev. Mr. White's Three Letters*. He claimed, in fact, that the Church of England was not even, properly speaking, a state Church, but 'really a parliamentary church'; not 'an ally, but a mere creature of the state. It depends entirely upon the acts and authority of parliament for its very essence and frame.' That situation was insupportable, he believed, because 'the subjection to higher powers, and obedience to magistrates, which the scriptures enjoin Christians, relates only to civil, not at all to religious matters. Christianity is so far from enjoining, that it actually forbids, obedience to civil governors in things of a religious nature.'[27]

Towgood's influential polemic has been described as 'a classic compendium of nonconformist argument'. *The Dissenting Gentleman's Answer* was reprinted several times in Ireland, for example,[28] and its strictures, particularly on the proper functions of the magistrate, were reiterated many times by the advocates of toleration during the debates in the British parliament, on subscription in the 1770s and on the repeal of the Test and Corporation Acts in the late 1780s. John Wilkes denied 'that the civil magistrate has the least concern with the salvation of souls, or that any power of that nature is delegated to him'. Charles James Fox asserted that 'religion should always be distinct from civil government'.[29]

Yet times had changed since Towgood wrote. In the first place, new measures of toleration were introduced. In 1779 English and Welsh dissenting teachers were relieved of the obligation to subscribe to thirty-five articles, while the following year their Irish counterparts could celebrate the repeal of the Sacramental Test. The spectre of Quakerism no longer haunted the ruling elites. A small and increasingly insular (and prosperous) community, the Quakers continued to record their 'sufferings', mainly the distraint of property, but between 1759 and 1789 only one of their number was imprisoned for the non-payment of tithe.[30] The long tortuous dismantling of anti-Catholic legislation had also begun. Penal laws remained on the statute books, to be sure, and the petitions for repeal of the Test and Corporation Acts in 1787, 1789 and 1790 provided 'the classic issue on which the Anglican doctrine of the state was attacked, analysed and defended'.[31] Advocates of toleration, moreover, deployed a rhetoric of enlightenment that would never have occurred to an old-style Presbyterian like Towgood. 'As a liberal and enlightened nation,' lamented one MP, 'it was a matter of great reproach to this country that its established church still retained the prejudices of barbarous times, and continued to practice intolerance and persecution . . .'[32] Examples of this genre could be multiplied.

There is no doubt either about where Towgood, who had warned against the spread of infidelity, would have stood in the furore about free-thinking and revealed religion which tracked the rhetoric of enlightenment. One opponent of further toleration decried 'the alarming progress of atheism, and the multiplicity of atheistical opinions which were daily issued from the press'; another discerned denials of revelation and 'the immateriality of the soul'; and the alleged blasphemer and libertine John Wilkes proved only too ready to confirm their worst fears. Wilkes rejected the proposition that atheism was on the increase, but acknowledged that deism, 'sound pure deism, has made rapid progress, not only in this island, but in every part of the continent. It is almost become the religion of Europe.' Conservatives opposed even minor alterations to the law, including subscription for dissenting teachers, on the principle that *any* breach in the bulwarks of orthodoxy and authority threatened to break open the floodgates of change, with unforeseeable and catastrophic results. Once again Wilkes – admittedly a rather extravagant figure – obliged the Cassandras. 'I wish,' he announced in an astonishing hymn to complete religious freedom, 'to see rising in the neighbourhood of a Christian cathedral, near its gothic towers, the minaret of a Turkish mosque, a Chinese pagoda, and Jewish synagogue; with the temple of the sun, if any Persians could be found to inhabit this island, and worship in this gloomy climate.'[33]

The Age of Enlightenment was also the age of Lord North and of 'powerful Trinitarian reassertion' and reaction.[34] The Bishop of Cloyne, Richard Woodward's bestseller, *The Present State of the Church of Ireland* (1786), offered

[1 8 2] a forceful polemic in defence of establishment.[35] The Test and Corporation Acts were not repealed (before 1827). The French Revolution proved to be the real watershed, though. In a system where Church and state were inextricably linked, the issue of toleration had always had inescapable political and constitutional implications, and from the time of the Wilkesite agitation in the 1760s Dissenters had achieved a high profile in radical politics. The revolution now demonstrated just how dangerous that activism could be. Edmund Burke, who earlier in his career evinced sympathy with the cause of toleration, shifted to outright opposition in 1790. There were now 'strong and warrantable grounds,' he warned, 'of serious apprehensions for the church's safety'. 'The leading preachers among the dissenters were avowed enemies of the Church of England . . . they acknowledged their intentions and that thence our establishment appeared to be in more serious danger than the Church of France was in a year or two ago.'[36] The age of counter-revolution had begun.

Why was Burke so resolute in defence of the Church? Why were the 'theological politicians', as he called them, also 'political theologians'? At the most straightforward level the answer lies in the structure of the near-confessional state: there is nothing surprising about the fact that Dissenters were prominent in movements seeking to reform a system that discriminated against them. In practical terms the defeat of Jacobitism allowed them room to manoeuvre in what was now a securely Protestant state. That is one reason that many Dissenters stirred from their political quiescence after the 1750s. The centrality of the Church to Burke's conception of an ordered society, and the presumed threat to good authority posed by the Dissenter intelligentsia, may also be attributed to heterodoxy of the Socinian, Arian and Unitarian varieties, which J.C.D. Clark considers 'conceptually basic' to the radical project. Clark is worth quoting at length on this. 'A consequence of the denial that Christ exercised divine authority', he writes,

> was that He could not institute a priesthood descending by apostolic succession and exercising its mediatory powers by virtue of divine right . . . if even the Church could not claim divine institution, the state was still more obviously secular . . . mankind was free to amend or reject its ecclesiastical and political hierarchy in the name of reason, conscience or utility.[37]

Clark, in other words, identifies radical ideology primarily with Rational Dissent; with the likes of the scientist Priestley and the natural rights theorist Richard Price, precisely the people whom Burke had in his sights. It is entirely consistent with Clark's thesis too, that Thomas Paine, the author of the 1790s' most celebrated radical manifesto *Rights of Man*, should also write that decade's most notorious deist tract, *The Age of Reason*. Many radicals, of course, do not fit into this model; just as many Dissenters displayed little interest in politics at all, radical or otherwise. Some prominent radicals and reformers, such as the founder of the Yorkshire Association, Christopher Wyvill, were churchmen (if only just). Radical ideology moreover drew on intellectual resources – the ancient constitution, the 'Norman Yoke', contract theory and so on – which were entirely secular. But perhaps the most persuasive modification of Clark's elegant thesis is to be found in the work of J.E. Bradley, who suggests that 'while some so-called "rational" Dissenters derived their political views in part from their heterodox theology, the common heritage of a radically separated polity was *controlling* for both the "rational" and the orthodox alike . . . radical political theory was thus grounded primarily in polity, and only secondarily in theology'.[38]

'Glad tidings of salvation': Methodism and revival

Methodism, the most astonishing eruption in the eighteenth-century history of religion, was an anomaly. Is it best defined as a movement, a church or a sect? Did it belong to the dissenting tradition, or to the evangelical wing of the Church of England? One bishop deemed Methodism the 'old Puritan fanaticism revived'. In Wales, the site of its greatest, most enduring, success, it drew 'on the tough, deep roots of Welsh nonconformity'. And yet the same movement has been identified as 'a sign of the intellectual vitality and strength of orthodox churchmanship'![39] It is certainly true that the 'founder' of Methodism, John Wesley, was schooled in a High Church ethos, and that he remained a loyal son of the Church of England until his dying days in 1791. Feared and reviled at the time for its appeal to the lower classes and to the spirit of 'enthusiasm', far from overturning good government and social order, Methodism is frequently assigned a decisive function in Britain's avoidance of revolution in the 1790s.[40]

Although the story of the Methodist revival might logically begin in the Welsh valleys and with Howell Harris, it makes equal sense to pinpoint its origins in the High Church environs of Oxford where, in 1729, Charles Wesley and other students formed the 'Holy Club'. The club's members included Charles's brother, John, and, slightly later, George Whitefield. As the name suggests, these young men took their religion seriously, striving

[1 8 4] after 'inward holiness' through, for example, the study of devotional liter-ature and spiritual autobiography, notably the writings of Thomas à Kempis. In the mid-1730s both Whitefield and John Wesley ministered in the American colonies, where Wesley first encountered the pietistic German Moravian communities. Back in England a Moravian minister, Peter Bohler, persuaded Wesley that instantaneous conversion was scriptural, and on 24 May 1738 he experienced personal conversion or rebirth. In his own terms he became a Christian. Wesley later visited the Moravians in Germany, while across the Atlantic Jonathan Edward's America stood on the brink of the 'Great Awakening'. Methodists participated in a transcontinental revival.

It was an evangelical revival, conducted by itinerant preachers. Upon his return from America Whitefield met Wesley in London, then travelled to Wales and opened a correspondence with Harris – the connection would prove an important one. But Whitefield took the crucial initiative on 17 February 1739 by preaching in an open field to thousands of 'largely unchurched miners' from Kingswood colliery near Bristol. Just over a month later when Wesley arrived at Bristol he remarked that 'I could scarce recon-cile myself at first to this strange way of preaching in the fields.'[41] Less troubled by novelty, Whitefield, by all accounts a mesmerising public orator, quickly discovered that he had hit upon a winning formula. In May that year he preached to tens of thousands gathered in Moorfields and in Kennington in London. Wesley began to record hundreds of personal conversion narrat-ives in his journals. During the early 1740s Methodist societies spread across the country at an incredible rate.

Undoubtedly Wesley himself would have attributed this spectacular harvesting of souls to the workings of the Holy Spirit – although that raises questions about the Spirit's comparative inactivity before and after. Success may also be attributed to Whitefield's energy and eloquence in winning converts and to Wesley's energy and organisational skill in translating that voluntary human raw material into a flexible associational movement. But the main explanation of success lies surely in what might be termed the sociology – and geography – of Methodist recruitment. 'Methodists in gen-eral,' according to one critic, 'were composed of the lowest of the people.'[42] That typical perception, however, disguises an often highly specific appeal. Methodism attracted certain categories of people more than others: women, particularly unmarried young women, were well represented within its ranks; so too were industrial workers, the coal-miners of Kingswood and the north-east, the tin-miners of Cornwall or the tradesmen of the woollen manufactures of Yorkshire, for example.

The 'unchurched' condition of the Kingswood colliers to whom Whitefield reached out in 1739 provides a clue to the reasons for the rapid expansion of the movement. Methodism appears to have filled a collective spiritual vacuum; to have plugged the gaps, as it were, left by an established Church unable to keep pace with demographic growth and change. In that sense it can be read as a function of the social dislocations caused by early industrialisation. Methodist preachers, moreover, invited the hostility of parochial clergy by tactlessly denouncing the shortcomings of existing pastoral care. It is not surprising therefore that local clergymen and their allies in the magistracy frequently connived in the riots against these turbulent evangelists and their meeting houses.[43] With its emphasis on rebirth, rebaptism and salvation by faith, Methodism made a direct emotional appeal to the neglected which, to its opponents, smacked of excess and 'enthusiasm'. It also stood accused of placing lurid stress upon the punishment of sin, of operating what the nineteenth-century historian W.E.H. Lecky called an 'appalling system of religious terrorism'.[44]

The causes of popular religious revival will always be difficult to ascertain with any certainty, but in the case of mid-eighteenth-century Britain it is clear that it owed more to an evangelical *style* than to doctrine. That much is clear because whereas England, Wales, Scotland and, to a lesser extent, Ireland each witnessed revivals, the doctrinal accent shifted in the different national contexts. Whereas Whitefield was Calvinist, Wesley was Arminian. Both travelled and preached extensively in Wales, Scotland and Ireland, but both trimmed their doctrinal sails to the prevailing national winds. Wesley, especially, silenced his doubts about predestination during his missions outside England.

The revival, then, in which 'the people called Methodists' played a vital role, was a truly British phenomenon. In Calvinist-Presbyterian Lowland Scotland it took the form of an extraordinary outpouring of religious fervour, mass conversions and two enormous outdoor gatherings addressed by Whitefield on 11 July and 15 August 1742, at Cambuslang five miles south-east of Glasgow. The parallels with the Methodist experience in England are striking. Seventy-five of the 110 recorded conversions were of women. There was, likewise, a preponderance of 'lower-class' participation in the revival and open hostility towards it among the propertied. The Glasgow professor, Adam Smith, had Cambuslang at the back of his mind, perhaps, when he later wrote of 'the delusions of enthusiasm and superstition, which, among ignorant nations, frequently occasion the most dreadful disorders'.[45]

[1 8 6]   Revival made its most spectacular advances in Wales. The revival's leaders, Griffith Jones and Howell Harris, built on sturdy foundations. Between 1699 and 1727 the Society for Propagating Christian Knowledge (SPCK) established ninety-six charity schools in Wales. In sharp contrast to its Scottish counterpart, the SSPCK, which spurned Gaelic as a medium for proselytising, the SPCK also distributed large quantities of Bibles in the Welsh language.[46] By March 1739 Harris boasted some thirty religious societies in South Wales; by the end of 1740 the figure had risen to sixty-four; by 1750 there were an estimated 433 such societies in Wales and the Borders.[47] Howell, like his colleague Whitefield in whose London 'Tabernacle' he preached in the 1740s, was Calvinist, and his achievement traded on the ethos of Welsh Old Dissent. At the same time it seems likely that his achievement was so much greater and more enduring than that of his seventeenth-century forerunner, Vavasor Powell, because he remained within the framework of the established Church.

Despite official anxiety and occasional accusations to the contrary, the charge of political radicalism never attached to Methodism in the way it stuck to Restoration dissent and to some of its eighteenth-century heirs. Wesley himself condemned Wilkes in the 1760s and the insurgent American colonists in the 1770s. During the 1790s, as noted earlier, Methodists were conspicuously loyal. Still, the importance of Methodists as a counter-revolutionary bulwark must remain in doubt, particularly when the numbers are taken into account: 72,000 in the British Isles in 1791.[48] The comparatively small scale of the movement is further underlined when it is recalled that there were probably more Catholics in England, let alone the British Isles, at this time; a fact about which the Methodists were deeply concerned.

The return of the Catholic Question

John Wesley proclaimed a High Church allegiance, but shared the Dissenters' antipathy to popery. He even visited the anti-Catholic demagogue Lord George Gordon in prison. Similarly, his followers were believed to be prominent among the Gordonite anti-Catholic petitioners in 1780.[49] But in this respect the Methodists were merely reflecting, not leading, public sentiment – or more precisely a section of it, because it is one of the paradoxes of the later eighteenth century that, as anti-Catholicism declined among the 'enlightened' of polite society, it retained – even tightened – its tenacious grip upon popular culture.

Certain Catholics of a pragmatic bent had, since the time of the Restoration, sought a legal or political accommodation with the Protestant state. These usually took the shape of proposed formularies or tests, such as the abortive Remonstrance promoted by the Irish Dominican friar Peter Walsh in the 1660s, which repudiated the temporal authority of the Pope. English Catholics attempted to devise loyalty oaths acceptable to the state in the 1690s and again after the Hanoverian succession in 1714.[50] Such manoeuvres were virtually doomed to failure, however, so long as the Jacobite threat persisted. The eclipse of Jacobitism after 1746 thus opened up fresh opportunities for 'Catholic relief', as it became known, from the civil disabilities imposed by the penal laws. No one perhaps understood better the intimate connection between the Jacobite cause and anti-Catholicism or more clearly perceived the new possibilities of legal amelioration presented by the defeat of that cause than the Irish Catholic activist Charles O'Conor.

O'Conor, a County Roscommon landowner, belonged to one of the few Catholic families that had escaped the 'shipwreck' of 1691. Scholar, anti-quarian and founder, with Thomas Wyse and John Curry, of the Catholic Association in the late 1750s, through his many (usually anonymously pub-lished) pamphlets he played a pivotal role in raising and articulating the case for repealing at least some of the penal laws. By his antiquarian researches O'Conor hoped to establish the antiquity of native Gaelic civilisation and thereby refute the charge of Irish (Catholic) barbarism; by seeking to exor-cise the 'myth' of the 1641 massacres O'Conor and his collaborators tried to demonstrate that it was now safe to admit their co-religionists to the benefits of civil liberty. His main polemical strategy, however, consisted in assimilat-ing the cause of Catholic relief to the rhetoric of whiggery, Saxon and British liberties, and tolerance.

Writing in the persona of a liberal Protestant, he declared in 1755 that 'the time proper for exhibiting the case of the Roman-Catholics of Ireland appears to be at hand'. The Pretender had been routed; the Protestant Interest was secure; Jacobitism, and therefore the Catholics, no longer posed a threat. It was manifestly unjust, moreover, to punish Catholics for the actions of their ancestors. Even more importantly, Catholic loyalty to the civic magistrate and lawful prince constituted 'an active religious principle'; contrary to popular belief they were not obliged to obey the Pope in tem-poral affairs. Echoing the arguments advanced by Abernathy on behalf of the Presbyterians in the 1730s, O'Conor insisted that the Catholics should be rewarded for good behaviour. By 1771 he could refer to 'a period of eighty years, uninterrupted from foreign hostility or domestic rebellion'. Finally,

[1 8 8] he predicted that dismantling laws that impeded the sale and acquisition of property would mobilise untapped economic resources.[51]

O'Conor thereby supplied a vocabulary of supplication and a fund of arguments which were recycled in other pamphlets, in petitions and addresses, in Scotland and in England, as well as in Ireland, up to the 1790s. Some at least in governing circles and in either parliament were at last prepared to listen. Colin Haydon has shown how anti-Catholicism, a central feature of English political culture since the age of Elizabeth, became increasingly unfashionable in polite society in the Age of Enlightenment.[52] Certainly, the extent to which a discourse of enlightenment, toleration, liberality and modernity peppered the parliamentary debates on relief measures in the 1770s and 1780s is striking. In that sense O'Conor was correct in asserting that the time to make the Catholic case appeared to be at hand. Some of his other arguments were likewise vindicated. The first penal laws to be repealed, in 1772, 1778 and 1782, concerned mortgages and leases. And the speed with which the Jacobite clans were integrated into the British army testifies to the obliteration of Jacobitism as a psychological barrier to political accommodation (although the rigorous suppression of the Scottish episcopalian Church does suggest another story). Nevertheless there could be little effective response to Charles James Fox's observation in 1780 that 'the Pretender was out of the question', still less to Wolfe Tone's announcement eleven years later that 'the man is dead; there is no Pretender'.[53]

The burial of the Pretender, the spread of more liberal attitudes, the imperatives of economic growth and the regrouping and rising self-confidence of the Catholic communities in these islands all help to explain the progress of Catholic relief measures from the 1770s onwards; however, the most decisive reasons for that progress lay elsewhere, in the logic of imperial expansion and military necessity. The classic example of the impact of empire on the Catholic Question is the Quebec Act. In 1763, when Britain acquired French Canada at the end of the Seven Years War, it acquired thereby jurisdiction over a large Catholic population – a reality duly acknowledged under the terms of the 1774 Act which recognised Roman Catholicism as the established religion of the province. It is roughly at this time too that, with a view to the need to police and defend the empire, His Majesty's ministers in London began to cast a covetous eye upon rich untapped reserves of Catholic manpower within the realm.

In an era of imperial and great power rivalry, near endemic war and the emergence of the military fiscal state, 'anachronistic' confessional barriers to army recruitment were being removed across Europe.[54] Already during the Seven Years War an estimated 6,000 Catholic Highlanders saw 'foreign [1 8 9] service' in the British army, mainly in India and the West Indies. In 1770 General Burgoyne introduced a Commons motion designed to ease the recruitment of Catholics by devising a 'simple oath' of loyalty, and in 1778 the army did, in fact, purge its required oath of its anti-Catholic clause. Negotiations were opened between the government and Bishop Hay in Scotland and Bishop Challoner in England.[55] The Irish parliament had meanwhile enacted its own simple oath in 1775. The scene thus seemed set fair for the gradual readmission of Catholics to the political nation. But Challoner for one remained cautious. Events would prove him right.

Neither the pragmatic considerations of the generals and ministers, nor the more secular outlook of the ruling elites, effected a corresponding shift in wider public opinion, and the first attempts to implement Catholic relief met with fierce resistance. In Ireland the grounds for Protestant resistance were clear. Catholics were a dispossessed majority, with a history – albeit in the seventeenth century – of rebellion, and Protestant estates, as the Lord Chancellor, John Fitzgibbon, reminded his co-religionists in 1789, were founded on 'an act of violence'. It was not in Ireland, however, but in Scotland and England with their small Catholic minorities that strong out-of-doors opposition to proposed relief measures was first mobilised.

There is no necessary relation between prejudice and fear on the one hand and the numbers of the despised outgroup on the other, as the experience of anti-semitism shows; still, Catholic numbers (actual, alleged and imagined) did figure in the debates about relief. The size of the Catholic communities in Scotland, England and Wales had grown steadily, though modestly, from c. 80,000 in 1700 to c. 110,000 in 1778 (in a population of just over seven million); but in a pre-statistical age there could be no agreement about this explosive issue. Some nonconformists in particular were convinced that Catholicism was on the march. As the Bishop of Bath and Wells observed in 1780, 'an idea had got into the world, that the number of Papists had very much increased of late years', whereas, in his view, 'the exact reverse was the fact'. Lord North likewise asserted that 'Popery had been in decline since the revolution, nay, it had declined within the last twenty years'. Moreover, he added – accurately – the contingent of Catholic peers had been drastically reduced.[56]

Incessant head-counting provided one prop for anti-popery; traditional Protestant fears and hostility – or, in the words of Edmund Burke, 'bigotry and fanaticism'[57] – provided the others. A mere ten years before the first

[1 9 0] English Catholic Relief Act of 1778 two Catholic chapels were burned down during election riots in Preston.[58] Traditional xenophobia played its part too, and nothing, perhaps, better illustrated the international character of *Roman* Catholicism than the foreign embassy chapels in London. Nor could all the vapouring about liberality and enlightenment hide from the vigilant Protestant eye the continuing companionship of popery and tyranny: significantly, the Quebec Act had combined the establishment of the Catholic religion with government by royal prerogative. Since popery never changed, it followed that toleration jeopardised the Protestant constitution.

On 1 May 1778 the English and Scottish Catholics presented an address (drafted by Burke) to parliament. Legislation rescinding restrictions on Catholic ownership and inheritance of land passed the Lords on 22 May and received the royal assent on 3 June. The Irish parliament followed suit in August. Only the English laws were repealed at Westminster, however. Standing the argument for extending the English militia provisions north of the border on its head, it was now pointed out that as the relevant Scottish penal laws pre-dated 1707, repeal would subvert Scotland's 'ecclesiastical constitution' and contravene the terms of the Act of Union. More ominously, popular anti-Catholic agitation within Scotland escalated.[59] In late January and early February 1779, rioters attacked Catholic chapels in Edinburgh, Glasgow, Peebles and Dundee, prompting the Scottish Catholic leadership to withdraw its application for relief for fear of provoking an even greater backlash. John Wilkes, true to his Scotophobic form – and without apparent irony – complained of 'a British parliament . . . controlled in their [sic] proceedings by an Edinburgh mob'.[60] He could not have foreseen that it was London, not Edinburgh, that posed the real danger.

The Scottish agitation resulted in the formation of the Protestant Association led by the virulently anti-Catholic Lord George Gordon. In parliamentary circles Gordon had the reputation of a crank. 'The noble lord had got a twist in his head,' remarked one MP, 'a certain whirligig which ran away with him, if anything relative to religion was mentioned.'[61] In the summer of 1780 he earned the reputation of a sulphurous demagogue. During 1779 and early 1780 the Protestant Association organised a stream of petitions to parliament, which thousands signed, against popery and for a repeal of the Relief Act. This campaign, which stood no chance of success, reached its calamitous climacteric on 2 June when a crowd of around 60,000 accompanied Gordon to Westminster to support his bill for securing the Protestant religion.

The 'Gordon riots', which erupted that day, lasted until 12 June and were the longest and most violent street disturbances in London's (and Britain's) history. Rioters burned down Catholic chapels, including those belonging to the Sardinian and Bavarian embassies. They looted distilleries; broke into Newgate prison and released its inmates; attacked the home of the Lord Chief Justice, Lord Mansfield, and launched an assault, which was repulsed, on the Bank of England. Perhaps as many as 450 people were killed; a further twenty-five were afterwards hanged. Both the initial cause of the riots and much of the property targeted by the crowd demonstrate the persisting vitality of popular English anti-popery. The targets and victims were not exclusively Catholic, however, and historians have detected a strong undercurrent of social protest in these events.[62] Contemporaries, too, were as struck and horrified by the destruction of property as by the onslaught on popery, and, ironically, if the riots had any outcome it was to discredit the reform movement. Here was proof, if proof were needed, of the perilous folly of embroiling the common people in politics.

In Ireland the Catholic and reform questions became even more directly linked. It was during the early 1780s, indeed, that after almost a century of political inaction Irish Catholics, organised into the Catholic Committee, re-emerged as a significant political force. In terms of politics and public life, to be sure, the penal laws had decimated the Catholic community. They had also effected further transfers of landed property into Protestant hands, and produced a steady trickle of Catholic converts to the established Church. Yet it is now clear that these successes masked a Catholic resurgence.[63] Some Catholic families like the O'Conors of Roscommon, or the Bellews in County Galway, managed through a variety of stratagems to cling on to their estates, but the real basis of Catholic renewal lay in trade and in the growth of a new Catholic 'middle class'.

The leadership of the Catholic Committee, originally founded by O'Conor, Wyse and Curry, soon passed to the remnant of the Catholic nobility – Lords Kenmare, Fingal and Gormanston – and, like their aristocratic counterpart in England, Lord Petrie, these men were cramped by the weight of social respectability and the restraints of political loyalty into a tame rhetoric of supplication. The challenge to the *status quo*, when it came, came from within the Protestant nation: Charles Lucas in the 1740s; the volunteer movement in the 1770s. Similarly, the reopening of the Catholic Question, when it happened, owed as much to the more advanced reformers among the Volunteers as it did to the Catholics themselves. It owed very little indeed to Fingal and his colleagues who always erred on the side of caution.

After the 'constitution of 1782' had been won, a number of Volunteers, based mainly in Dublin and east Ulster, and 'Patriot' MPs, notably Henry Flood, pressed on for parliamentary reform. That new departure alienated some of the more conservative members of the Volunteer–Patriot axis, such as Henry Grattan; clearing a space, in the process, for the radicals. The Dublin 'tribune', James Napper Tandy, entered into his heyday. The Volunteer–reform movement thus split over the issue of how far it should go, and indeed, over how hard it should push – the Volunteer convention at Dungannon, County Tyrone, in 1782, had persuaded the legislature of the timeliness of asserting its 'independence', but how safe would it be to permit further 'out-of-doors' pressure to be applied to a sovereign parliament? An even more divisive issue then intruded: ought not the Catholics to be included in the proposals for reform?

Certain Volunteer companies were in favour of reaching out to their Catholic fellow countrymen on the grounds of political expediency – potentially, Catholics offered a huge accretion of numbers to the ranks of the reform movement – and justice; some companies, in fact, began to admit Catholics and, in contravention of the penal laws, to arm them. Other reformers, Flood among them, opposed any *political* amelioration. Catholics, affirmed the future United Irishman William Drennan in 1784, were still unfit for liberty.[64] It was at this point too that a new breed of Catholic politician, sympathetic to reform, more assertive than the aristocratic old guard and represented by the Dublin businessmen Richard McCormack and John Keogh, appeared on the public stage for the first time. The demands of the Volunteer convention, held in Dublin in November 1784, were rebuffed by parliament, while the delegates failed to reach agreement on the Catholic Question. That question and parliamentary reform were then shelved. But what must, at the time, have seemed an epilogue to the 'constitution of 1782', turned out, in the event, to be a prologue to the tumultuous 1790s.

The shock-wave known as the French Revolution transformed Irish and British politics by awakening radicals and reformers to new senses of change and possibility. In Ireland revolution in Catholic France demonstrated to those Protestants who wished to see it that Catholics were not merely fit for liberty but capable of achieving it. However, many, perhaps most, Protestant reformers still hesitated at the psychological Rubicon of granting full civil rights to Catholics, and the deadlock over the issue was not broken until Wolfe Tone published his brilliant pamphlet, *An Argument on Behalf of the Catholics of Ireland* (1791) aimed directly at an Ulster Presbyterian audience.

One consequence of the *rapprochement* that followed was the formation, in [193] Belfast, in October 1791, of the first Society of United Irishmen.

Whitehall took a rather jaundiced view of Belfast as a nest of disaffection, and the startling, tentative alliance broached there between Catholic and Dissenter caused serious alarm in London. 'There is no evil,' remarked Lord Grenville, 'that I should not prophesy if that union takes place.'[65] By some timely new instalments of Catholic relief, the British government (if not its client Dublin administration) hoped to conciliate the majority population, win its loyalty and remove it from the embrace of the radicals. From its standpoint the Catholic Committee drew encouragement from the introduction of the so-called 'Mitfort Act' which ended the double tax for English Catholics in 1791. Late that year, taking advantage of these new more favourable circumstances, and assisted by the lobbying in London of Edmund Burke, the committee renewed its campaign for the repeal of the penal laws.

The responsible minister, Henry Dundas, proved responsive to the Catholic case – he also piloted Relief Acts for Scottish episcopalians and Catholics in 1792. In Ireland he cajoled the reluctant Lord Lieutenant, Westmorland, and the 'friends of government', into sponsoring a Relief Act. The provisions of the 1792 Act were in themselves quite modest: besides the blow to Irish Protestant morale delivered by Dundas's (and William Pitt's) 'desertion', the real significance of that episode lay in the nature of the Catholic agitation and in the ferocity of Protestant resistance. Ever ready to please those in authority, in October 1791 the Catholic Committee old guard led by Lord Kenmare publicly distanced itself from the 'extremist' stance of the middle-class Dubliners. Times had changed, however, and the Dubliners orchestrated a popular nation-wide anti-Kenmare campaign which confirmed the new men in their leadership, shattered the conventions of social deference and, by mobilising lower-class Catholics, amounted to a sort of social revolution.

Meanwhile the anti-papist rhetoric which disfigured the debates on the relief bill robbed the Act, when it came, of the conciliatory effect for which Pitt had hoped. Dublin Castle patronage could secure a majority of votes in the Irish parliament; it could not change the hearts and minds of Irish MPs on this most divisive of issues. After the 1792 Act the Catholic Committee decided to step up their agitation; in particular they chose to answer the accusation of unrepresentativeness made during the parliamentary debates by holding countrywide delegate elections to a national convention. Protestant hardliners in turn elaborated the doctrine of Protestant Ascendancy.

[1 9 4]   After the convention, held in Dublin in 1792, a delegation including John Keogh, and the committee's agent, the United Irishman Wolfe Tone, travelled to London to petition the throne. Once again the Pitt government proved responsive. If anything, as war with France loomed, the logic of inoculating Irish Catholics against Jacobin infection by offering concessions seemed, to the British government, more urgent than ever.

The 1793 Relief Act, extending the franchise to Catholic forty-shilling freeholders in the counties, was a major piece of legislation which, for the first time since the 1680s, breached the Protestant monopoly of political power and struck at the foundations of the confessional state. The Catholic Question had not been settled, of course – that accolade must go to the Emancipation Act in 1829 which allowed Catholics to sit in (the United Kingdom) parliament. But the importance of 1793 should not be under-estimated. The implications of the Act itself, and the manner of the agitation that secured it, unnerved Irish Protestants. Legislative union now presented itself as a way of converting a menacing Irish Catholic majority into a permanent British minority. By similar reasoning union likewise offered the possibility of Catholic emancipation without Catholic power. Both arguments duly emerged in 1799–1800.

Radicalism and reaction: the 1790s

The Society of United Irishmen, the most formidable radical (and later, revolutionary) movement in these islands during the 1790s, sought, in Wolfe Tone's celebrated phrase, to unite Catholic, Protestant and Dissenter,[66] and in practice drew its membership from all three of Ireland's main denominations. It was much more, therefore, than a political expression of religious dissent. Nevertheless the historian A.T.Q. Stewart's description of the movement as 'a Presbyterian initiative' has much to recommend it.[67] Not all of Ulster's Presbyterians were radicals, nor were all United Irishmen Presbyterian; but the movement was founded in the Presbyterian 'capital', Belfast; its newspaper, *The Northern Star*, was likewise launched in Belfast in January 1792 and edited by a Presbyterian lay elder, Samuel Neilson, and, most tellingly perhaps, a number of Presbyterian ministers were active in the ranks right down to and during the 1798 rebellion. The United Irish 'Presbyterian initiative' thus appears to provide a classic example of the standard political radical–religious dissent equation.

The sources of Ulster Presbyterian politicisation and disaffection are not difficult to trace. Presbyterians, after all, had laboured under the yoke of an Erastian–episcopal state since the 1660s; under the terms of the notorious sacramental test they had been excluded from the corporations between 1704 and 1780; Presbyterian marriages were denied legal status. If that burden of discrimination seems mild when compared with the plight of the Catholics, the feelings of resentment that second-class citizenship is bound to cause were no less real for that. As late as 1792 *The Northern Star* invoked the memory of Queen Anne's reign and Presbyterian sufferings under 'the galling restraints of a proud [High Church] ascendancy'.[68] Traditional Presbyterian hostility to prelacy, and to the privileges enjoyed by the established Church, were also registered by the polemical replies of the Revd William Campbell and (the future United Irishman) the Revd Samuel Barber, to Woodward's *Present State of the Church of Ireland* in the 1780s, and by the attacks on worldly bishops and on tithes in the pages of *The Northern Star*.

In addition Presbyterians were primed for politicisation by the participatory, quasi-democratic structures of their Church, by a culture of doctrinal debate and by the high levels of literacy typical of Bible-centred religion. None of those preconditions determined the content or direction of politicisation, however, and in rural Ulster the appeal of radicalism tended to diminish as the distance from Belfast increased. The strength of radicalism, or later in the decade of republicanism, among Presbyterians was also related to the local sectarian geography. The United Irish movement flourished in Antrim and Down where Catholics were in a minority; it made less headway in those counties, such as Armagh or Tyrone, where the denominations were more finely balanced. Indeed, even those Presbyterian radicals who were nominally pro-Catholic took the view that in an age of enlightenment and revolution Catholicism – the epitome of *ancien régime* superstition – had gone into irreversible decline.

There was nothing 'natural' about Presbyterian attachment to radicalism, as both the retreat from the United Irish cause after 1798 and the range of political opinion within the community during the 1790s both demonstrate. Some of the United Irish leaders, such as Tone and Arthur O'Connor, were deists, but they belonged to the Church of Ireland. Thus the 'Presbyterian initiative' does not appear to have originated, as J.C.D. Clark might suspect, in heterodoxy, but rather, as J.E. Bradley would surmise, in 'heteropraxis' – in a confirmed opposition to episcopacy and a state Church. The primacy of issues of Church polity over theology in shaping political outlooks is further

[196]   suggested by the contrast between the Ulster and the Scottish Presbyterian experience in the 1790s.

Scotland produced a considerable parliamentary reform movement, the Friends of the People, in 1792–3, which was ruthlessly suppressed by the courts. Scotland also produced a Society of United Scotsmen later in the decade, although that organisation can be seen as an extension of the much bigger Irish revolutionary movement. In short the comparative lack of civil disturbance in the 1790s appears to confirm contemporary perceptions that the Scots were by then, in T.C. Smout's words, 'an uninflamable people'.[69] And yet if Presbyterians are, to quote an historian of the Ulster variety, 'inherently radical', or as the United Irish leader Thomas Addis Emmet put it, 'almost republicans from religion',[70] how then are we to account for the absence of large-scale political turmoil during that most unsettled of decades, in that most Presbyterian of countries, Scotland? Part of the explanation, explored earlier, is that, as committed unionists operating in a country where the union had taken root, the Friends of the People were unable and unwilling to appeal to the sort of national sentiment which the United Irishmen exploited to such effect. Another part of the answer, surely, has to do with the fact that in Scotland Presbyterians belonged to the *national* Church, by law established, whereas in Ireland Presbyterians were Dissenters.

The Moderate regime, associated with the names of William Robertson, Hugh Blair, Alexander Carlyle and others, which dominated the General Assembly of the Church of Scotland from 1752 has been subject to the same accusations of worldliness and spiritual torpor as the eighteenth-century Church of England, and for broadly the same reasons. The Moderates valued learning and distrusted 'enthusiasm' and the experiential style of religion dear to their contemporary critics in the 'popular party' and to their nineteenth-century evangelical detractors.[71] The Scottish and English cases were different, however, in that the Moderates, at least nominally, rejected as Erastian the imposition of the 1712 Patronage Act which provided for the presentation of ministers by lay patrons, either local gentry or the crown. The popular party opposed the arrangement outright, insisting instead upon the traditional primacy and prerogatives of the congregation in 'calling' its own minister. Francis Hutcheson addressed this issue in his pamphlet, *Considerations on Patronage. Addressed to the Gentlemen of Scotland* (1735, reprinted 1773), and, like all good Presbyterians, he found the procedure objectionable. Significantly, though, he was not prepared to follow the lead of sterner men, such as Ebenezer Erskine, who upheld the 'divine right of the people in the choice of their pastors', maintaining rather that 'the populace are by no means the fittest and best judges of ministerial qualifications'.[72]

Hutcheson went to the heart of the matter. Despite their theoretical problems with patronage the Moderates were in practice satisfied with a system that, in their view, promoted a learned and socially respectable clergy. Since, in effect, the *status quo* suited them, it is not surprising that in politics Moderates tended towards conservative positions. During the American war, for instance, and in marked contrast to English Dissenters, Ulster Presbyterians and the Scottish popular party, the Moderates supported the government against the colonists. During the 1790s Moderates were likewise in the vanguard of reaction against the French Revolution and its doctrines. But it is impossible to determine the extent to which they reflected popular attitudes on this. While the Moderates controlled the General Assembly for just over fifty years, they did so by a narrow margin, and there is evidence furthermore that they were out of step with the laity. As the 'Dundas party at prayer' they dutifully supported Catholic relief in 1792, whereas it is probable that the republication of Robert Fleming's *Rise and Fall of the Papacy* (1701, reprinted 1793) more accurately registered Scottish public opinion at the time. On the other hand the comparative political stability of Scotland in the 1790s does suggest that in preaching loyalty, obedience and the superior blessings of the British constitution, the 'Moderate pulpit' did reach receptive ears.

The 'Anglican pulpit' broadcast the same message in England, while Anglican clergy played their part in the loyalist associations that sprang up in 1792 and after. The ideology of anti-Jacobin, anti-Paineite popular loyalism of the sort pioneered by John Reeves's Association for the Preservation of Liberty and Property against Levellers and Republicans drew on a variety of non-religious sources, including xenophobia, patriotism and traditional antipathy to France. Edmund Burke and other less sophisticated, but perhaps in terms of immediate propaganda value, more effective, 'conservatives' also mounted a sustained ideological defence of the British virtues: respect for tradition, the rule of law, property rights and so on. Revolutionary France by way of contrast stood as a warning of the dangers of rash innovation. Violence, social collapse and the levelling of property and class distinctions were, in the conservative view, the inevitable consequence of tampering with the 'natural' order of things. And if a headcount of loyalists and radicals in the 1790s is taken as the yardstick, then the conservatives won the argument.[73]

Loyalist ideology contained an important religious element as well, in both an aggressively Protestant and in the wider Christian sense. For among the many Jacobin vices to be resisted was their irreligion. On that score at least the Irish (and all other) Catholic bishops and the British government were at one.[74] Rallying to the defence of the *ancien régime* of which they formed an integral part, the Churches invoked the divine sanction of the existing social hierarchy, proclaimed the duty of obedience to lawful authority; preached the Christian virtue of resignation to one's assigned lot in this world (especially for the poor) and reminded their flocks of man's reward in the hereafter. That kind of moral teaching as a palliative to the hard realities of economic and other inequalities is exemplified, above all, by the writings of the evangelical (and Tory)[75] Hannah More, the sales and dissemination of whose one-penny *Cheap Repository Tracts* far outstripped Thomas Paine's *Rights of Man*. In Britain the generalised Christian counter-attack on 'French' principles also had a robust Protestant side: the much-celebrated British constitution – self-evidently, to its champions, the envy of the world – was a *Protestant* constitution. The Protestant character of militant loyalism was even more pronounced in the deeply divided society of Ireland. There the Dublin corporation formulated the doctrine of Protestant Ascendancy in 1792; three years later lower-class Protestants in County Armagh in Ulster formed the explicitly sectarian Orange Order,[76] which grew rapidly into one of the most formidable (and certainly the most enduring) popular loyalist movements in these islands.

During the 1790s Britain and Ireland were rocked by political crises on a scale not witnessed since 1688–91. In terms of 'radical' disaffection such unrest had not been experienced since the 1640s. Some historians have argued that in this decade Britain came within an ace of revolution.[77] In Ireland there is no doubt that that was the case. Over 30,000 people perished in the United Irish-led republican insurrection of 1798. Unsurprisingly the radical, reform and revolutionary movements of the late eighteenth century have long stirred the interest of historians. But historiographical fashions change, and much has changed indeed since E.P. Thompson acknowledged in a postscript to the 1967 edition of his classic book, *The Making of the English Working Class*, that 'we have almost everything to find out about' 'the flag-saluting, foreigner-hating, peer-respecting side of the plebeian mind'.[78] Since then the study of British conservatism and loyalism has become a small boom industry – which has fallen prey to the usual revisionist occupational hazard of over-compensation. Nevertheless it must be conceded that what was once treated as the quintessentially revolutionary decade must now be treated as *the* counter-revolutionary decade as well; and in that counter-revolution the Churches played a leading role.

Notes

1. Clark, J.C.D., 1985, *English Society 1688–1832: Ideology, Social Structure and Political Practice during the Ancien Régime*, Cambridge, opens with the sentence 'This is a revisionist tract.'

2. Hempton, David, 1996, *Religion and Political Culture in Britain and Ireland, from the Glorious Revolution to the Decline of Empire*, Cambridge, 1. 'Seldom,' observes Ian D.L. Clarke, 'has an ecclesiastical party been condemned by posterity quite so mercilessly as the "Moderates" ' of the Scottish General Assembly in the second half of the eighteenth century: 'From protest to reaction: the Moderate regime in the Church of Scotland, 1752–1805' in Mitchison, R. and Phillipson, N.T. (eds) 1970, *Scotland in the Age of Improvement*, Edinburgh, 200. An analogy might be drawn here with the way in which later 'heroic' images of Restoration Dissenters and Covenanters were shaped by their early eighteenth-century memorialists such as Edmund Calumny and Robert Wodrow.

3. Hempton, *Religion and Political Culture in Britain and Ireland*, 2.

4. *Ibid.*, 12.

5. The phrase is Gordon Rupp's: 1986, *Religion in England, 1688–1791*, Oxford, 17.

6. Walsh, John, Haydon, Colin and Taylor, Stephen (eds) 1993, *The Church of England c. 1689–c. 1833: From Toleration to Tractarianism*, Cambridge, 55–8.

7. Towgood, Micaiah, 1745, *Serious and Free Thoughts on the Present State of the Church and Religion*, London, 7, 20.

8. Burke, Edmund (6 February 1772) in Langford, P. (ed.) 1981, *The Writings and Speeches of Edmund Burke*, ii, Oxford, 361.

9. Black, Jeremy, 'Confessional state or elect nation? Religion and identity in eighteenth-century England' in Clayton, A. and MacBride, I. (eds) 1998, *Protestantism and National Identity: Britain and Ireland c. 1650–c. 1850*, Cambridge, 54.

10. *The Parliamentary History of England*, xxviii (8 May 1789), 27.

11. Clark, 'Orthodox Anglican political theology', in *English Society*, 216–35.

12. Bradley, J.E. 1989, 'The Anglican pulpit, the social order, and the resurgence of Toryism during the American Revolution', *Albion*, 21: 361–88; Vincent, Emma, 'The responses of Scottish Churchmen to the French Revolution, 1789–1802', *SHR*, 73: 191–215.

[200] 13. Albers, Jan, '"Papist Traitors" and "Presbyterian Rogues": religious identities in eighteenth-century Lancashire' in Walsh, J., Haydon, C. and Taylor, S. (eds) 1993, *The Church of England* c. *1689–c.1833*, Cambridge, 328–9; Seed, John, '"A set of men powerful enough in many things": Rational Dissent and political opposition in England, 1770–1790' in Haakonssen, Knud (ed.) 1996, *Enlightenment and Religion: Rational Dissent in Eighteenth-century Britain*, Cambridge, 148.

14. Quoted by Albers in '"Papist Traitors" and "Presbyterian Rogues"', 322.

15. *The Parliamentary History of England*, xx (speech of Sir Roger Newdigate, 10 March 1779), 246.

16. Langford, P. (ed.) 1981, *The Writings and Speeches of Edmund Burke*, ii, Oxford (6 February 1772), 362. For Chillingworth see Fitzpatrick, Martin, 'Latitudinarianism at the parting of the ways: a suggestion' in Walsh, J., Haydon, C. and Taylor, S. (eds) 1993, *The Church of England*, c. *1689–c. 1833*, Cambridge, 212–13.

17. See Gascoigne, John, 1989, *Cambridge in the Age of the Enlightenment*, Cambridge.

18. Rupp, *Religion in England*, 277; Clark, *English Society*, 228.

19. Abernathy, John, 1720, *Religious Obedience Founded on Personal Persuasion. A Sermon Preach'd at Belfast the 9th. of December 1719*, Belfast, 3–4.

20. Langford, *Edmund Burke*, ii (6 February 1772), 362.

21. Fitzpatrick, 'Latitudinarianism at the parting of the ways', 213.

22. This episode is summarised by Michael Watts in 1978, *The Dissenters: From the Reformation to the French Revolution*, Oxford, 372–5.

23. Abernathy, *Religious Obedience*, 17, 38. For accounts of the subscription controversy see Steward, A.T.Q., 1993, *A Deeper Silence: The Hidden Origins of the United Irishmen*, London, 74–80; MacBride, Ian, 1998, *Scripture Politics, Ulster Presbyterianism and Irish Radicalism in the Late Eighteenth Century*, Oxford, 43–52.

24. MacBride, *Scripture Politics*, 42, 46–8.

25. My discussion of Latitudinarianism draws freely on Seed, '"A set of men powerful enough in many things"', and on Fitzpatrick, 'Latitudinarianism at the parting of the ways'.

26. Abernathy, 1731, *The Nature and Consequences of the Sacramental Test Considered, with Reasons Humbly Offered for the Repeal of it*, Dublin, 16–19.

27. Towgood, Micaiah, 1746, *The Dissenting Gentleman's Answer to the Rev. Mr. White's Three Letters*, 14–15.

28. Towgood's entry in the *Dictionary of National Biography* claims classic status for his polemics. For the Irish reprints see MacBride, *Scripture Politics*, 97–8.

29. *Parliamentary History of England*, xx (speech of Wilkes, 17 March 1779), 309, and xix (speech of Fox, 8 May 1789), 28.

30. Ditchfield, G.M., 'Ecclesiastical policy under Lord North' in Walsh, J., Haydon, C. and Taylor, S. (eds) 1993, *The Church of England c. 1689–c. 1833*, Cambridge, 237.

31. Clark, *English Society*, 253.

32. *Parliamentary History of England*, xx (speech of Sir Henry Hoghton, 10 March 1779), 239.

33. *Parliamentary History of England*, xx (speeches of Sir W. Bagot, Sir Roger Newdigate and John Wilkes, 10 March and 20 April 1779), 241, 243, 246, 312.

34. Ditchfield, 'Ecclesiastical policy under Lord North'.

35. Kelly, James, 'The genesis of "Protestant Ascendancy": the Rightboy disturbances of the 1780s and their impact on Protestant opinion' in O'Brien, G. (ed.) 1989, *Parliament, Politics and People*, Dublin, 93–127.

36. *Parliamentary History of England*, xxviii (speech of Burke, 2 March 1790), 234–9.

37. Clark, *English Society*, 281.

38. Bradley, J.E., 1990, *Religion, Revolution and English Radicalism: Nonconformity in Eighteenth-century Politics and Society*, Cambridge, 4, 138. Italics added.

39. Watts, *The Dissenters*, 436; Rupp, *Religion in England*, 454; Clark, *English Society*, 235.

40. Historians who have ascribed a counter-revolutionary role to Methodism include W.E.H. Lecky, Elie Halévy and E.P. Thompson.

41. These events are recounted in Rupp, *Religion in England*, 339–79.

42. *Parliamentary History of England*, xxi (speech of Spencer Stanhope, 20 June 1780), 707.

43. Rupp, *Religion in England*, 372–4, 378.

44. Lecky, W.E.H., 1878, *History of England in the Eighteenth Century*, London, ii, 582.

45. Smout, T.C., 1982, 'Born again at Cambuslang: new evidence on popular religion and literacy in eighteenth-century Scotland', *P&P*, 97: 114–27, Smith cited 118.

[202] 46. Mandelbote Scott, 'The bible and national identity in the British Isles, *c.* 1650–*c.* 1750' in Clayton, A. and MacBride, I. (eds) 1998, *Protestantism and National Identity: Britain and Ireland c. 1650–c. 1850*, Cambridge, 169, 174.

47. Rupp, *Religion in England*, 455–8; Watts, *The Dissenters*, 397.

48. Watts, *The Dissenters*, 404.

49. *Parliamentary History of England*, xxi (speech of Spencer Stanhope, 20 June 1780), 707.

50. Duffy, Eamon, ' "Englishmen in Vaine": Roman Catholic allegiance to George I' in 1982, *Studies in Church History*, vol. 11: *Religion and National Identity*, Oxford.

51. [O'Conor, Charles] 1749, *A Counter-appeal to the People of Ireland*, Dublin; *idem*, 1755, *The Case of the Roman-Catholics of Ireland. Wherein the Principles and Conduct of that Party are Fully Explained and Vindicated*, Dublin, iii, 19–20, 37–8, 42, 50; *idem*, 1756, *The Principles of the Roman-Catholics Exhibited*, 14; *idem*, 1771, *Observations on the Popery Laws*, 11–12.

52. Haydon, Colin, 1993, *Anti-Catholicism in Eighteenth-century England, c. 1714–80: A Political and Social Study*, Manchester.

53. *Parliamentary History of England*, xx (Speech of Fox, 20 June 1780), 706; Tone, 1791, *An Argument on Behalf of the Catholics of Ireland* in Moody, T.W., McDowell, R.B. and Woods, C.J. (eds) 1998, *The Writings of Theobald Wolfe Tone*, i, Oxford, 122.

54. Black, Jeremy, 'Confessional state or elect nation?' in Clayton, A. and MacBride, I. (eds) 1998, *Protestantism and National Identity: Britain and Ireland c. 1650–c. 1850*, Cambridge, 69–72.

55. Johnson, Christine, 1983, *Developments in the Roman Catholic Church in Scotland, 1789–1829*, Edinburgh, 16, 20.

56. Towgood, *The Dissenting Gentleman's Answer*, 36; Fitzpatrick, 'Latitudinarianism at the parting of the ways', 218–19; *Parliamentary History of England*, xxi (speeches of Lord North, 20 June 1780, and Bishop of Bath and Wells, 3 July 1780), 705, 759.

57. *Parliamentary History of England*, xxi (Burke, 20 June 1780), 709.

58. Albers, ' "Papist Traitors" and "Presbyterian Rogues" ', 329.

59. Donovan, R.K., 1987, *No Popery and Radicalism: Opposition to Roman Catholic Relief in Scotland, 1778–1782*, New York and London.

60. *Parliamentary History of England*, xx (Wilkes, 15 March 1779), 281.

61. *Parliamentary History of England*, xxi (speech of Mr Turner, 11 April 1780), 386–7. [2 0 3]

62. The classic formulation of this interpretation is Rudé, George, 'The Gordon riots: a study of the rioters and their victims', reprinted in Rudé, 1970, *Paris and London in the Eighteenth Century*, London, 268–92.

63. Wall, Maureen, 1989, *Catholic Ireland in the Eighteenth Century: Collected Essays of Maureen Wall* (ed. Gerard O'Brien) Dublin; Power, Thomas and Whelan, Kevin (eds) 1990, *Endurance and Emergence: Catholics in Ireland in the Eighteenth Century*, Dublin.

64. Lawless, J., 1818, *The Belfast Politics Enlarged; Being a Compendium of the Political History of Ireland, for the Last Forty Years*, Belfast, 187–9.

65. Grenville to Westmorland, 20 October 1791, *HMC Dropmore Ms* ii, 213–14.

66. That is Catholic, Anglican and Presbyterian.

67. A.T.Q. Stewart uses the phrase in 1977, *The Narrow Ground: Aspects of Ulster, 1609–1969*, London, 102; for a detailed discussion of the Presbyterian provenance of the United Irish movement see Stewart, *A Deeper Silence*.

68. *The Northern Star*, 22–26 September 1792.

69. See the comments of Thomas Malthus quoted in McFarland, E.W., 1994, *Ireland and Scotland in the Age of Revolution*, Edinburgh, 31.

70. Elliott, Marianne, 1985, *Watchmen in Sion: The Protestant Idea of Liberty*, Derry, 11; MacNevin, William J., 1807, *Pieces of Irish History*, New York, 9.

71. My discussion of the Moderates draws on Clark, I.D.L., 'From protest to reaction: the Moderate regime in the Church of Scotland, 1752–1805' in Mitchison, R. and Phillipson, N.T. (eds) 1970, *Scotland in the Age of Improvement*, Edinburgh, 200–24; Fitzpatrick, Martin, 'The enlightenment, politics and providence: some Scottish and English comparisons' in Haakonssen (ed.) *Enlightenment and Religion* and Allan, David, 'Protestantism, Presbyterianism and national identity in eighteenth-century Scottish history' in Clayton, A. and McBride, I. (eds) 1998, *Protestantism and National Identity: Britain and Ireland c. 1650–c. 1850*, Cambridge, 182–205.

72. Fitzpatrick, 'The enlightenment, politics and providence', 73–6.

73. For conservative argument in the 1790s see Christie, I.R., 1984, *Stress and Stability in Late Eighteenth-Century Britain*, Oxford; Dickinson, H.T., 1977, *Liberty and Property*, London; McDowell, R.B., 1944, *Irish Public Opinion*, London.

[204]   74.   Keogh, Daire, 1993, *'The French Disease': The Catholic Church and Radicalism in Ireland, 1790–1800*, Dublin.

75.   More named her two cats 'Passive obedience' and 'Non-resistance'!: Clark, *English Society*, 242.

76.   Smyth, Jim, 1995, 'The Men of No Popery: the origins of the Orange Order', *History Ireland*, 3 (3).

77.   The case for the nearness of revolution is put most forcefully by Roger Wells in 1983, *Insurrection: The British Experience, 1795–1803*, Gloucester.

78.   Thompson, E.P., 1968, *The Making of the English Working Class*, London, 916–17.

9

UNITING THE KINGDOMS:
THE BRITISH–IRISH UNION

The integration – or 'internal colonisation' – of Wales, Scotland and Ireland into an English political, economic and cultural framework accelerated during the eighteenth century, although the nature and pace of that integration varied greatly from country to country. Wales, while it sustained a strong linguistic distinctiveness, particularly in the more 'remote' north, was the most thoroughly assimilated. The SPCK, it is true, distributed Welsh-language bibles, but these were printed in London. The abolition of the Council of Wales in 1689, like the abolition of the Scottish Privy Council in 1708, replaced an instrument of royal authority with more direct rule from Westminster. The principality's twenty-seven 'increasingly anglicised' and London-based MPs (fewer than the number of representatives from Cornwall) never cohered into a solid phalanx or parliamentary national interest group. 'Welshmen in London celebrated St. David's day ... Yet they would also refer to themselves as English in a way Scotsmen would never have done. Being Welsh was not part of their political culture, except on the rare occasions when it proved a useful propaganda weapon.'[1] Some minor differences in the legal system remained; but the Church of England was the Church of Wales too, and for most of the eighteenth century, the initial successes of Methodism notwithstanding, the great nonconformist revival lay safely in the future. Moreover the Methodists, it is worth recalling, at first met with stiff resistance in Wales as well as in England.

Scotland occupied an intermediate position, on the integration spectrum, between Wales and Ireland. It retained its own distinctive Church and law. Scottish MPs were digested by Westminster for the most part smoothly, although occasionally, and in contrast to their Welsh counterparts, they proved capable of acting in concert in defence of a perceived national interest. Twenty-three of the twenty-five Scots members voted for a Scottish militia bill in 1760, for example. On the other side of the balance sheet North Britons were bound ever more closely to South Britons by free trade, joint participation in the imperial project and the British army, the ironing out of some of Scotland's legal particularism by the post-Culloden 'reform' legislation, and the auto-anglicisation of the Lowland literati. The pace of integration was also speeded up by improved communications. More and better (often turnpike) roads and greater ease of travel facilitated the 'picturesque' tourist, the new taste for the 'sublime' in nature, and the descriptive literature of writers like William Gilpin whose books, published in the 1780s, familiarised 'metropolitan' readers with the beauties of such 'remote' corners of the kingdom as the English Lake District, the Scottish Highlands and north Wales.[2]

Ireland too had its share of tourists, notably the agricultural improver Arthur Young, whose *Tour of Ireland, 1776–1779* has earned him the eternal gratitude of social and economic historians. Young, admittedly, saw and heard things in Ireland that 'make an Englishman stare',[3] but just how different was the host country from its 'sister kingdom'? English stereotypes of the impoverished, popish, potato-eating peasant and the claret-swilling, improvident squire suggest that, from an English standpoint at least, the Irish were less than fully assimilated to the superior metropolitan civilisation. Late eighteenth-century Patriot politicians – and subsequently historians – likewise stressed what divided Ireland from England/Great Britain by reading the 'constitution of 1782' as the culmination of an unfolding national struggle to win legislative 'independence'. The Patriots and Volunteers, like Charles Lucas before them, *did* assert Ireland's constitutional autonomy, of course; and in the 1790s the United Irishmen advanced to outright republican separatism; the Whig teleological version of eighteenth-century political history is not completely wrong, therefore. It is only part of the story, however.

In 1782 an astute Dublin publisher marked the repeal of Poynings' Law and the Declaratory Act by reissuing William Molyneux's celebrated defence of the rights of the Irish legislature, *The Case of Ireland Being Bound by Acts of Parliament in England, Stated* (1698). But, awkwardly, *The Case* included a reference to the advantages of an Anglo-Irish union – 'an happiness', lamented Molyneux, which 'we can hardly hope for'. The publisher's political antennae were as finely tuned as his commercial sense, though, for he simply suppressed the offending passage.[4] To Daniel Corkery's 'hidden Ireland' of Gaelic civilisation, it seems, we might juxtapose the 'hidden history' of eighteenth-century unionism.[5]

The eighteenth-century discursive background to the union

Unionist discourse, such as there was, touched upon the 'hidden Ireland' only when pro-unionists claimed, rather implausibly as it later turned out,

that a union of Britain and Ireland would strengthen the Protestant Interest [2 0 7]
and fatally weaken the grip of Catholicism on the benighted popish natives.
Unionist and anti-unionist opinion, that is, was generally the affair of a
handful of British political economists and politicians and of the (exclusively
Protestant and English-speaking) political nation in Ireland. At the beginning of the century spokesmen for that political nation usually described themselves as English. By 1782 they had generally come to see themselves as
unhyphenated Irish. The fashioning, and appropriation, by Irish Protestants
of an Irish identity has been traced earlier, and is a critical factor in both
Anglo-Irish relations and interdenominational politics; but, like the (closely
related) national struggle for legislative independence, it is only part of the
story. Outside Ulster, with its large Scottish settlement, the term 'British'
never caught on in Ireland.[6] And yet it is striking that Charles Lucas (who
sometimes signed himself 'Britannicus') and the Catholic spokesman Charles
O'Conor both invoked the British derivation of the constitutional rights to
which they appealed. Anti-unionists and 'Patriots' were not separatists.

After the Irish parliamentary addresses soliciting union, in 1704, 1707
and 1709, were pointedly ignored by Queen Anne and her ministers, the
pursuit of legislative union with Great Britain fizzled out as a practical political
option. The prevailing orthodoxies of mercantilist political economy insisted
that under free trade conditions (consequent upon union) a cheap-labour, low-
cost economy like Ireland's would enjoy a competitive edge in England's
overseas and domestic markets. That argument also applied to Scotland before
1707, but political and international security considerations – in other words
the necessity, in London's view, of guaranteeing the Hanoverian succession
in the northern kingdom – overrode perceived national economic self-interest.
In 1720 when Westminster wished to assert control over Ireland, as it had
secured control over Scotland in 1707, it simply introduced the Declaratory
Act (6 Geo. 1), underlining thereby the already existing subordination of the
Dublin parliament.

British hostility – laced with indifference – towards an Anglo-Irish union
rendered Irish advocacy fairly pointless. Robert, Viscount Molesworth,
endorsed the idea of union in the foreword to his edition of *Franco-Gallica* in
1720; Arthur Dobbs recommended it in his *Essay upon the Trade of Ireland*
(1729–31)[7] and a few scattered references to the issue can be picked up here
and there; but for the most part in the three decades or so after 1709 Irish
politics and Irish political ideology moved along different channels. The rise
of Protestant nationalism, exemplified by the Wood's Ha'pence episode in
the mid-1720s, nudged 'unionism' off the political agenda. As late as 1764

[2 0 8]   'A Lover of Union' complained in the press that the topic 'is become excluded even from common table discourse, and superficial bottle talk', although, ironically enough, his letter succeeded in provoking a lively exchange of views in the pages of *The Freeman's Journal*.[8]

In 1756 while in exile in England, Charles Lucas, who, according to one interpretation, played a 'pivotal role in the transition to republican separatism', called for an 'effectual union' between Ireland and Britain on the Scottish model. By 1760, however, he considered that option a 'most violent and desperate remedy'[9] – at the end of the previous year, after all, the Dublin crowd, educated in the rhetoric of national rights by Lucas himself and, more cynically, by the Speaker, Henry Boyle, during the money bill affair of the mid-1750s, had rioted outside (and inside) the parliament on College Green, incited by (false) rumours that a union was about to be imposed.[10] Even though union was not, at that stage, back on the political agenda, the rumours took hold, stirred by speculation in the press and by the pro-union public pronouncements of Lord Hillsborough before the riots.[11] As Irish antipathy to the idea of union increased, British opinion became more amenable. Union had not yet entered the realm of practical politics but, thanks in part to Hillsborough, it had re-entered Anglo-Irish political discourse.

In 1751 Hillsborough, a senior Irish aristocrat, active in British – and later imperial – politics, published anonymously *A Proposal for Uniting the Kingdoms of Great Britain and Ireland*. His pamphlet sparked off a minor controversy at the time, prompting at least three replies, including an intellectually cogent response from Nicholas Archdall, MP for County Fermanagh, entitled *An Alarm to the People of Great Britain in Answer to a Late Proposal Showing the Fatal Consequences of Such an Union*. Pro- and anti-union pamphleteering, of widely varying conceptual quality, continued from then on, right down to the flood-tide of printed polemic unleashed in late 1798, but Hillsborough's otherwise average effort is important for two reasons. First, it registers a shift in British attitudes towards a union with Ireland, and second, it provides a sort of compendium of standard unionist arguments.

During the eighteenth century the new political economy began to erode the traditional opposition to union of the British exporting and manufacturing sectors. Between the 1740s and 1780s Matthew Decker, Malachy Postlethwayt, Adam Smith and Josiah Tucker, like the Irish 'commonwealthmen' Henry Maxwell and Arthur Dobbs before them, all insisted that union and free trade would benefit Britain economically, as well as Ireland. That was the economic incentive. Politically, union began to appear more attractive to the British government as the most effective means of securing an insubordinate colony, striving after 'independency'; for what Lucas in the 1740s and the Volunteers and Patriots in the 1770s and 1780s termed political and constitutional equality, to British eyes looked like a loss of control. It is no coincidence, perhaps, that Hillsborough wrote in the wake of the Lucas agitation.

The arguments in favour of union set out in the *Proposal for Uniting the Kingdoms* and elsewhere, before and after, were mainly economic. By way of increased, unfettered commerce between Britain and Ireland, and between Ireland and the colonies, union, claimed its proponents, would generate economic growth. In addition it would reduce taxes, by ridding Ireland of the expense of a separate parliament, attract foreign Protestant merchants and manufacturers, lured by rich economic opportunities, and, in the process, so weaken the popish interest that 'Ireland would in a few years be a Protestant nation'. Union would strengthen Britain and the British empire, check French ambitions in Europe and America, increase the population, create full employment, drain the bogs, reclaim mountainy wastes (and 'mountineers'), and reduce the consumption of claret! Moreover, if any remained sceptical about the likely benefits of union they need only look to the Scottish experience since 1707.[12]

The major arguments against a union were political and, in essence, nationalist. Justice, geography and policy, according to this position, demanded that Ireland should enjoy full equality with her sister kingdom, and not be incorporated into a larger political entity where the voice of her representatives would be drowned out like that of the Scots. Besides the fact that distance and the sea rendered the whole project impractical, there were, in addition, economic objections. A union would increase taxes, depopulate the countryside and devastate Dublin, robbing it of its resident gentry which would, inevitably, decamp to London. Moreover, since the situations of Scotland before 1707 and Ireland in mid-century were so unlike, the Scottish experience of union was irrelevant.[13]

Opinion on the matter within British and Irish political circles was moving steadily in opposite directions. The more that Irish politicians and pamphleteers asserted their constitutional rights, the more anxious the British government became that 'independency' or separation was their actual and ultimate objective. Thus as the Volunteer–Patriot campaign for 'free trade' gathered pace in 1779, senior British politicians began, for the first time, to explore the possibility of a legislative union as the way forward in Anglo-Irish relations.[14] However, Buckinghamshire, the Lord Lieutenant of the day, urged the utmost caution 'upon so nice a subject'. 'The idea of a projected union,' he wrote later, is 'best calculated to excite the indignation of the Dublin

[2 1 0] rioters.' Sir George Macartney sent to Ireland by Lord North in late 1779 to sound out Irish opinion reached an even bleaker conclusion: 'the idea of a union at present,' he warned, 'would excite a rebellion'.[15]

There were committed unionists in Ireland in the 1780s, such as the first commissioner of the revenue, John Beresford, the future Lord Chancellor, John Fitzgibbon, and the (English) under-secretary at Dublin Castle, Thomas Waite, but, on that score, the political tide ran strongly against them. The year 1782 marked the apogee of Protestant nationalism. In 1785 when Pitt attempted a 'final adjustment' to Anglo-Irish relations by proposing a set of 'commercial propositions' which would harmonise duties between the two kingdoms, the Irish parliament rejected the proposal on the *political* grounds that it would infringe Irish sovereignty.[16] Then the apparent fragility of the Anglo-Irish connection was further underlined by the regency crisis in 1788–89 when only the king's timely recovery prevented the Irish parliament from appointing the Prince of Wales regent of the kingdom of Ireland. The following year a little-known Dublin lawyer on the fringes of Whig politics, Theobald Wolfe Tone, published a pamphlet, *Spanish War!*, concerning a diplomatic quarrel between Great Britain and Spain, in which he argued that Ireland was both entitled and obliged to remain neutral.[17] The prediction of the Lord Lieutenant, the Duke of Rutland, in 1784 that 'without an union Ireland will not be connected with Britain in twenty years',[18] appeared to be on course.

Crisis and union: 1790–1800

Protestant nationalism, based on the autonomy of the Irish parliament, acted as the main barrier to a union. But Protestant nationalism was conditional upon Protestant Ascendancy. Thus as soon as that ascendancy was threatened by the admission of Catholics to the political nation Protestant opposition to a union began to wilt. Rather than face the prospect of an eventual Catholic take-over of 'their' parliament, some Protestants now preferred to abandon that institution in favour of a United Kingdom whose permanent Protestant majority would guarantee Protestant power. If the events of 1779 convinced the British ruling elite of the desirability of union, then the events and Catholic Relief Acts of 1791–93 had a formative impact on Irish Protestant opinion. However, although rumours about the British government's intentions began to circulate,[19] Pitt made no attempt at this point to further his objective, judging presumably – and correctly – that the idea had not yet garnered sufficient support in Ireland to assure success. The true significance of the aftershock experienced by conservative Protestants in 1793 is that for the first time attitudes towards union within both the British and Irish political elites began to move in the same direction.

Far from viewing the granting of limited political rights to Catholics as presenting a terrible dilemma, Protestants of a radical persuasion in the United Irish movement actively campaigned for relief alongside parliamentary reform. But in that respect also 1793 proved to be a turning point. Dublin Castle set its face against any more concessions on either the reform or Catholic questions. Indeed, as in Scotland and England, demands for reform were met by new repressive legislation and the prosecution of radicals in the courts. That trend was immeasurably strengthened, moreover, by Britain's entry in 1793 into the war against revolutionary France. At a stroke domestic reformers, long tarred with the epithet 'Jacobin', were transformed into potential fifth columnists. Volunteering and conventions were outlawed and in 1794 government suppressed the Dublin Society of United Irishmen. In early 1795 the ill-fated lord lieutenancy of Earl Fitzwilliam dashed hopes of a fresh instalment of Catholic relief. The crisis deepened, and violence escalated, as thwarted radical and Catholic activists, many of whom were already predisposed to more militant action, embarked upon an overtly revolutionary, republican strategy.[20]

Union offered one possible response to what amounted to a security and law and order crisis. Similarly, union offered a possible solution to the still festering Catholic Question. But before the summer of 1798 the possibility remained speculative. In the meantime Dublin Castle reacted to the spread of disaffection and armed republican organisation with ever more coercion, the suspension of habeas corpus, the Draconian Insurrection Act and, eventually, martial law. It took the bloody rebellion, which broke out in late May 1798, to wrench the idea of union finally from the realm of speculation into the domain of practical politics. Pitt acted swiftly. On 28 May, 'the day after' he heard the news from Ireland, the prime minister wrote to the Lord Lieutenant, Camden, 'cannot crushing the rebellion be followed by an act appointing commissioners to treat for an union?'[21] So close was the connection between rebellion and union, in fact, that (the evidence of Pitt's adept opportunism notwithstanding) it gave rise to the legend that the British government had deliberately provoked an insurrection in order to provide a pretext for imposing a union.

Although Pitt simply grasped the opportunity that presented itself, an armed uprising by tens of thousands of Irish 'Jacobins' clearly exposed the

[2 1 2]   failure of 'Protestant Ascendancy'. After the immediate security crisis had passed, a more lasting solution was in order. What particularly alarmed the British government was French involvement, first, in the abortive Bantry Bay expedition of December 1796, then in General Humbert's landing at County Mayo in August 1798. Ireland, once again, had offered a 'backdoor' into Britain for her continental enemies. First and foremost the union was designed to shut that door. As the Marquis Cornwallis, a dedicated imperial servant, who had replaced Camden as Lord Lieutenant, and Lake as commander-in-chief, explained at the height of the rebellion:

> The question of union was brought forward upon the principle that the independent legislatures had a tendency to separate, that the independent legislatures of Ireland and England had shown that tendency, and that the effects of it were felt in divisions at home and attempts of invasion abroad . . . the evils proposed to be cured by an union are, religious divisions, the defective nature of the imperial connexion, and commercial inequalities.

Elsewhere, both he and Pitt referred repeatedly to 'the empire at large', 'the security of the empire' and even 'perhaps the salvation of the British empire'.[22]

The anti-union pamphleteer William Drennan understood that motive very well. Pitt, he declared, had decided 'for the indefinite prolongation of the war'; union was 'a military idea', conceived by 'a council of war' to render 'Ireland a more productive war contribution' and 'concentrate the military force of the empire'. 'France,' he states, 'wishes to assimilate abroad. Britain hastens to consolidate at home.'[23] This was scarcely a state secret. Under-secretary Edward Cooke, whose pamphlet *Arguments For and Against an Union* effectively launched the public debate, wrote that:

> France well knows the principle and the force of incorporations. Every state which she unites to herself, she makes part of her empire, one and indivisible . . . but as we wish to check the ambition of that desperate and unprincipled power, and if that end can only be effected by maintaining and augmenting the power of the British empire, we should be favourable to the principle of union, which must consolidate its resources.[24]

But whereas Cooke viewed 'consolidation' as an imperial strategic necessity, Drennan believed that it would dangerously increase executive power and convert 'the whole country . . . into a great barrack'.[25]

Concern for imperial security also lay behind the attempt to resolve the Catholic Question by way of union, because sectarian animosities were identified as the root cause of that mass disaffection which, in turn, the French were able to exploit. Cornwallis remained 'fully convinced that until the Catholics are admitted into a general participation of rights (which when incorporated with the British government they cannot abuse) there will be no peace or safety in Ireland', and to that end sought to 'make a union with the Irish nation' rather than a (Protestant) 'party' within it. The union-supporting Earl of Shannon arrived at his position from a rather different route. 'If we have not a union,' he remarked, 'it is inevitable that the papists will succeed here, and if that is the case, and the parliaments remain separate [then] . . . the papists will work a separation.'[26] Cornwallis's chief secretary, Viscount Castlereagh, secured the public neutrality of the Catholic hierarchy on the issue; the Lord Lieutenant, however, underestimated the strength of opposition to Catholic relief among senior Irish politicians. Crucially, the insertion of a 'Catholic clause' in the proposed bill was resisted by the otherwise staunch unionist the Lord Chancellor, Lord Clare. In these circumstances the British government decided to proceed without it, while holding out a promise to the Catholics of a relief bill after the union had passed.

As rebellion raged in Ireland, government ministers in London were busy drawing up detailed memoranda on the possible shape of a union and the strategy for obtaining it. 'Pitt's first move, with Grenville and Auckland, was to look at the union with Scotland.' Under the instruction of the home secretary Portland, an historian, John Bruce, began a search of the records of Anglo-Scottish relations. In early August the former Irish Lord Lieutenant, Camden, send his analysis to Pitt.[27] During the autumn a succession of Irish politicians, including Clare, John Beresford, the Speaker John Foster and Sir John Parnell, travelled to London for consultations. By October rumours about an intended union began to circulate in the Dublin and London press. Then on 1 December the government opened the public debate with Edward Cooke's anonymously published *Arguments For and Against an Union*.

Cooke's pamphlet had an explosive impact as anti-unionists rushed into print. Over the next eighteen months or so extensive newspaper coverage and bitter polemic kept the union before the public eye. 'Pamphlets are raining down upon us,' wrote Drennan. 'Pamphlets swarm,' stated Cooke. 'Pamphlet writing is such a rage at present,' reported the *Freeman's Journal* in January 1799, 'that all classes are scribbling upon the union. It is a common question in the streets, are you writing a pamphlet against the union?' And, in fact, a modern scholarly bibliography of union political literature lists over 320 items (not including handbills).[28] The other main expressions of out-of-doors opinion were conveyed by public meetings, resolutions and declarations, beginning with the Irish Bar, a majority of whom voted against the proposed union in early December.

Union headed the legislative programmes of the British and Irish parliamentary sessions which opened in late January 1799. At Westminster the ensuing debate offered the likes of Pitt, Dundas and Lord Minto the occasion for set-piece speeches, a number of which were subsequently published in pamphlet form for distribution in Ireland. The opposition, led in this instance by Richard Brinsley Sheridan, was heavily outnumbered and, in the event, outvoted. In College Green it was a different story. There the union bill was defeated by 107 votes to 105. Unionist opinion had gained ground steadily among Protestant conservatives since at least 1792, and the levers of patronage at Dublin Castle's command usually ensured a ministerial majority in parliament, but even that combination proved insufficient to overcome the opposition coalition on the day.

The key to the opposition strength lay precisely in the fact that it represented a coalition of views and interests. The first of these was Dublin city, and the rejection of the union met with jubilation on the streets outside parliament. As in 1759 anti-unionists insisted that the abolition of the Irish parliament would diminish the city's prestige and devastate its economy. Radicals like Drennan, and Whig stalwarts like Henry Grattan, Lord Charlemont and the Duke of Leinster, opposed it on 'national' and Patriot grounds. Speaker Foster and leading Orangemen such as George Ogle and John Cladius Beresford opposed it in defence of Protestant Ascendancy. The Orange Order adopted a formal neutrality, but most Orangemen were, in practice, against a union that, in their view, would extinguish 'their' parliament. The Catholics as a body were ostensibly neutral as well, and although a majority were probably in favour of union, a significant minority were not, especially those living in or near Dublin,[29] including a then little-known young lawyer named Daniel O'Connell. 'Never,' observed Drennan, 'was there a stranger conjunction of political planets than now occurs.'[30]

Support for a union drew on equally diverse sources. The Catholic hierarchy, clergy and probably most of the laity were generally in favour, although there is little evidence of enthusiasm. Totally reversing their colleagues' reasoning, the stridently anti-Catholic Orangemen Sir Richard Musgrave and Dr Patrick Duigenan saw in union the best chance of maintaining Protestant Ascendancy. In contrast to the Dubliners, Cork – and other – merchants viewed the prospect of union in terms of commercial opportunity. Even some United Irishmen welcomed the measure. Since the number of Irish MPs was to be reduced from 300 to 100 at Westminster that would entail the abolition of most of the borough seats. The Act of Union, in other words, could be reasonably construed as a sweeping act of parliamentary reform.

Far away in America, the United Irish exile Archibald Hamilton Rowan
commented, 'I am almost sent to coventry here by the Irish, for my opinions
concerning a union.'[31] After a decade on the cutting edge of political conflict,
and unmoved by the likely fate of a discredited Dublin parliament, most
Ulster Presbyterians stayed out of the fray. Strange conjunctions indeed!

After the defeat in parliament of the original bill, government in London
and Dublin was determined to press on. Traditional accounts of what followed
concentrate on the use of 'corruption' to secure a parliamentary majority, and
there is no doubt that patronage – peerage promotions, employments (and
dismissals of the recalcitrant), sinecures and straightforward bribes – was
liberally exchanged for votes. 'It will not surprise you,' Cornwallis told Pitt,
'that every man in this most corrupt country should consider the important
question before us in no other point of view that as it may be likely to promote
his own private objects, or ambition, or avarice',[32] and in that sense the Irish
union is rivalled only by the Scottish as a grand-scale political 'job'. Like the
Scottish case, however, jobbing provides only a partial explanation of what
happened. As David Wilkinson has recently reminded us, only twelve MPs
who voted against the union in 1799 subsequently changed their votes. Most
of the government's largesse, that is, was dispensed to *retain* support.[33] The
government, moreover, invested much time, effort and resources in the mobilisation of public opinion.

Cornwallis identified 'the direction of the public sentiment [as] superior in
importance to every other object'. Even after it appeared that a union was almost
inevitable 'because we had a majority in the House of Commons', he cautioned
that it would be a mistake 'to suppose that a measure so deeply affecting the
interest and passions of the nation can be carried against the voice of the
people'.[34] Dublin Castle and its supporters thus competed with the opposition:
subsidising newspapers, disseminating pamphlets, orchestrating county meetings, eliciting resolutions and collecting signatures. Cornwallis himself toured
extensively, receiving union addresses in person. By February 1800, Castlereagh
could claim in parliament that after the first union bill had been knocked back,
'government felt it their duty then to say that they would not bring that measure forward, until its introduction should be justified by the public sentiment:
and the event has justified the expectation'. The chief secretary had employed
a narrow definition of the 'public', to be sure, which he defined variously as
those with a stake in the country and 'the great body of landed property'.[35]
The evidence suggests, furthermore, than in terms of signatures the anti-
unionists won the numbers game.[36] Yet it had never been a one-sided debate;
the government had done enough to lend credence to Castlereagh's claims.

[216]   In and out of parliament the arguments ran along well-worn lines. Speech-makers and writers opposed national and constitutional rights to the promise of an equal share in the benefits of British civilisation; some predicted economic prosperity, others, economic ruin; Catholics were assured that their remaining grievances would be redressed; Protestants were warned that only a union with Great Britain could guarantee their privileges and safety. One theme, pertinent to a British perspective on the debate, has been somewhat neglected – the Scottish comparison. Pitt's 'first move', as we have noted, entailed a search of the records concerning the Anglo-Scottish union. During the summer of 1798 Sylvester Douglas at the Home Office compiled materials relating to 1707, including reports of proceedings in the Scottish parliament, extracts from Defoe's *History of the Union* and, 'to complete the collection' some months later, a copy of Henry Maxwell's 1704 pamphlet *An Essay Towards an Union Between Ireland and England*. Defoe's book was republished in Dublin in 1799, while the other materials were forwarded to Cornwallis and Castlereagh as ammunition in the paper war.[37]

Whereas Douglas thought the coincidence between the Scottish and Irish arguments 'quite extraordinary', anti-Unionists either dismissed the Anglo-Scottish example as irrelevant or drew negative inferences from it. Some dwelt on the 'dragooning' of Scotland into a union and upon her political humiliation and under-representation thereafter. Critics cited the malt tax as a breach of the treaty and an instance of bad faith, or pointed to English contempt for the Scots in their midst who, 'in spite of all their pains in asserting themselves to Britons', are constantly reminded of their non-English status.[38] But for the most part Scotland figured in the debates as a prosperous and peaceful country which had patently benefited from the union. Edinburgh's undeniable growth since 1707 proved particularly useful to the advocates of an Irish union because – at least to those still open to persuasion – it provided an effective riposte to the prophets of Dublin's doom. Indeed, since no one could deny that Edinburgh had flourished in the previous fifty years or so, anti-unionists were thrown back onto the position that it did not necessarily follow that this had resulted from the union. Would it not have happened anyway? they asked.[39]

Eighteen months of persistent government out-of-doors campaigning and parliamentary management paid off. The second union bill passed the House of Commons on 7 June and the House of Lords on 13 June 1800. On 1 August it received the royal assent. The Irish parliament had voted for its own demise and on 1 January a new political and constitutional entity, the United Kingdom of Great Britain and Ireland, came into existence. It was a deeply flawed arrangement. Perhaps it had been damaged at the outset by [2 1 7] the manner of its making. Perhaps, as Richard Brinsley Sheridan remarked, 'a union effected by fraud, by intrigue, by corruption, by intimidation, would ultimately tend to endanger the connexion between the two countries'.[40] It is certainly true that nineteenth-century Irish nationalist politicians and historians later amplified Sheridan's attack, but then similar accusations were made about the way in which the Anglo-Scottish union had been carried, and Scotland remained firmly wedded to the United Kingdom. Moreover, in the years immediately after 1800 opponents of the union such as John Foster, Henry Grattan and the Orange Order accommodated themselves to the new dispensation with remarkable speed. Perhaps, as the Victorian historians W.E.H. Lecky and J.A. Froude believed, the union had come too late. If it had come earlier, in 1707 for example, before the rise of Irish nationalism, it might have worked. Then there was the failure to resolve the Catholic Question. The Irish Catholic Question, in fact, now became Britain's Irish Question, and in that form it bedevilled British politics for the next thirty years.

At the beginning of 1801 *The Scots Magazine* carried the following report:

> On January 1 it was intended, as given out in the general orders by Major-General Vyse, that all the Volunteer corps of this city [Edinburgh] should have assembled and fired a *feu de joye*, in celebration of the union with Ireland, which took place this day; but the badness of the day prevented.
>
> The Lord Provost and magistrates, very judiciously issued a proclamation, prohibiting illumination, in respect of the pressing circumstances of the times.

The omens were not auspicious.

Notes

1. Thomas, P.D.G., 1998, *Politics in Eighteenth-century Wales*, Cardiff, 2–7.

2. Brewer, John, 1997, *The Pleasures of the Imagination: English Culture in the Eighteenth Century*, London, 633–58.

3. Hutton, A.H. (ed.) 1892, *A Tour in Ireland, 1776–1779* (2 vols), London, ii: 54.

4. Kelly, P.H., 1988, 'William Molyneux and the spirit of liberty', *Eighteenth-century Ireland*, 3: 143.

5. The outstanding exception to this neglect of unionist opinion is James Kelly, 1987, 'The origins of the Act of Union: an examination of unionist opinion in

Britain and Ireland, 1650–1800', *IHS*, 25: 236–63; and 'Public and political opinion in Ireland and the idea of an Anglo-Irish union, 1650–1800' in
Boyce, D.G., Eccleshall R. and Geoghegan, V. (eds), (forthcoming) *Political
Thought in Ireland*, ii, London. I am grateful to Dr Kelly for letting me read this
paper in advance of publication.

6. Arthur Dobbs, however, used the phrase 'the British Protestant inhabitants of
Ireland': [1730], 'An essay on the expediency of a union betwixt England and
Ireland', NLI Thom Ms 1.

7. Dobbs also wrote an unpublished essay advocating union, see n. 6 above.

8. *Freeman's Journal*, 26–30 June, 11–18, 21–25 August, 2–8 September 1764.

9. Murphy, Sean, 1994, 'Charles Lucas: a forgotten Patriot?' *History Ireland*, 2:3,
29; Lucas, Charles, 1756, *An Appeal to the Commons and Citizens of London by
Charles Lucas the Last Free Citizen of Dublin*, London, 8; Kelly, 'The origins of the
Act of Union', 248, n. 55.

10. Murphy, Sean, 'The Dublin anti-union riot of 3 December, 1759' in O'Brien
(ed.) 1989, *Parliament, Politics and People*, Dublin, 49–68.

11. *Faulkner's Dublin Journal*, 20–24 November 1759, *Belfast Newsletter*,
27 November 1759.

12. [1751, Hillsborough] *A Proposal for Uniting the Kingdoms of Great Britain and
Ireland*, London and Dublin, 12 and *passim*. Dobbs, Arthur, 'An essay on the
expediency of a union betwixt England and Ireland', *Freeman's Journal*, 26–30
June, 21–25 August 1764; 1772, *Justice and Policy: An Essay on the Increasing
Growth and Economies of our Great Cities . . . Also Considerations upon the State of
Ireland . . . by a Freeholder in Ireland, and a Stockholder in England*, Dublin, 53.

13. Archdall, Nicholas, 1751, *An Alarm to the People of Great Britain in Answer to
a Late Proposal Showing the Fatal Consequences of Such an Union*, Dublin; 1759,
*A Dialogue Between a Protestant and a Papist; Concerning the Late Strange Reports
of an Union, and the Seditious Consequences of Them*, Dublin; *Freeman's Journal*,
11–12 August 1764.

14. Kelly, 'The origins of the Act of Union', 251–4.

15. Buckinghamshire to Lord George Germain, 23 August 1778, *HMC Stopford-
Sackville Ms*, I: 251–2; O'Connell, M., 1965, *Irish Politics and Social Conflict in
the Age of the American Revolution*, Philadelphia, 163; Macartney to Lord North,
8 January 1780 in Bartlett, Thomas (ed.) 1978, *Macartney in Ireland 1768–
72, A Calendar of the Chief Secretaryship Papers of Sir George Macartney*, PRONI,
Belfast, 325.

16. The complex history of Anglo-Irish relations in this period is unravelled by James Kelly in 1992, *Prelude to Union: Anglo-Irish Politics in the 1780s*, Cork.

17. Reprinted in Moody, T.W., McDowell, R.B. and Woods, C.J. (eds) 1998, *The Writings of Theolbald Wolfe Tone*, i, Oxford, 50–63.

18. Rutland to Pitt, 16 June 1784 in Lord Mahon (ed.) 1890, *The Correspondence Between William Pitt and the Duke of Rutland*, London, 19.

19. For example William Drennan to Martha McTier, February and, 29 September 1792, 26 March 1793, in Chart, D.A. (ed.) 1931, *Drennan Letters*, Belfast, 77, 91, 145.

20. The historiography of Ireland in the 1790s has expanded rapidly in recent years. See e.g. Elliott, Marianne, 1982, *Partners in Revolution: The United Irishmen and France*, New Haven; Smyth, Jim, 1992, *The Men of No Property: Irish Radicals and Popular Politics in the Late Eighteenth Century*, Houndsmills; Curtin, Nancy, 1994, *The United Irishmen: Popular Politics in Ulster and Dublin, 1791–1798*, Oxford; Whelan, Kevin, 1996, *The Tree of Liberty: Radicalism, Catholicism and the Construction of Irish Identity, 1760–1830*, Cork.

21. Ehrman, John, 1996, *The Younger Pitt: The Consuming Struggle*, London, 171; Pitt to Camden, 28 May 1798, in Aspinal, A. (ed.) 1967, *The Later Correspondence of George III*, iii, Cambridge, 68.

22. Cornwallis to Lord Ely, 13 January 1799; Cornwallis to Major Gen. Ross, 21 January 1799; Cornwallis to Portland, 28 January 1799; Pitt to Cornwallis, 26 January 1799 in Ross, Charles (ed.) 1859, *Correspondence of Charles, First Marquis Cornwallis*, London, ii, 37–40, 53–7.

23. Drennan, William, 1799, *Letter to the Right Honorable William Pitt*, Dublin, 4, 6–9.

24. Cooke, Edward, 1798, *Arguments For and Against an Union Between Great Britain and Ireland Considered*, Dublin, 9.

25. Drennan, *Letter*, 19.

26. Cornwallis to Ross, 30 September 1798, *Cornwallis Corr.* ii, 414–15; Robert Johnson to Lord Downshire, 19 February 1799, PRONI, Downshire Papers, 607/G/75. For an up-to-date account of the Catholic Question and the union, see Bartlett, 1992, *Fall and Rise*, Dublin.

27. Ehrman, *The Younger Pitt*, 173; Camden memorandum [July/August 1798, undated] CUL. Add. Ms. Pitt Papers 6958/2379. For a Namierite account of the high political, parliamentary and administrative history of how the union was carried, see Bolton G.C., 1966, *The Passing of the Irish Act of Union: A Study in Parliamentary Politics*, Oxford.

[2 2 0]   28.   Drennan to Mrs McTier, 6 December 1798, *Drennan Letters*, 283; Cooke to Castlereagh, 15 December 1798, *Memoirs and Correspondence of Viscount Castlereagh*, i, 43–4; *Freeman's Journal*, 12 January 1799; McCormack, W.J., 1996, *The Pamphlet Debate on the Union Between Great Britain and Ireland, 1797–1800*, Dublin; for the paper war and public opinion, see Smyth, Jim, 'The Act of Union and "public opinion"' in Smyth, Jim (ed.) 2000 *Revolution, Counter-Revolution and Union: Ireland in the 1790s*, Cambridge.

29.   Catholic ambivalence or hostility towards union was noted by the Catholic Bishop of Meath, Plunkett, and by Leonard McNally: Bishop of Meath to Castlereagh, 29 October 1799, *Castlereagh Corr.*, ii, 438; 'JW' (McNally) to Downshire, 20 February 1799, PRONI. Downshire Papers, 607/G/76.

30.   Drennan to McTier, 25 January 1800, *Drennan Letters*, 297–8.

31.   1848, *AutoBiography of Archibald Hamilton Rowan*, Dublin (reprinted Shannon, 1972), 340–3, 350.

32.   Cornwallis to Pitt, 7 December 1798, *Cornwallis Corr.*, iii, 7–8.

33.   Wilkinson, David, 1997, 'How did they pass the union?', *History*, 82: 229.

34.   Cornwallis to Portland, 22 June 1799; Cornwallis to Ross, 21 January 1800, *Cornwallis Corr.*, iii, 104–6, 167–8.

35.   *Parliamentary Register of Ireland 1800* (Speech of Castlereagh, 5 February 1800), 146.

36.   Henry Grattan Jnr (a frankly partisan source) gives the figures as 187,000 signatures against union and 7,000 in favour: Grattan, 1839, *Memoirs of the Life and Times of the Rt. Hon. Henry Grattan*, London, v, 50–1.

37.   Douglas to Cornwallis, 16 October 1798, NLI. Union Correspondence Ms 882 f. 329; Douglas to Castlereagh, January 1799, *Castlereagh Corr.*, ii, 125–6.

38.   Drennan uses the term 'dragooned' in a letter to his sister, Martha McTier, in August 1796, *Drennan Letters*, 235; Drennan, 1799 *Letter to Pitt*, 35; anon., *No Flinching, or A Preserving Opposition to the Measure of an Incorporate Union* . . . Dublin, 3–4; Bushe, Charles Kendle, 1798, *The Union. Cease Your Fuming or, the Rebel Detected*, Dublin, 18–19.

39.   Bushe, *The Union*, 18; *The Parliamentary History of England*, xxxiv (speech of R.B. Sheridan, 23 January 1800), 299.

40.   *Parliamentary History of England*, xxxiv (speech of R.B. Sheridan, 23 January 1800), 213.

AFTERWORD

I f Mark Twain did not coin some lethal and amusing epigram about the folly of historians writing generalising epilogues, he should have. This is especially true where such reflections include prediction, for there is no reason that an historian's predictive abilities should be any more reliable than, say, the forecasts of Kremlinologists in the early 1980s. On the other hand, the cautionary tale of the Kremlin-watchers illustrates how the pressure of current events can alter our understanding of the past. The 'break-up' or reconfiguration of post-imperial Britain in the late 1990s – the establishment of devolved assemblies in Scotland and Wales and Northern Ireland, the creation of all-Ireland and Irish–British institutions, and the uncertain direction of their development, together with the equally uncertain implications for sovereignty of closer integration into the European Union – inevitably prompts a fresh look at the making of the United Kingdom. Because the indissolubility of the union of 1801 was never beyond question, in retrospect the contingent elements in its passing were never obscured – quite the reverse. At the time, however, when the union of 1707 was considered 'a complete success', 'a triumph of legislative wisdom' and 'a lasting monument of successful British statesmanship', its very 'success' and assumed permanence, observed A.V. Dicey in 1920, 'concealed from the thinkers of to-day the all but insuperable obstacles which opposed its creation'.[1] In 2001 it is no longer possible to be so complacent either about the making of the union or about its survival.

The other great hazard with historical generalisation is hindsight. By concluding that the omens for the future of the Act of Union between Great Britain and Ireland in 1801 were inauspicious, I alluded to its ultimate 'failure'. The reasons for that failure are usually located in the history of nineteenth-century Anglo-Irish relations, specifically in the thirty-year postponement of Catholic emancipation, and in the perceived culpability of the British government in the great famine which decimated Irish society after 1845.[2] After George III's initial veto, Catholic emancipation had to be fought for and won rather than freely given, and in the course of the struggle Daniel O'Connell mobilised a Catholic nation that learned to distinguish itself more sharply than ever from Protestant Britain.[3] It is no accident that the emancipation campaign of the 1820s was followed by a campaign for repeal of the union in the 1830s and 1840s. 'Repeal', however, was ill defined – the O'Connellites seem to have envisaged a return to 'Grattan's parliament' – and did not extend to separation. The famine, it could be argued, had an even greater negative political impact on the union than did the protracted rearguard defence of Protestant Ascendancy. Famine may be an act of God; famine relief is a function, among other things, of political will; and the manifest unwillingness of the central government to respond adequately to the Irish disaster – its persistence in treating it as a local catastrophe rather than as an imperial calamity – exposed fatally the emptiness of unionist rhetoric. Quite simply, people asked at the time, would Westminster or Whitehall have stood by while Yorkshire starved? To many in Ireland the answer and the conclusion were not in doubt.

The presentation of Ireland within the context of the United Kingdom as 'an entirely exceptional case'[4] did not proceed solely from political considerations. Political analysis in fact often rested on deeply held assumptions about 'cultural identity'. Ireland, in that view, never was (and perhaps never could have been) fully integrated into the metropolitan polity and culture. The Irish, or at least, since race and religion were by now routinely conflated, the Catholic Irish, did not (perhaps could not) become British. The most fundamental cause for the failure of the union, in other words, could be traced to the unbridgeable incompatibility of different 'national characters'[5]. During the nineteenth century Irish as well as English writers carried representations of the great divide between the 'Saxon' and the 'Celt' to new levels of pseudo-scientific refinement and literary caricature, but there was nothing new about stereotyping the Irish as wild, barbarous, violent, verbose, improvident, hard-drinking and so on. Such stereotypes were firmly in place at the time of the union and scarcely augured well for the sort of 'moral unity' that, held Dicey, eventually consolidated the union of England and Scotland.[6] Britain and Ireland by contrast never achieved 'an identity of interests [or] community of feeling'.[7]

A further flaw in the fabric of union resided in the manner of its making. The accusations of jobbing, corruption, bribery and fraud levelled at government by anti-unionists at the time enjoyed a long afterlife. Sir Jonah Barrington's *Rise and Fall of the Irish Nation* (1833) is the foundation text of a small genre of polemical literature which sports book titles such *The Story of the Union, as Told by its Plotters*, with chapter titles such as 'A Carnival of Corruption'.[8] But what effect, if any, did the tainted reputation of the union's origins have on public opinion? The least that can be said is that it provided the repealers and the home-rulers with ammunition. That 'political crime', declared one pamphleteer in 1830,

> which has distinguished the memory of its guilty perpetrators by a most
> unenviable perpetuity of infamy. Can any measure so effected, be looked
> upon as comprehending the essence of a perennial existence? Does it not
> rather contain in its very origin and birth the first principle of decay, and seeds
> of an early dissolution. Can that which is engendered in corruption have any
> pretensions to immortality? It was moreover, in simple truth, an act of
> downright plunder and spoilation, effected by a mixture of fraud and violence.[9]

And yet to treat the union as doomed from the start is to indulge a nationalist teleology towards Ireland every bit as Whiggish as the unionist teleology of those who once celebrated the 'statesmanship' of 1707 and the 'moral unity' of Scotland and England. Several of the principal causes identified as inimical to the union project in Ireland also applied to Scotland in 1707. The Scots, like the Irish – and the Welsh – were then and later held in contempt by their southern neighbours; similarly the passing of the Scottish union was notoriously attributed to the greasing of greedy Scottish palms with 'English gold'; indeed in its earlier years the Scottish union appears to have been even more unpopular and more precarious than was the Irish union in the first years of the nineteenth century. Conversely, a number of the reasons often adduced for the eventual success of the Anglo-Scottish union applied equally to Ireland, notably the job opportunities afforded by the British army and the British empire.[10] Finally, if the counter-factual reasoning usually implicit in historical causal analysis is made explicit, then the horizons of possible outcomes widen and once more the prospects for the union do not appear so bleak. We can only speculate, for example, on the changed course of Anglo-Irish relations if, say, George III had suffered a prolonged mental break-down in 1801, as he did in 1788 and would again in 1810, and Pitt had thus been able to push through Catholic emancipation.

'British history' of the sort advocated by J.G.A. Pocock has perhaps still to be written. The conceptual and technical difficulties remain, but the conceptual gains have, nonetheless, been great. The writing of English history is in robust good health, but as changes in the titles of university curricula in the past decade or so suggest, it no longer stands as a synonym for British history. Anglocentric history will not do. The Whig epic of the inexorable triumph of parliament, Protestantism, industry and empire – in which 1707 if not 1800 plays a part – will not do either. If anything is clear from the growing historiography of 'British history', it is that British identities were 'constructed' or 'invented' and that the making of the United Kingdom was contingent. As one practitioner in this emerging field recently declared, he is 'British by chance';[11] and, as every Kremlinologist knows, what is constructed can be deconstructed, what is invented can be reinvented. United Kingdom watchers live in interesting times.

Notes

1. Dicey, A.V., 1920, *Thoughts on the Union between England and Scotland*, London, 347–8; see also Weir, Ron, 'The Scottish and Irish unions: the Victorian view in perspective' in Connolly, S.J. (ed.) 1999, *Kingdoms United? Great Britain and Ireland since 1500: Integration and Diversity*, Dublin, 60–2.

2. For a survey of post-union opinion see Kennedy, Liam and Johnson, David S., 'The union of Ireland and Britain, 1801–1921' in Boyce, D.G. and O'Day, Alan (eds) 1996, *The Making of Modern Irish History: Revisionism and the Revisionist Controversy*, London, 34–70.

3. Dicey believed that the 'terrible error' of not introducing Catholic emancipation sooner 'was fatal to the chance that the union between Great Britain and Ireland might be as successful as the union between England and Scotland': *Thoughts on the Union between England and Scotland*, 267.

4. The phrase is John Redmond's, quoted in Kendle, John, 1989, *Ireland and the Federal Solution: The Debate over the United Kingdom Constitution, 1870–1921*, Kingston and Montreal, 81.

5. Deane, Seamus, 'Irish national character 1790–1900' in Dunne, Tom (ed.) 1987, *The Writer as Witness: Literature as Historical Evidence*, Cork, 90–113.

6. Dicey, *Thoughts on the Union between England and Scotland*, 295–6. Negative English perceptions of Ireland at the time of the union are discussed by Thomas Bartlett in *Acts of Union: An Inaugural Lecture Delivered at University College Dublin on 24 February 2000*, Dublin, 7–14.

7. 1830, *The Legislative Union between Great Britain and Ireland Considered . . . by Aristharchus*, Dublin, 13.

8. Barrington, Sir Jonah, 1833, *The Rise and Fall of the Irish Nation*, Paris; Dennehy, William F., 1891, *The Story of the Union, as Told by its Plotters*, Dublin.

The chapter title is in McDonnell, Bodkin M., 1904, *Grattan's Parliament, Before and After*, London.

9. *The Legislative Union between Great Britain and Ireland Considered . . . by Aristharchus*, 16–17.

10. Bartlett, *Acts of Union*, 14–18; Irish participation in empire took some unlikely turns: see Kerr, Donal, 'Under the union flag: the Catholic Church in Ireland' in 1989, *Ireland after the Union: Proceedings of the Second Joint Meeting of the Royal Irish Academy and the British Academy*, Oxford, 40–3.

11. Davies, Norman, 1999, *The Isles: A History*, Oxford, v.

APPENDIX

Kings and queens of England, Scotland and Ireland 1660–1800

Charles II	(1649)1660–85
James VII (of Scotland) and II	1685–88 (1701)
William III	1689 (–1696 with Mary) –1702
Anne	1702–14
George I	1714–27
George II	1727–60
George III	1760–1820

The Stuart line

James VII and II	1685–1701
James VIII and III (the Old Pretender)	1701–66
Charles III (the Young Pretender)	1766–88

British prime ministers, 1707–1800*

Earl of Godolphin	(of England 1702) 1707–10
Robert Harley, Earl of Oxford	1710–14
James Stanhope	1714–21

* The term 'Prime Minister' is anachronistic. Although Sir Robert Walpole is often referred as the first Prime Minister, 'First Minister' might perhaps be more accurate, and while one or two of these ministers held offices such as Secretary of State, almost all of them were First Lord of the Treasury.

Sir Robert Walpole	1721–41
Sir John Carteret	1742–44
Henry Pelham	1744–54
Duke of Newcastle	1754–56
William Pitt (the Elder, later Chatham)	1756–57
Duke of Newcastle	1754–62
Earl of Bute	1762–63
George Grenville	1763–65
Marquis of Rockingham	1765–66
Earl of Chatham	1766
Duke of Grafton	1767–69
Lord North	1770–82
Marquis of Rockingham	1782
Earl of Shelburne	1782
Duke of Portland	1783
William Pitt (the Younger)	1773–1801

Secretary of State for Scotland 1709–46

Duke of Queensberry	1709–13
Earl of Mar	1713–14
Duke of Montrose	1714–16
Duke of Roxburghe	1716–25
Vacant	
Marquis of Tweeddale	1742–45

Lords Advocate of Scotland 1660–1800

Sir George Lockhart	1658–61
Sir John Fletcher	1661–64
Sir John Nisbet	1664–67
Sir George Mackenzie	1667–81
Sir John Dalrymple	1681–88
Sir George Mackenzie	1688

[228]

Sir John Dalrymple	1689–92
Sir James Stewart	1692–1709
Sir David Dalrymple	1709–10
Sir James Stewart	1711–13
Thomas Kennedy	1714
Sir David Dalrymple	1714–20
Robert Dundas	1720–25
Duncan Forbes	1725–37
Charles Erskine	1737–42
Robert Craigie	1742–46
William Grant	1746–54
Robert Dundas (jnr)	1754–60
Thomas Miller	1760–66
James Montgomery	1766–75
Henry Dundas	1775–83
Henry Erskine	1783
Illay Campbell	1784–89
Robert Dundas	1789–1801

Lord Deputies and Lords Lieutenant of Ireland 1660–1800*

Lord Robartes	1660
1st Duke of Ormond	1662–64
Earl of Ossory	1664–68
1st Duke of Ormond	1668–69
Lord Robartes	1669–70
John, Baron Berkeley	1670–72
Earl of Essex	1672–77
1st Duke of Ormond	1677–85
2nd Earl of Clarendon	1685–87
Earl of Tyrconnell	1687–91

* In the absence of the Lord Deputy or Lord Lieutenant, Ireland was governed by three locally appointed Lords Justices.

Sir Henry Sidney	1692–95
Henry Capell	1695–96
Earl of Galway	1697–1701
Earl of Rochester	1701–03
2nd Duke of Ormond	1703–07
Earl of Pembroke	1707–08
Earl of Wharton	1708–10
2nd Duke of Ormond	1710–13
Duke of Shrewsbury	1713–14
Earl of Sunderland	1714–17
Viscount Townsend	1717
Duke of Bolton	1717–20
Duke of Grafton	1720–24
Lord Carteret	1724–30
Duke of Dorset	1730–37
Duke of Devonshire	1737–45
Earl of Chesterfield	1745–46
Earl of Harrington	1746–50
Duke of Dorset	1750–55
Duke of Devonshire	1755–57
Duke of Bedford	1757–61
Earl of Halifax	1761–63
Earl of Northumberland	1763–65
Viscount Weymouth	1765
Earl of Hertford	1765–66
Earl of Bristol	1766–67
Viscount Townsend	1767–72
Earl of Harcourt	1772–76
Earl of Buckinghamshire	1776–80
Earl of Carlisle	1780–82
Duke of Portland	1782
Marquis of Buckingham	1782–83
Earl of Northington	1783–84
Duke of Rutland	1784–87
Marquis of Buckingham	1787–90
Earl of Westmorland	1790–95
Earl Fitzwilliam	1795
Earl of Camden	1795–98
Marquis Cornwallis	1798–1800

[230] Sources

Cook, Chris and Stevenson, John, 1988, *British Historical Facts, 1688–1760*, New York; Cook and Stevenson, 1980, *British Historical Facts, 1760–1830*, Hamden, Conn.; Pickrill, D.A., 1981, *Ministers of the Crown*, London; Moody, T., Martin, F.X. and Byrne, F.J. (eds) 1984, *A New History of Ireland*, ix, *Maps, Genealogies, Lists: A Companion to Irish History, II*, Oxford.

GLOSSARY

Arianism Anti-Trinitarian heresy which holds that Christ is not consubstantial (i.e. does not share the same substance) with God the Father.

Cameronians 'Extreme' Scottish Covenanter followers of Richard Cameron.

Cavaliers Term applied to royalist MPs in the 1661 English parliament and to the crypto-Jacobite faction in the 1702 Scottish parliament.

Covenanters Scottish Presbyterians who refused to accept any ecclesiastical settlement not based on the Solemn League and Covenant (1643).

deism Belief in God but not in divine revelation.

Erastianism The doctrine of state supremacy in the Church.

Fifth Monarchists Militant millenarian Protestant sect.

Jacobites Those who continued after 1688 to recognise James II and VII and his heirs as the legitimate kings of England, Scotland and Ireland.

Latitudinarianism The allowance, chiefly among Church of England divines, of free inquiry in religious matters, combined with a relaxed attitude towards inter-Christian differences over inessential outward forms such as liturgy and ceremonial.

Moderates Eighteenth-century Scottish Presbyterian ministers who sought to distance themselves from the excesses of the past, promote a more 'rational' ethos and to serve the post-union Hanoverian state.

non-jurors Church of England bishops and clergy who, after 1688, refused to recognise the legitimacy of William of Orange or his successors.

out-of-doors Outside parliament, usually used to denote 'public opinion' or extra-parliamentary agitation.

Presbyterians This usually refers to members of the Presbyterian churches. In 1660, however, it may also denote those 'moderate' MPs who had been expelled from parliament in 1647, and who generally sought a 'middle way' between republicanism and monarchy.

Protestors Also known as 'Remonstrants', a minority faction – dating from a split in the General Assembly of the Church of Scotland in 1650 – who were Covenanters and republican.

Resolutioners The majority faction after the 1650 split of Scottish Presbyterians who remained committed to a covenanted king.

Rump Informal designation of the 'Long Parliament' after Pride's Purge in 1647. The Rump was itself expelled by Oliver Cromwell in 1653, then recalled again in 1659 only to expelled once more by the army. Recalled a third time by General Monck in 1660 the surviving 'excluded members' purged in 1647 were finally readmitted and the restored 'Long Parliament' promptly dissolved itself to make way for a Convention parliament.

Socinianism Anti-Trinitarian Heresy which rejects the divinity of Christ.

Squadrone *Squadrone Volante* (Flying Squadron) nickname of the influential group of pre- and post-union Scottish MPs led by the 2nd Marquis of Tweeddale.

Subscription The requirement for clergymen to 'subscribe' to formulae which defined Christian orthodoxy, in the case of the Church of England the thirty-nine articles, in the case of dissenters, the Westminster Confession of Faith (1643). Those who argued for the sufficiency of scripture and thus refused to submit to any 'man-made' standards were known as non-subscribers.

Unitarians Late eighteenth-century anti-Trinitarians, mainly but not exclusively of dissenter origin.

FURTHER READING

The historiography of the 'new British history' has already developed certain distinct characteristics. First, few areas of historical inquiry have generated so much reflection so quickly. Manifestos calling for new, more integrative, approaches to the histories of these islands, together with critical and review essays – sceptical as well as affirmative – addressing the question 'What is British history?' are almost as numerous as substantive pieces about 'what actually happened'. Second, the typical format for 'British' history thus far is not the single-author monograph or textbook (although there are fine examples of both), but the essay collection, comprising contributions from specialists in the history of each of the four nations. Expecting any individual historian to master four national archives is, after all, a tall order. And finally, while there have been some excellent and stimulating forays into modern and medieval British history, most work in the field has focused on the early modern period. The reasons for that, presumably, have to do with the intense interaction between the three kingdoms in the sixteenth and seventeenth – particularly the mid-seventeenth – centuries, and the pivotal importance of the eighteenth century for the emergence of senses of Britishness.

The most influential essays on the possibilities of a three-kingdom framework are J.G.A. Pocock's 'British History: a plea for a new subject', *Journal of Modern History*, 47 (1975) and 'The limits and divisions of British history', *American Historical Review*, 87: 2 (1982) – in the latter of which he tries to get around Irish nationalist objections to the term 'British' by coining a new term: the 'Atlantic Archipelago'. Several other historians have since had their say, but for a recent report on the state of the discussion see the contributions to AHR Forum: 'The new British history in Atlantic perspective', *American Historical Review*, 104: 2 (1999). A different, pre-Pocockian, and ultimately anglocentric model (betrayed by the use of the 'f' word in the subtitle) is suggested by the American sociologist Michael Hechter in *Internal Colonialism: The Celtic Fringe in British National Development, 1536–1966* (London, 1975). Murray G.H. Pittock, *Inventing and Resisting Britain: Cultural Identities in Britain and Ireland, 1685–1789* (Houndsmills, 1997) is an *engagé* intervention from the standpoint of a literary scholar. A European perspective is offered by J.H. Elliott: 'A Europe of composite monarchies', *Past and Present*, 137 (1992); while Jack P. Greene deals with many of the relevant issues within an 'Atlantic' context in *Peripheries and Center: Constitutional Development in the Extended Polities of the British Empire and the United States, 1607–1788* (Georgia, 1986).

[2 3 4]   Hugh Kearney, *The British Isles: A History of Four Nations* (Cambridge, 1988), Keith Robbins, *Great Britain: Identities, Institutions and the Idea of Britishness* (London, 1998) and, on a tighter chronological scale, David Smith, *A History of the Modern British Isles 1603–1707: The Double Crown* (Oxford, 1998) provide general accounts which attempt to practise what so many have preached. Most recently, Norman Davies' hefty tome *The Isles: A History* (Oxford, 1999) takes the long view; vigorous and sweeping, it 'necessarily presents', as the author admits, 'a very personal view of history'. On the other hand, Linda Colley, *Britons: Forging the Nation, 1707–1837* (New Haven, 1992), Colin Kidd, *British Identities before Nationalism* (Cambridge, 1999) and Alexander Murdoch, *British History 1660–1832: National Identity and Local Culture* (Houndsmills, 1998) focus specifically on questions of identity. Volumes of essays that cover a wide range of topics from a variety of angles include A. Grant and K. Stringer (eds) *Uniting the Kingdom? The Making of British History* (London, 1995); S. Ellis and S. Barber (eds) *Conquest and Union: Fashioning a British State 1485–1720* (London, 1995); B. Bradshaw and P. Roberts (eds) *British Consciousness and Identity: The Making of Britain, 1533–1707* (Cambridge, 1998); B. Bradshaw and J. Morrill (eds) *The British Problem* c. *1534–1707: State Formation in the Atlantic Archipelago* (Houndsmills, 1996); G. Burgess (ed.) *The New British History: Founding a Modern State, 1603–1715* (London, 1999); R.G. Asch (ed.) *Three Nations – A Common History? England, Scotland, Ireland and British History* c. *1600–1920* (Bochum, 1991) and S.J. Connolly (ed.) *Kingdoms United? Great Britain and Ireland since 1500: Integration and Diversity* (Dublin, 1999).

Of course the secondary literature on the British and Irish 'long eighteenth century' is vast, especially for England. What follows, therefore, is merely a brief list of those titles that are particularly relevant to the themes explored in this book. For the Restoration the best place to begin is R. Hutton, *The Restoration in England and Wales, 1658–1667* (Oxford, 1987). Events in Ireland have now, at last, received meticulous reconstruction in A. Clarke, *Prelude to Restoration: The End of the Commonwealth in Ireland, 1659–1660* (Cambridge, 1999). A detailed account of the transition in Scotland is provided by F.D. Dow, *Cromwellian Scotland, 1651–1660* (Edinburgh, 1979). The English ecclesiastical settlement is covered by I.M. Green, *The Re-establishment of the Church of England, 1660–1663* (Oxford, 1978). Anglo-Scottish relations before and up to the union are analysed by Brian P. Levack, *The Formation of the British State: England, Scotland, and the Union, 1603–1707* (Oxford, 1987), and John Robertson (ed.) *A Union for Empire: Political Thought and the British Union of 1707* (Cambridge, 1995). In the case of eighteenth-century Scotland, R. Mitchison and N. Phillipson (eds) *Scotland in the Age of Improvement* (Edinburgh, 1970) has aged remarkably well, although for an up-to-date survey see Tom Devine and J.M. Young (eds) *Eighteenth-century Scotland: New Perspectives* (East Linton, 1999). No serious student of eighteenth-century England can afford to ignore J.C.D. Clark, *English Society, 1660–1832* (Cambridge, 1985) – a revised edition of which is due at the time of writing. More than any other scholar, Clark has restored religion to the central place in political, cultural and intellectual history where it belongs. An altogether different sort of book which surveys an admirable range of topics is Paul Langford's *A Polite and Commercial People: England 1727–1783* (Oxford, 1992). Kathleen

Wilson, *The Sense of the People: Politics, Culture and Imperialism in England, 1715–1785* (Cambridge, 1995) examines the domestic impact of imperial expansion. The most stimulating contribution to Irish history in this period in recent years is undoubtedly S.J. Connolly's *Religion, Law and Power: The Making of Protestant Ireland, 1660–1760* (Oxford, 1992). Historical writing on eighteenth-century Wales is comparatively slim when placed beside the available literature on the medieval period, or the nineteenth century, as a glance at the contents of *The Welsh History Review* will confirm; but see P.D.G. Thomas's thorough (in the Namierite idiom) *Politics in Eighteenth-century Wales* (Cardiff, 1998), and more generally, Philip Jenkins, *A History of Modern Wales, 1536–1990* (London, 1990).

The study of Jacobitism is a growth industry which threatens to repeople these islands with covert Jacobites around every corner. Only Robert Walpole now seems safe from unmasking. A strong narrative treatment of the undeniable strain of Jacobitism is offered by Bruce Lenman, *The Jacobite Rebellions in Britain, 1689–1746* (Aberdeen, 1995), while Paul Monod's *Jacobitism and the English People, 1688–1788* (Cambridge, 1989) is an innovative essay which tracks the subculture of Jacobitism across many media and unexpected manifestations. Breandán Ó'Buachalla's formidable excavation of Irish Jacobite sentiment, *Aisling Ghéar, na Stiobhartaigh agus an tAos Leinn, 1603–1788* (Dublin, 1996) is, at any rate for the time being, unavailable in English translation. Among the many works devoted to religion in the 'long eighteenth century' Ian McBride and Tony Clayton (eds) *Protestantism and National Identity: Britain and Ireland* c. 1650–c. 1850 (Cambridge, 1998) relates most directly with the sorts of issues raised in this book. Finally, it says something of the priorities of Irish – and, indeed, for different reasons of English – historians that for many years the only full-scale monograph on the 1800 Act of Union was G.C. Bolton's *The Passing of the Irish Act of Union* (Oxford, 1966) but – as the recent publication of Patrick Geoghegan's *The Irish Act of Union: A Study in High Politics 1798–1801* (Dublin, 1999) suggests – the combination of the bicentenary of the union and the infiltration of four-nations perspectives seems set to rectify that neglect.

INDEX